¡TEQUILA!

¡TEQUILA!

DISTILLING THE SPIRIT OF MEXICO

MARIE SARITA GAYTÁN

Stanford University Press
Stanford, California

Stanford University Press
Stanford, California

Printed in the United States of America on acid-free, archival-quality paper

Library of Congress Cataloging-in-Publication Data

Gaytán, Marie Sarita, author.
   ¡Tequila! : distilling the spirit of Mexico / Marie Sarita Gaytán.
   pages cm
   Includes bibliographical references and index.
   ISBN 978-0-8047-8807-6 (cloth : alk. paper) — ISBN 978-0-8047-9307-0 (pbk. : alk. paper)
   1. Tequila—Mexico—History. 2. Alcoholic beverages—Mexico—History. 3. Drinking of alcoholic beverages—Mexico—History. 4. National characteristics, Mexican. I. Title.
   TP607.T46G39 2014
   663'.50972—dc23

                                                              2014010117

ISBN 978-0-8047-9310-0 (electronic)

Typeset by Thompson Type in 10/14 Minion

CONTENTS

ILLUSTRATIONS

¡TEQUILA!

INTRODUCTION

Every November, toward the end of the month, the residents of Tequila, Mexico, celebrate the *Feria Nacional del Tequila*, the National Fair of Tequila. The two-week event culminates on December 12, the feast day of the Virgin of Guadalupe, and includes *charreadas* (Mexican rodeo), cockfighting, carnival rides, firework displays, art exhibits, and musical performances. Like most annual fairs, the festivities are marked by the return of family members from other parts of the country and the United States. Preparations begin the week before the festival: The main square is populated with ornate stages, banners are draped on streetlights, and promotional posters are liberally affixed to the doors of small businesses. Once Saturday arrives, street vendors with balloons, cotton candy, and churros set up shop all along the perimeter of the large plaza in front of the local Catholic Church, St. James the Apostle. As its bells ring, every hour on the hour, excitement flows through the streets of the centuries-old town.

With the exception of the municipal website, there is little outside publicity for the yearly festival—even in the nearby state capital, Guadalajara, the nation's second-largest city, located just forty-five minutes south, the event goes relatively unnoticed. I arrived to the inaugural parade as floats, marching bands, Aztec dancers, and *charros* (cowboys) on horseback started lining up on the pageant route. At the end of the procession, a truck pulled a midsized stage from which Miss Mayahuel and members of her court waved to gathering onlookers. Clapping and cheers abounded, a cannon exploded—boom!—

and the procession began. When the parade finished, loudspeakers repeatedly played the 1958 song by The Champs, "Tequila," and the large crowd eagerly waited for the mayor to signal the start of the next stage of the celebration.

As important and anticipated the festival is for residents of Tequila, almost no one thinks of it when they hear the word *tequila*. Outside of Mexico, tequila is likely to conjure images of rowdy celebrations, body shots, or heavy hangovers. It is a drink to consume quickly—an effective means to an inebriated end. Within Mexico, tequila is often associated with weddings, birthdays, or just drinking with friends; in other words, tequila is frequently thought of as a libation to commemorate a range of noteworthy and quotidian festivities. Sometimes it is shot, but most often it is sipped. Beyond when and how it is consumed, tequila, as a complex cultural commodity, is first and foremost about people—and in this case, about the people of Mexico.

This book explores the political, economic, and social relations of tequila as a symbol of national identity, an emblem of resistance, a touristic destination, and its link to a rural town that is associated with its namesake. Tequila, like all commodities, is dynamic, active, and relational—it is promoted and interpreted by a diverse range of groups and individuals. Even with its many potential meanings, one association holds true above all others: Tequila is a preeminent marker of *lo mexicano*, or what is commonly known as Mexicanness. Curiously, there are dozens of distilled drinks that, like tequila, reflect aspects of Mexico's rich history: *bacanora* from the state of Sonora, *sotol* from the state of Chihuahua, *mezcal* from Oaxaca and Zacatecas, and *raicilla* from Jalisco, to name a few. So what is so special about tequila? Why is tequila the enduring symbol of Mexicanness? Tequila has not always been the nation's drink. Over the years, tequila manufacturers, consumers, government officials, authors, performers, and movie producers have each strengthened tequila's ties to *lo mexicano*. This book will show that the close association between *lo mexicano* and tequila was hardly a given, despite contemporary representations that portray it as such (see Map 1 and Figure 1).

Stories that emphasize an object's intrinsic ties to national identity are far from neutral. Instead, claims of authenticity tend to hide more than they reveal. For every aspect of national unity that tequila is said to represent, there are numerous untold tales of exclusion and struggle. Simply put, over the last two centuries, tequila has meant different things to different groups of people. Mexican elites initially dismissed tequila as backward and cheap—preferring instead to drink cognac and other European beverages—while the poor and

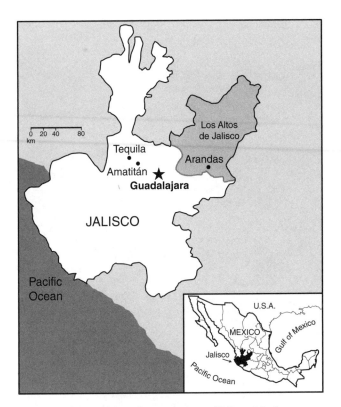

MAP 1. The tequila-producing regions of Jalisco, Mexico.

working classes embraced it as a symbol of resistance against the privileged classes. These associations would also evolve through cinema, in literature, on the radio, and within legislative measures. New meanings of tequila gained momentum through everyday channels where the components of *lo mexicano* were continually being forged.

Tracking Tequila

Analyzing tequila's production and consumption casts important light on some of the unfamiliar actors and episodes that influence—often behind the scenes—attributes of Mexicanness. Unraveling tequila's iconic reputation enables a better understanding of how the nation's sense of self evolved for both powerful and ordinary people. Commonplace items, such as bottle labels, provided clues that helped shape some of my initial queries. I wondered, for

FIGURE 1.   Field of blue agave in Tequila, Mexico. Photo by
Gwyn Fisher.

example, why images of the revolution played such an important role in contemporary tequila branding and advertising. This question, and others like
it, led me to a broader set of materials that provided information on tequila's
lesser-known travails, and, in the case of the revolution, its connection to the
infamous General Pancho Villa. Why was Pancho Villa heralded, in *corridos* (ballads) especially, as a tequila drinker? Given this popular association,
I started to consider how song lyrics and films from Mexico's "Golden Age"
of cinema (c. 1936–1969) could fill in some of the details that seemed nowhere
to be found, but that were often hinted at, in earlier historic works on tequila.

Over the course of two years, and then later during several follow-up visits
to Mexico, I talked to hundreds of individuals about tequila. During infor-

mal conversations in places like tequila-themed markets, the gym, or even on the city bus, I discovered that people had a lot to say about the topic. For instance, while in line for food at the *tianguis cultural* (a weekly artisanal market), a vendor told me of the rumors surrounding the beloved *ranchera* singer, Lucha Reyes, whose song "*La Tequilera*" (the female tequila drinker) served as a soundtrack for women who unapologetically drank tequila. In addition to the circumstances of her untimely and tragic death, there was also talk that the singer was a lesbian.

My interviews with individuals involved with formal aspects of tequila's culture (for example, tequila company owners, tour guides, agave farmers) likewise resulted in a treasure trove of information. Details such as learning about the increasing infighting among producers—especially the debate over whether officials should allow the manufacture of flavored tequila (for example, mango and strawberry)—deepened my understanding of the tensions inherent in the politics of tequila in the present day. As a participant observer, I spent a great deal of time in Tequila, Amatitán, Arandas, and Guadalajara, in particular locales where people interacted with tequila. For example, I took dozens of tequila distillery tours, attended formal tasting events, regulatory meetings, and tequila-themed conferences; I even enrolled in a university-sponsored tequila studies diploma program. I also hung out in cantinas and tequila-themed bars, oftentimes with friends but sometimes by myself. I frequented tequila-themed restaurants that offered tequila-based appetizers, desserts, and meals in addition to a large tequila selection. Whenever a free minute presented itself, I took written notes in my journal or on a napkin and sometimes audio-recorded my observations either at my table or in the bathroom.

I began this project initially thinking that I would focus on tequila's place in modern-day Mexico—I would spend most of my time in distilleries, talking to members of the official group that oversees the industry, the Tequila Regulatory Council—charting the spread of tequila's global popularity. I very quickly realized that such an approach was myopic; the meanings associated with tequila required a step back in time. Surprisingly, a deeper understanding also required a step across national borders. Heeding the insight of anthropologist Arjun Appadurai, I decided to follow tequila as a "thing in motion"[1] and consider the broad scope of its uses and values. I allowed myself (often reluctantly) to be surprised by the attributions, motivations, and human transactions that enhanced it with meaning.

When I one day typed the word *tequila* in a U.S. newspaper archive search engine, I discovered that it had its own history in the United States. Tequila had a transnational trajectory for more than a century before its formal entrée into the global marketplace. In the United States, tequila was endowed with divergent meanings, sometimes described as diabolical and sometimes proclaimed as distinguished. Journalists, scientists, and temperance activists warned of tequila's wicked and immoral attributes, while late-nineteenth- and early-twentieth-century immigrant entrepreneurs ran ads in Spanish-language newspapers announcing the arrival of their tequila shipments. Based on this information, I decided to expand the scope of my study and incorporate aspects of tequila's travels, which included analyzing magazine and newspaper articles and talking to American-based ethnic Mexican tequila drinkers. Applying a cross-border lens allowed me to better understand the contours of national and cultural identity. As I discovered, there was more to tequila than I expected.

Tequila and *Lo Mexicano*

No ordinary drink, tequila uniquely reflects Mexican society by linking the past to the present and transcending class boundaries, writes Alberto Ruy-Sánchez Lacy, editor of the popular book series, *Artes de Mexico*.[2] Echoing this enthusiasm, noted cultural critic Carlos Monsiváis describes tequila as embodying the visceral and symbolic aspects of what it means to be Mexican. Tequila, he muses, imprints *lo mexicano* wherever and whenever it is poured. In his words, tequila defines "the nation at play."[3] For these and other Mexican historians, writers, and poets, tequila is heralded as exemplifying and provoking a range of powerful sentiments: "temperance and excess, joy and sorrow, health and sickness, the celebration of life and the consummation of death."[4] To be sure, no other drink is as renowned or celebrated within Mexican popular culture.

Tequila is synonymous with the attributes that comprise what Mexican scholars (and other writers) call *lo mexicano*. *Lo mexicano*, or what I will interchangeably refer to as Mexicanness or *mexicanidad*, represents an idea, a sensibility, and the fiction that there exists a collective, unified Mexican national consciousness. The notion that there is one true way of being Mexican is an essentialist ideal that, although oftentimes reflecting well-intentioned sentiments, forecloses on diversity. Yet there is something intrinsically human about the quest for authentic identity. Whether it is about being part of a *genuine* ethnicity or being able to identify someone as a member of a *real* cultural group, we frequently employ ideas, like *lo mexicano*, as undeniable markers of reality. Much like sociological accounts that examine race or gender as social constructs—that is, as blurred categories that become distinct only through steady interaction and repetition—ideas of *lo mexicano* are actual in their ability to shape daily life despite their socially created qualities. The historical and present-day aspects of *lo mexicano* form what I call a *symbolic economy of identity*—a web of characteristics, relations, meanings, symbols, and intuitions that are understood to comprise Mexicanness.[5] Among its features are ideas associated with places, skin colors, languages, sexualities, emotions, costumes, dances, songs, actors, writers, foods, and drinks.

Cultural critics have long detailed the diverse attributes that comprise Mexicanness. Writers such as Octavio Paz and Samuel Ramos famously trace Mexican uniqueness to the psychic costs associated with the Spanish conquest and the birth of mestizo (people of combined European and indigenous descent) identity. Broadly speaking, Paz and Ramos focus on attributes such as treachery, isolation, and inferiority as influencing the Mexican personality and infringing on the country's ability to cultivate a "universal culture" that could "appropriately express [the nation's] spirit."[6] Other authors, such as Fredrick Turner, turn their attention away from assessing cultural shortfalls and analyze the structural dynamics that shape aspects of *lo mexicano*. Turner observes that foundational events such as the conquest, independence, and the revolution initiated significant changes in how Mexicans identified. Evidence of a new nationalism became apparent when mestizos and indigenous groups, once excluded in artistic, cultural, and political realms, were incorporated—at least partially—in dialogues of national cohesion. For Turner, the postrevolution period signified a turn toward egalitarianism that uplifted and unified the nation.

Skeptical of the consensus surrounding patriotic sagas, sociologist Roger Bartra warns against narratives that connect Mexican identity to the nationalist myths that emerged from the revolution. As he sees it, reflections on *lo mexicano*—especially those that developed within this postrevolution era—most often endorse the dominant political culture at the expense of less powerful actors. Authoritative accounts support a version of Mexicanness that is far from progressive, creative, or inclusive. Bartra further argues that when using metaphors to describe the "essence" of a unique Mexican imaginary, competing political and philosophical schools of thought erred in portraying Mexicans as collectively "melancholic."[7] Two separate representations of Mexicans—the first as timid, childlike, and lazy up until the revolution; and the second as violent, sentimental, and evasive as a result of modernization—relied on static but powerful stereotypes that later influenced the behavior of individuals and, in some cases, entire sets of people.

Sentiments and connotations of *lo mexicano* are often mobilized to fulfill particular political and economic agendas. At the same time, there are many possibilities associated with how people negotiate Mexicanness. For as much as large tequila companies strive to align themselves with certain accounts of *mexicanidad*, articulations of *lo mexicano* do not simply reflect top-down orientations. Indeed, even influential appropriations are diverse and contingent; they are capable of eliciting spontaneous emotion and signifying resistance.[8] Drinking a chilled shot of tequila in a large chain restaurant on Cinco de Mayo, a Chicana consumer may at once feel a sense of cultural refinement through her brand choice, feel a connection to her Mexican heritage, or feel empowered as a woman, bucking traditional stereotypes associated with tequila. All of these sentiments are possible because the meanings drawn from tequila are not solely reflective of individual taste, nor are they exclusively driven by tequila advertisers. People aren't monolithic: They draw on varied references and recognize different environmental cues when it comes to evaluating meanings associated with tequila.[9]

Place and Product

Tequila is named after its town of origin, Tequila, in the western state of Jalisco. The word likely comes from the Náhuatl *téquitl*, meaning work, duty, job, or task, and *tlan*, which means place.[10] Founded by the Spanish in 1530, the town of Tequila became exclusively associated with the drink only in the latter part of the nineteenth century. In the same period, the building of new roads better connected the town to surrounding communities and technological advancements in distillation made the drink more widely available. Deforestation of the valleys in and around Tequila in the nineteenth century enabled the expansion of agave harvesting. Strides made in packaging, especially the 1903 invention of the automated glass bottle-blowing machine, significantly boosted the industry's reach.[11] After Mexico gained independence from Spain in 1821, distilleries began to open in greater numbers in Tequila and in the neighboring towns of Amatitán and Magdalena. Over 100 operations were established, including well-known makers still in business today such as Viuda de Romero in 1852, Herradura in 1861, Orendáin in the 1870s, San Matías in 1886, and Centinela in 1904. The tequila industry continued to develop throughout the twentieth century.

The Mexican Revolution, perhaps more than any other period, is widely seen as endorsing and popularizing tequila. Historian José María Muriá explains that, when General Porfirio Díaz was overthrown in 1911, so too (at least temporarily) was the accompanying Francophilia that he and other elites espoused. Once the old regime was ousted, the entire country searched for "native expressions and customs to guarantee the strengthening of Mexican identity."[12] Tequila, it seemed, would emerge as one such expression and custom. The government itself participated in the portrayal of tequila as an evolving national icon; however, their efforts were challenged at home and abroad.

During the 1940s and 1950s, radio and cinema became new sites for struggles over tequila's representation, as the booming Mexican entertainment industry devoted a great deal of time and space elevating its image.[13] Radio advertising campaigns proclaimed that tequila was "a good, healthy drink," and the successful musical variety show *Noches Tapatías* was sponsored by Sauza Tequila for its twenty-five-year-run.[14] It was cinema, however, that most profoundly promoted the *ranchera* (western) genre (and consequently tequila) as central to Mexican identity. Anthropologist Alfonso Alfaro notes that, during this period, Mexicans of all social classes embraced the idea of the *rancho grande*—an idyllic setting with bougainvillea-draped buildings, fighting roosters, and sprightly horses. The bucolic beauty of this imagery tapped into the nation's nostalgic pulse as it sought to embrace modernity and its citizens began to express a new, shared understanding of Mexicanness.[15]

Cinema shaped stereotypes about Mexico by diffusing images of new cultural icons and objects on a massive scale never before possible. Central to the new repertoire of oft-repeated storylines was tequila's role as a "macho" drink. Movie directors and scriptwriters, in seeking to ensure that scenes were filmed in an authentic way, relied heavily on images of *charros*, ranchers, gunslingers, gamblers, drunkards, and Casanovas, each with "a bottle of tequila to hand."[16] Mexican cinema, and the songs, movie stars, and printed posters it produced, were important sites for amplifying tequila's notoriety and linking it to traditional notions of feminine and masculine *mexicanidad*. Although it was primarily male actors who imbibed—often too much—in local cantinas, at fiestas, and rodeos, female performers on and off screen drank tequila and challenged traditional mores that it was unladylike to drink in public.

Tequila's ubiquity in Mexican cinema heightened its ties to Mexican identity both within and outside of the nation. On the legislative front, industrialists began initiating steps to conserve tequila's association as an exclusively Mexican drink. In 1949, the first official norm (DGN-R9/64) was published outlining the formal definition of tequila and specifying its conditions of production. However, it was not until the ratification of the Lisbon Agreement in 1958, which created an international system of protective measures for appellation of origin products (goods that are trademarked as originating from a certain country or region), that a legal precedent was set for the preservation of foodstuff from particular places. Modeled on the French system of terroir, in Mexico, intellectual property designations are known as denominations of origin (DOs), and in 1974 the Mexican government awarded tequila the nation's first DO.[17] A number of other officially recognized safeguarding procedures followed: In 1994, the Official Mexican Standard for Tequila was established to regulate tequila's agricultural, industrial, and commercial processes. That same year, the Tequila Regulatory Council was formed to ensure that the policies outlined by the official standard were being observed and to promote tequila's culture, quality, and authenticity. Additionally, state administrators and industry elites have vigorously sought tequila's protection through numerous multilateral negotiations by demanding formal acknowledgment of tequila as a uniquely Mexican product.

The 1990s was a remarkable decade for the tequila industry; global sales more than doubled, making it the fastest growing liquor category in the world.[18] Within Mexico, from 1995 until 1999, national sales increased 120 percent.[19] A combination of factors contributed to its significant growth, including the institutionalization of stronger international protection measures. A transformed image, one that underscored quality, appealed to a broader field of drinkers, especially middle- and upper-class consumers, within and outside of Mexico.[20]

One result of the boom in sales was an unexpected agave shortage. Exacerbated by a fungal plague (*Fusarium oxisporum*), severe winter conditions in 1997, and shifts in the number of mature agave plants in any given year, from 1997 to 2000 the blue agave population decreased by 50.7 percent.[21] Together, increased demand and the agave shortage prompted a rise in the price of tequila, drawing global media attention.[22] The unforeseen jump in cost (between 60 and 70 percent) placed tequila in the price range of premium spirits like cognac and scotch. Yet not even rising prices could dampen tequila's popularity and close association with Mexican identity. During the height of the agave shortage, ethnobiologist Dr. Ana Valenzuela-Zapata of the University of Guadalajara explained to the *Boston Globe*, "Tequila has always been identified with national pride for us . . . It's hard for us to admit that our national product is in danger, but this is a problem that's getting worse."[23] If anything, the international media attention elevated tequila's reputation as a Mexican product, codifying its role as a symbol of *lo mexicano*.

Tequila's rising international popularity sparked a revived interest within Mexico in the places and people associated with its origin. Tourism became a new avenue of economic development for Tequila and neighboring Amatitán, home to the nation's three largest companies (Jose Cuervo, Sauza, and Herradura). By 1997, there were organized distillery tours and the Tequila Express, a train journey from the city of Guadalajara to the grounds of Herradura's hacienda, San José del Refugio. In addition to serving tequila-based drinks, the train offers live mariachi music and a generous selection of traditional Mexican cuisine. As part of the day's itinerary, tourists walk the distillery grounds and are introduced to the *jimador* (the loyal agave harvester) and Mayahuel (the Aztec agave goddess), two icons that have recently been incorporated into tequila's evolving mythical narrative. Other companies, such as Jose Cuervo, have sought to tap into the lucrative tourism industry. In 2003, it opened Mundo Cuervo—or Cuervo World. Included on its theme park–like grounds are a fully operating distillery, lush gardens, a concert venue, a bar, and a high-end boutique with artisanal offerings from around Mexico. Cuervo also established its own train line in 2012—the Jose Cuervo Express—which, like the Tequila Express, includes a guided tour and live entertainment. New sightseeing venues and excursions stoke touristic desire for a comfortable and old-fashioned encounter at the same time that they commodify ideas of Mexicanness within an otherworldly rural environment.

Taking a train tour to the tequila region is quite costly. However, the steep price tag has not deterred middle- and upper-class Mexican tourists, willing to pay upwards of several hundred dollars to take their families on a nostalgic journey to the Jaliscan countryside. Ironically, tequila was once widely considered a "common" or "cheap" drink, but its reputation has steadily evolved into a product that elicits patriotic pride. The shift from its lowbrow to respectable, and in some cases highbrow, status took place in part because of the formal and informal measures that established new paths for its national and global legitimacy. The formation of government-supported tequila associations, together with the subsequent legislation they endorsed, has shaped the perception of tequila as something other than unrefined.[24] Informal measures coalesced with the recognition of these formal validating bodies. For example, the creation of the Mexican Academy of Tequila Tasters—an organization of professional tequila tasters—also helped transform its image. With approximately seventy elected members, the group conducts blind taste tests and then ranks each product. The Mexican Academy of Tequila Tasters exclusively judges tequila made of 100 percent agave, as opposed to tequila *mixto*, made of 51 percent agave and 49 percent other sugars. In other words, only tequila made of 100 percent agave is deemed worthy for review. This led distillers to emphasize their pure agave products, further boosting the spirit's image.

Long-established cultural institutions contributed to the legitimization of tequila's shifting reputation. For example, in 2005–2006, the University of Guadalajara offered its first-ever diploma program in tequila studies. The five-month-long course was titled *El Tequila: Su Cultura y su Entorno* (Tequila: Its Culture and Surroundings) and met for eight hours a week. The class was co-taught by university professors from Guadalajara who specialized in a range of disciplines—sociology, cinema studies, anthropology, and biology. We were thirteen students in total, ten men and three women whose ages ranged from eighteen to sixty-five. Most had grown up in the state of Jalisco and were taking the class to improve their knowledge of tequila for business purposes. Some owned their own tequila brands, while others wanted to start their own companies; one classmate volunteered with a well-known charitable organization and taught Mexican culture classes to North American Christian missionaries; another worked as a university administrator and frequently enrolled in classes that interested him. That tequila was important enough to merit its own regimen of study by the nation's second-oldest university was so intriguing that a local newspaper ran a cover story.

Mexican officials and industry elites enthusiastically participated in the formal recognition of tequila's new status. The acquisition of place-based designations, such as the esteemed UNESCO World Heritage title for the Tequila-Amatitán valley, and the introduction of local tourism initiatives fashioned increasingly robust ideas pertaining to tequila's ties to modern Mexican identity. By pursuing protective international and domestic initiatives, Mexican state agencies and powerful tequila industrialists established legitimacy, asserted authority, and affirmed their role as defenders of both the nation and the tequila industry.

To be sure, a new standard of excellence was being applied to tequila, but it left little room for critique of or divergence from authoritative endorsements. In the process, less powerful groups of people, such as small-scale distillers, agave farmers, and the communities involved in the production of tequila were largely excluded from the financial gains that came along with its new standing. Big companies profited while poverty in the region increased.

Despite corporate efforts to portray tequila as a potent and long-standing symbol of Mexican identity—as a means of legitimizing their reputations and forwarding their own advertising agenda—consumers' impressions of tequila do not always align with official viewpoints. Formal truths seldom translate neatly to the real-world truths of people's lived experiences.[25] Tequila drinkers employ various strategies to interpret, critique, support, and engage with marketing strategies and dominant myths connected to the product. The shared codes of cultural identity communicated by tequila consumers—in Mexico and the United States—offer a glimpse into the diverse connotations that express and affirm what it means to be Mexican in the contemporary period.

Theorizing Things

Tequila is a thing, an object, a product that is manufactured and sold in the marketplace—what researchers refer to as a commodity. Although often conceptualized in broad or abstract terms, commodities like tequila are "rich with meaning and affect."[26] They create distinctions, establish difference, and tell us something about "who we are [and] how we connect to one another."[27] Consequently, how people relate to commodities is deeply rooted in the human experience. A source of meaning in people's daily interactions, commodities highlight the interplay between local culture and transnational contexts. Through them, people enact resistance, back the status quo, and assert individual and national identity.

However, the idea that commodities—and what people do with them—illuminate the complexities associated with industrial development and everyday life is relatively recent. For example, Daniel Miller contends, that while often overlooked by scholars, consumption is actually "the vanguard of history" and vital for the "radical rethinking of areas of already acknowledged importance such as economies and politics."[28] Commodities and consumption, Miller and others tell us, provide alternative perspectives on human motivation and enable greater exploration of both the social aspects of desire and the structural mechanisms that regulate taste. In short, today consumption is increasingly considered "good for thinking and acting in a meaningful way."[29]

Arjun Appadurai examines how things circulate, acquire meaning, and lose value under globalization and within specific historical milieus. By treating goods as though they are capable of leading social lives, Appadurai argues that the social dimension of stuff provides "glimpses of the way in which desire and demand, reciprocal sacrifice, and state power interact to create economic value in specific social institutions."[30] He asserts that commodities act as carriers of social history and cultural biography, easily transforming their meanings over time. Commodities and their consumption reflect more than just the exchange and creation of symbolic messages, as some scholars once claimed.[31] Instead, by attributing agency to things, Appadurai holds that consumption does not flow in one direction only—messages are sent and received simultaneously by consumers. As he sees it, we should follow objects because "their meanings are inscribed in their forms, their uses, their trajectories." By doing so, we are better able to "interpret the human transactions and calculations that enliven things."[32]

By following tequila's trajectories, I engage with interdisciplinary concerns central to the study of material culture and national identity. A growing body of research by anthropologists and historians demonstrates that studying objects is a way of acquiring a deeper understanding of the human dimensions of globalization, the ties that link the worlds of consumers and producers, and the expressions of individual and collective identities.[33] Although these and other scholars would agree that a commodity is a socialized thing and that consumption is "subject to social control and political redefinition,"[34] very little is known about their significance in shaping the dynamics of race, class, gender, and sexuality, some of the most critical aspects of everyday life. With a few exceptions, sociologists have been slow to contribute to discussions of commodities and consumption. One of my primary objectives is to begin to think more comprehensively about the *sociality* of things in relation to their uses and meaning-making attributes—such as the symbolic reinforcement of racial differences in pulque taverns in the colonial period or in setting out to prove one's heteronormative manliness by drinking in excess while in a cantina in Guadalajara.[35]

Analyzing seemingly inconsequential things like tequila offers an alternative panorama into people's alliances, struggles, and convictions—human experiences that sometimes fall between the cracks of traditional empirical engagement. Following tequila as it acquires and diffuses meaning allows for a greater understanding of how competing political ideologies and shifting economic priorities influence what a nation holds true about itself. Furthermore, tracking tequila's rise as Mexico's spirit provides a new vantage point, not only for understanding the intricacies of national identity but for gaining a greater appreciation of those views and voices of less powerful individuals who also contribute to the evolution of Mexico. The following chapters examine the circumstances that brought tequila to national prominence and keep it there in the present day.

FERMENTING STRUGGLES

Pulque, Mezcal, and Tequila

In 2003, the National Institute of Anthropology and History, in collaboration with state officials and the National Chamber of the Tequila Industry (NCTI), began the lengthy process of seeking U.N. Educational, Scientific and Cultural Organization (UNESCO) World Heritage recognition for the Amatitán-Tequila valley. Jalisco Secretary of Culture Sofía González Luna contributed the following statement to the official application:

> The cultural profundity of the agave landscape and the production of tequila harkens back to the very foundation of our nationality—for it fuses the closeness to nature and the land of the indigenous populations with the transforming and fundamental spirit of the Spanish settlers. From this union the spirit of a new culture was born, giving rise to the traditions and values that now characterize the Mexican people.[1]

Like many of the individuals that I met over the course of this project, González Luna described tequila's linkages to nature, heritage, and the idea of *lo mexicano*—an enduring national symbol that seamlessly (and romantically) reflects the nation's mestizo legacy.

Contrary to popular belief, tequila was not always a celebrated—let alone obvious—icon of Mexican identity. For most of the country's history, the agave-based drinks, pulque and mezcal, better reflected people's preferences. Pulque is a fermented, mildly alcoholic drink (between 3 and 4 percent) that was consumed by diverse ethnic groups for centuries before the arrival of the

Spanish. Despite its far-reaching popularity, pulque's close association with native identity and urban unrest made it an unlikely contender to symbolize the modernizing nation. Mezcal is a distilled and high-proof spirit (between 35 and 55 percent) that—according to recent findings—might have been produced in limited quantities when the Spanish landed in New Spain.[2] As distillation technologies evolved,[3] mezcal became associated with qualities of progress that made it a more appealing alcohol alternative for the growing colonial population. Although mezcal's reputation increased steadily, it too would lack what sociologist Pierre Bourdieu refers to as the "symbolic capital" necessary to represent the nation.[4] By the mid-nineteenth century, a certain type of mezcal from the Tequila region of western Mexico started to acquire distinction and would soon be known simply as "tequila." The tequila industry's ties to the city of Guadalajara and the state of Jalisco—and their status as possessing more European cultural attributes than indigenous ones—bolstered its standing as a product in its own right. However, its newly acquired prestige would also face challenges as nineteenth-century elites aligned themselves with European values, practices, and goods. Here, I explore how, by the beginning of the revolutionary period, tequila was in the best position to become Mexico's national spirit.

Agave in Mesoamerica

Pulque, mezcal, and tequila derive from the agave, also known as the maguey,[5] or the century plant.[6] Indigenous legends recorded by Mesoamerican and Spanish clergy relate stories about the origin of agave, pulque, and their interconnections. For example, the fifteenth century pre-Hispanic Nuttall codex described seventeen types of agave used by the Mixteca.[7] Spanish chronicler Fray Bernardino de Sahagún noted that the Olmeca credited male gods, including Tepuztecatl, Quatlapanqui, Tliloa, and Papaztactzocaca, with inventing pulque.[8] In his classic study of alcohol in ancient Mexico, Henry Bruman explained that the Huaxteca of northeast Mexico referred to the drink gods collectively as Ometochtli, or "Two Rabbit." In total, there were over 400 celestial deities linked to the agave-based brew.[9]

A mysterious and nurturing natural resource, agave sustained human life and its association with the moon complemented the sun's instinctual, rhythmic relationship with Earth.[10] Various indigenous groups adopted the virtues associated with the moon and applied them to their daily routines.

Attesting to these deeply held connections, the name *Mexico* comes from the Náhuatl words *metztli* (moon), *xictli* (navel), and *co* (place).[11] However, some have suggested stronger etymological ties, claiming that *Mexico* comes from the Náhuatl word *me xitl co*, whereby the root word *metl* relates directly to the maguey's (agave's) association with the moon.[12] Thus, depending on the source, Mexico means "place in the moon's navel" or "place in the maguey's navel."[13]

In precolonial civilizations, agave served a vital function in the organization of everyday life. Cultivated in many regions throughout Mexico, agave is described as the "universal understory upon which the later food resources were superimposed."[14] More than a source of sustenance, agave fibers were used for building homes, roofs, and walls; its leaves (or *pencas*) were used for making plates, paper, and rope.[15] Early Mesoamericans planted agave to delineate tracts of land and prevent alluvial erosion;[16] in treeless or deforested areas it served as the primary source of construction material.[17] As one scholar aptly put it, agave "thrive[d] and sustain[ed] human life."[18] Spanish colonizers were impressed by its numerous uses. The sixteenth-century writer José de Acosta went so far as to describe agave as *"el árbol de las maravillas"*—or "the tree of wonders."[19] Fray Francisco Jiménez explained that "with this plant alone, it seems enough to provide all things necessary to human life."[20] In his second letter to King Carlos V, explorer Hernán Cortés discussed both agave and pulque by explaining that the natives made "syrup from a plant which in the islands is called maguey [agave] . . . and from this plant they also make sugar and wine, which they likewise sell."[21] Despite their initial admiration, early impressions soon wore thin as the *"indios"* (the Spanish for "Indians") started to cause problems for the new arrivals.[22]

In pre-Hispanic times, pulque (*octli poliuhqui* in Náhuatl) was a sacred mixture in Aztec culture that only the elderly, nursing mothers, and the ruling class were allowed to drink during religious festivals.[23] Pulque provided vitamins and minerals (vitamin C, vitamin B, and carbohydrates); it was also used for medicinal purposes. More important, it served as a source of potable water in arid areas where water was scarce or contaminated.[24] Regardless of pulque's nutritive and healing qualities, there were limits on how much people could drink. Regulations dictated the size and number of cups allotted to different groups of people; for example, the elderly and nursing mothers had to use small cups, while children used even smaller ones.[25] The penalty for drunkenness involved public humiliations such as head shaving and beatings;

for repeat offenses of drunkenness, the punishment was death. Indigenous populations were cognizant of the potential danger that alcohol posed for their societies and incorporated a number of restrictive measures.[26]

With two ethnically distinct sectors of governance, the *república de los españoles* (Spanish nation) and the *república de los indios* (Indian nation),[27] the Spanish initially limited their interaction with indigenous communities and considered many of their habits and practices "nauseating, savage, and diabolic."[28] The consumption of pulque, with its bitter flavor, sour smell, and phlegmy texture, was among the local customs the Spanish found offensive.[29] Pulque's central role in religious ceremonies and public celebrations also concerned the Spanish. Imbibed to commemorate births, weddings, funerals, and warriors' rites of passage, it was common for drinking celebrations to last for several days.[30] Pulque was an important aspect of cultural life, not only because of its spiritual significance but because its consumption strengthened community bonds.[31]

Initial colonial accounts were riddled with "fantastic, hyperbolic, or fabulous tales that mythified the American countryside and nature."[32] The Spanish meticulously documented flora and fauna and compared new objects to those found in Europe. Detailed descriptions resulted in new taxonomies and systems of classifications.[33] Consequently, codices—the texts produced under the supervision of Catholic clergymen (and often unacknowledged Nahua consultants)—legitimized the aspirations of colonial expansion at the same time that they narrated an epic tale of discovery. From the perspective of early Spanish settlers, who considered themselves *gente de razón* (people of reason), pulque's centrality in the lives of the indigenous, whom they considered *gente sin razón* (people without reason), was evidence of their inferiority and "the cause of virtually all sins and social problems."[34] For example, a report included in the *Recopilación de leyes de los reynos de las indias* (a set of governing laws and codes) stated that, when Indians drank pulque in moderation, their actions could be tolerated. However, when they mixed pulque with certain roots, the drink then "deprived them of their senses," "inflame[d] the body," and "sicken[ed], stupefie[d], and kill[ed] them with the greatest of facility."[35] More deplorable still, under the influence of this mixture they engaged in carnal acts, became violent, and committed idolatries.[36] Simply put, the Spanish viewed pulque as embodying the moral inferiority of the native population and encouraging civil disorder.

In spite of its nutritive qualities and its use in a range of drinking practices, pulque, according to this and numerous other historical references, reinforced ideas about Indian savagery and provided a context for the Spanish to justify their efforts at conquering the native population.[37] Although Spanish elites expressed concern over indigenous drinking, non-elite colonists distilled agave, producing their own versions of mezcal—or what was more popularly known as *vino de mezcal* (mezcal wine). European experimentation with alcohol was common practice throughout the colonial world, as water was laden with bacteria and often unsafe to drink.[38] Accustomed to consuming large amounts of wine, the Spanish brought grapes to Mexico but were initially unsuccessful at cultivating these crops.[39] Other circumstances, including "loneliness, unfamiliar surroundings, the threat of foreign invasions, epidemiological disasters" were among the many uncertainties that led early European colonists to drink.[40] That colonists drank frequently, and presumably also drank in excess, seemed to elicit little concern among officials who reported to the crown. For less affluent settlers, the high cost of imported alcoholic beverages likely encouraged experimentation with local raw materials such as sugar cane and coconut palm.[41] Even with the increased availability of domestic products, Spanish elites continued to hold onto their Old World drinking habits and exclusively drank imported wine and sherry.[42]

Documentation on the manufacture of mezcal during the colonial period details the taxes garnered and the names of those who applied for licenses. For instance, in 1608, the governor of Nueva Galicia (present-day Jalisco, Nayarit, and southern Sinaloa) imposed a tax on mezcal as a means of competitively protecting imported Spanish alcohol.[43] Beyond these records, very little is known about the production of mezcal and other distilled drinks during the first two centuries of colonial rule. What is known, however, is that by the early eighteenth century the commercial spirit industry began to emerge in Europe and in the Americas.[44] During this time, rum sales started to outpace beer and ale in the colony of New England.[45] In Mexico, improvements in distillation led to greater access to mezcal. These circumstances possibly contributed to the overall growth in mezcal production; however, unlike rum, mezcal did not surpass the popularity of pulque. Throughout the 1700s, the production of fermented and distilled agave products increased in scale and, for the latter, evolved into a commercial enterprise.

Adaptation, *Castas*, and Control

Spanish angst about alcohol consumption among indigenous and mestizo populations was tied to their concern about religious conversion, as a society that valued intoxication over abstinence was less likely to adopt the doctrines of Christianity. Missionaries aggressively set out to baptize natives, only to realize that they sometimes combined aspects of their former faiths with Christianity or reverted to their pagan practices.[46] The destruction of Mesoamerican temples and the initiation of baptism were not enough to fully or neatly indoctrinate the diverse ethnic communities into Christianity. As one Franciscan missionary explained, Yucatan Indians were "a simple people" who were "up to any mischief" because, in spite of the theological efforts of friars, they continued to partake in the rites and ceremonies that involved pulque.[47] Apprehension regarding religious conversion in relation to drinking habits during the colonial period was not limited to Mexico. Historian Frederick Smith reports that, in the Caribbean, indigenous populations (and later slave populations) were often described as more inclined to drunkenness, thievery, and idleness. Smith argues that these reports were likely embellished because missionaries needed to explain and justify their failure at converting the Carib to Christianity.[48] "Mischief" or not, native populations throughout the New World (to the dismay of the Spanish) negotiated the arrival of foreign religious doctrines into their cultural practices at their own pace. Not only did the Spanish miscalculate the ease with which religious adaptation would occur; they also underestimated pulque's spiritual, physiological, and ceremonial importance to native communities.[49]

Colonists' desire to convert the native populations was exceeded only by their aspiration to secure their social status. In Spain, the wealthy ate food that reflected their privileged position in society and distinguished them from those of different religious or ethnic backgrounds.[50] Food products that crossed the Atlantic to accommodate the colonizers' penchant for European ingredients included olive oil, capers, saffron, and fruits preserved in brandy.[51] Eating Spanish food rather than the local fare was not a simple indication of taste preference—social rank was intimately linked to what one consumed, especially in the anxiety-ridden colony. In ruling over a racially diverse populace, privileged Spaniards feared being perceived that they were "going native"—any hint of adopting indigenous customs could be interpreted as undermining the legitimacy of their status.[52] Increased cultural mixing threatened the regimented class and racial hierarchy. If elite colonists abandoned their Spanish heritage by consuming Indian beverages, it would be only a matter of time before strict class lines were challenged or, worse, eliminated.

Rigid class and racial boundaries loosened—but remained important—as creoles and Spanish lived and worked among diverse ethnic communities. The decreased ability to visually determine someone's class from his or her phenotype was especially troublesome. Intent on reinforcing their dominance, beginning in the eighteenth century, Spanish elites began commissioning a series of *casta* (literally, the Spanish for "caste") paintings that denoted an elaborate system of racial classification that emphasized Spanish superiority.[53] Originally, *castas* illustrated men and women of different races with one or two of their children. Also included were written descriptions that identified the race of their offspring. Portraying racial differences in a range of social circumstances and public spaces,[54] these taxonomies served as a cataloging system not just for subsets of people but for objects: flora, fauna, and food products.[55] *Casta* paintings were sent to Spain, where elites could whet their appetite for information about mysterious New World "others."[56] Like other exotic foodstuffs, such as corn and cacao, pulque was a common artistic subject through which racial hierarchies were solidified.

In 1822, one year after Mexican independence from Spain, *casta* designations were banned from official use in legal documents,[57] but nineteenth-century artwork continued to serve political functions, especially when it came to elevating the desired characteristics of the populace.[58] For example, José Obregón's 1869 painting, *The Discovery of Pulque,* depicts a pre-Hispanic legend in which King Tecpancaltzin is presented with a bowl of newly discovered pulque by Xochítl, a young peasant woman (see Figure 2). Accompanied (presumably) by her parents and trailed by a woman carrying an agave plant (standing on the far left), the scene metaphorically illustrates the relationship among nature, culture, and order within European aesthetic conventions. The light-skinned features of Xochítl and Tecpancaltzin suggest an attempt to visually "civilize" the native populations. Xochíl's genteel pose, together with her indigenous offering to the king, implies her sexual availability and willingness to comply with dominant power arrangements that delineate the colonizer from the colonized.[59] When represented as functioning

FIGURE 2. *The Discovery of Pulque* by José Obregón, 1869.
Source: De Agostini/Getty Images. Reprinted with permission.

members of society, indigenous people were depicted as living in the political and social structures similar to those of European culture. Under these
circumstances, "barbaric" Aztecs became orderly and noble subjects in the
artist's "classical spectacle."[60]

Nineteenth-century paintings and early observations by Spanish writers
reveal the intensity through which elites sought to assimilate indigenous populations within a familiar and hierarchal colonial framework. These examples
call attention to the deep symbolism attributed to pulque as the epitome of
indigeneity. Consequently, native people's consumption of pulque was seen
not as a choice but as evidence of their inherently aberrant dispositions—
traits that were used to justify Spanish superiority.[61] Although the Spanish
made every effort to force diverse ethnic communities "neatly into a European
world of laws and social relations," their attempts at full and swift indoctrina-
tion did not always work out as planned.[62]

Regulation, Women, and the Public Sphere

By the seventeenth century, pulque's strictly religious connotations had diminished. As it was no longer an exclusively indigenous product, the growing mestizo and mulatto population, in combination with non-elite Spanish colonists, imbibed the local brew and frequented *pulquerías* (pulque taverns). The commercial development of pulque ushered in new employment opportunities for women of different social backgrounds. A 1608 ordinance stipulated that no more than one law-abiding elderly Indian woman be licensed to sell pulque for every 100 customers.[63] Laws enacted in 1635 and 1639 specified that two women were permitted to sell pulque to the four Indian residential areas of Mexico City and one woman for towns within a five-league (approximately thirteen-mile) radius of the city.[64] In villages, peasant women were exclusively in charge of its distribution. If villages had few or no *pulquerías*, women sold pulque from the doorways of their homes.

Colonial elites continued to drink imported alcohol instead of pulque. However, selling the brew was another matter altogether. Illegal taverns, which comprised nearly half of all drinking establishments in Mexico City, were mostly run by married Spanish women known as *cuberas*. These *cuberas* purchased unsanctioned (that is, untaxed) pulque from customs officials or Indians who lived outside of the city and privately cultivated agave.[65] Indigenous and mestiza women skirted the authorities by buying sour pulque from legal *pulquerías*, adding it to *tepache* (a pineapple rind beverage), and reselling it as an alcoholic version of *tepache*. To the frustration of authorities, these clandestine operations not only evaded taxes but lowered the price of alcohol at illegal taverns, which reduced consumption at legal *pulquerías*.[66] Hence, the manufacture and sale of pulque enabled women of various backgrounds to tap into new economic and social possibilities; it also allowed women from the countryside to adapt to urban life and learn to navigate the challenges of colonial rule.[67]

Various legislative measures show that, to the likely disapproval of authorities, women frequented *pulquerías* as customers. Seen as centers of disorder and transgression, *pulquerías* attracted large crowds of "common" people, especially during religious festivals and holy days of obligation.[68] According to officials, excessive pulque consumption led to sexual indiscretions, including adultery and incest. To control such offences, the crown passed ordinances requiring the mandatory segregation of women and men consumers in *pul-querías*.[69] However, in 1752, colonial administrators ended this regulation because it became increasingly difficult to separate husbands and wives, fathers and daughters, and brothers and sisters.[70] Drinking pulque in clandestine places outside the view of authorities was a far greater danger than the threat of men and women socializing in a public space.

The mixing of opposite sexes in *pulquerías* was only one of many concerns that fueled the Spanish drive for full control of indigenous drinking habits during the early colonial period. Clerics preached against the local practice of drinking to stimulate vomiting and enacted laws forbidding the sale of alcohol to native peoples.[71] Spanish chroniclers spent a substantial amount of time documenting local drinking practices. One reason for their preoccupation is related to how the Spanish and native populations viewed alcohol and defined moderation. The Spanish equated grape wine as a sacred symbol of Catholic heritage—it embodied the customs of a culture that they aimed to honor and represent in the New World.[72] For example, one friar described wine as "a drink venerated and honored by Christ; and as the most noble of drinks, He chose to transform it into His most precious blood."[73] The Spanish also followed the Mediterranean custom of drinking with meals and being able to "hold" their liquor. Within this context, maintaining one's sober demeanor was associated with religious piety and the virtues of restraint. Indigenous populations defined moderation according to the appropriateness of an occasion (for example, ceremonial practices or religious rituals) rather than the amount of alcohol consumed. Hispanic studies scholar Tim Mitchell suggests that, within Aztec society, drinking rituals were actually "proestablishment" and legitimated the elite's governing role.[74] That drinking quite possibly supported—and did not challenge—the status quo was lost on the Spanish.

Condemnation and concern about native drinking habits was evident throughout the colonial period. The Spanish passed numerous laws restricting the sale and consumption of pulque and even went so far as to institute corporal punishment for the crime of inebriation.[75] Authorities often attributed indigenous insurrections to pulque. Instead of admitting to not providing enough grain for sustenance, colonial officials blamed the "seditious effects" of pulque as the reason why diverse ethnic populations rioted in central Mexico City.[76] Some officials even went so far as to make distinctions among different types of pulque. For example, Spanish scientists maintained that white, or pure, pulque was acceptable, but pulque mixed with roots was dangerous.[77] From this perspective, the mixing of ingredients, much like the mixing of different races, was seen as violating the crown's commitment to blood purity (*limpieza de sangre*)—a concept that ensured their authority over inferior racial groups (that is, *indios*, blacks, mestizos, and mulattos).[78]

The popularity of *pulquerías* continued to spread. In 1763 there were forty-five legal *pulquerías* in operation throughout Mexico City, most located on the outskirts where native peoples and poor mestizos resided.[79] Some establishments accommodated up to 600 people and included extensive seating areas that encouraged customers to assemble and relax.[80] *Pulquerías* were much more than places to consume alcohol; they played an integral role in the lives of the lower classes and served as sites of leisure, where locals could meet, gossip, sing, and drink with family and friends. Inside, neighborhood and working networks were formed and enhanced; class and ethnic solidarities were reinforced.[81] *Pulquerías* functioned as a supportive and restorative institution in a society burdened by concerns over employment, food, housing, and contagion, all while being ruled by a repressive and proselytizing colonial government.[82]

Drawing a steady set of returning customers, *pulquerías* likewise attracted food vendors and musicians; inside the establishments activities included dancing, card playing, and gambling.[83] Spanish authorities considered *pulquerías* dangerous not only because they were centers of depravity, disorder, and crime but also because a large number of male and female *indios*, mestizos, and mulattos congregated there.[84] *Pulquerías* were thus deemed "dark, ambiguous spaces" where members of the opposite sex could cavort in public and people from different race and class backgrounds could convene to ruminate over the hardships of life under colonial rule or, worse, plan subversive action.[85] According to some reports, officials had every right to be concerned: One document noted that a group of mulattos were overheard making the toast, "To our health and that next year we will be governing the kingdom."[86]

Mexico City officials sought to limit sales of pulque to licensed taverns and tried to control drinking and social interaction within *pulquerías*.[87] However, even when city ordinances prohibited gambling, dancing, and the selling of food, little heed was paid to the rules. Barely half of all drinking establishments in Mexico City were sanctioned by authorities, yet compared to the taverns in the countryside, drinking in the capital city was fairly well structured in terms of providing a stable supply for a steady stream of customers.[88]

Pulquerías in Mexico City sold enough pulque to serve 62,000 customers daily.[89] Although there is some debate over the accuracy of these claims,[90] it is safe to assume that Mexico City was "a growing, impersonal, socially and economically heterogeneous urban center"—where old-fashioned rural norms guiding what, when, and how much people drank were loosened.[91]

More than a place of refuge from the confines of village life, Mexico City attracted traders and a growing class of urban laborers who worked in the surrounding mining areas.[92] While poor residents—*indios*, mestizos, and mulattos—frequented *pulquerías*, "persons of honor and decency" who enjoyed pulque were unable to patronize the locales without being vilified by fellow righteous citizens.[93] Yet population growth created demand for more drinking establishments. During the late eighteenth century, the number of *pulquerías* remained stable while the number of *viñaterías* (locales that sold distilled liquor) rose significantly.[94] Initially, *viñaterías* were considered reputable establishments where Spaniards and creoles (those of Spanish lineage who were born in New Spain) could avoid the "coarse riffraff" who frequented *pulquerías*.[95] After they were legalized in 1796, the number of *viñaterías* went from 194 in 1784 to 593 in 1800 and then to 784 in 1807, an increase of 304 percent.[96]

Efforts to curtail drinking among the growing urban lower classes did not stop Spanish and creole elites from eventually entering the pulque market. The commercial production of pulque became worthwhile to the Spanish only when consumers with disposable incomes could expect return on their investment in equipment, labor, and land.[97] Much like their takeover of other traditional indigenous foodstuff such as cacao, the early to middle colonial period was marked by the Spanish securing their economic stronghold in the New World. Spanish elites extended their power by gaining control of the means of production even when the consumption of particular products was considered deplorable.[98] Of the many new cultural relations, responses, and encounters taking place during this period, one association remained clear and constant: Drinking pulque was synonymous with "backward" populations.

The Rise of Guadalajara

Regardless of measures to outlaw or restrict alcohol use, by the end of the eighteenth century officials had no choice but to accept its place in society. The failure of alcohol reforms, in combination with a growing class of agave and pulque *hacendados* (members of the landed class), prompted a shift in government strategy, one that moved from regulation to taxation. Agave cultivation and the alcohol trade were lucrative, especially for *hacendados* who had the resources to support every stage of the business, from growing agave to manufacturing spirits.[99] In 1811, Alexander von Humboldt observed that a proprietor who owned 30,000 to 40,000 agave plants was "sure to establish the fortune of his children," while nobles were making up to 46,000 pesos a year in profit from cultivation sales.[100] Increased yields resulted in considerable tax revenue for the crown.[101] What is more, the duty placed on pulque produced proceeds for war expenses, salaries for prison employees, and funds for street maintenance repairs.[102] Although these taxes primarily helped maintain colonial hegemony, they also funded more general infrastructural improvements. As the pulque market continued to develop in Mexico City and its surrounding areas, in the western part of the country the production of mezcal continued to evolve into a commercial enterprise.

Western Mexico in general, and the Guadalajara region in particular, emerged as an attractive urban alternative to Mexico City because of their diverse agriculture and large areas of undeveloped land. Guadalajara differed from Mexico City in the manner it was colonized and in the organization of its socioeconomic structure. Mexico City was a primarily indigenous urban center, while Guadalajara was historically associated with the provincial hacienda system.[103] Local indigenous populations swiftly succumbed to Nuño de Guzmán's violent two-year colonizing campaign (1530–1532) throughout Nueva Galicia (which included Jalisco). Historian Richard Lindley described his attack as particularly fierce: "His cruelty was so notorious that even his hardened military peers condemned the wholesale slaughter he perpetuated in the Northwest."[104] Guzmán's greed-driven pillage killed most of the local population while others fled, resulting in widespread loss of communal land rights. As a result, the remaining indigenous residents posed little challenge to the establishment of the colonial hacienda.[105] With its "vast tracts of abandoned, uncultivated land"[106] and semiarid climate, Guadalajara was characterized by the new and more self-sufficient hacienda system (large agricultural estates) rather than the *encomienda* system (forced system of labor enslavement) under which Spaniards were granted control over indigenous towns and the right to require tribute.

Throughout the eighteenth and nineteenth centuries, haciendas played a major role in rural social life, and often their populations surpassed those of towns. Even though they were located outside of urban areas, haciendas were integrally connected to the city through the trade of agricultural commodities and cash crops, including agave and tobacco. Among these products was the distilled agave spirit, mezcal. According to historian José Maria Muriá, in the early part of the seventeenth century Pedro de Tagle, Marquis of Altamira and Knight of the Order of Calatrava, moved to the town of Tequila and established a mezcal wine factory. Described as the "father of tequila,"[107] de Tagle is often heralded as the first person to introduce formal agave cultivation and mezcal production to the region.[108]

By the end of the eighteenth century, various incarnations of mezcal were produced for local use in areas across Mexico, from as far north as Sonora and as far south as Oaxaca, where there were plentiful supplies of agave. Sociologist Rogelio Luna observes that, during this same period, mezcal from the Tequila region experienced steady growth and started gaining a favorable reputation. In particular, he identifies three reasons that explain its expansion and increased popularity during this period. First, powerful hacienda owners and wealthy creoles were eager to invest in agave because of the low cost associated with its cultivation. Second, the undeveloped area near Tequila began to transform into a specialized region that offered an abundance of available resources and raw materials. Finally, the success of the booming mining industry in and around Guadalajara and the economic decline of cities like Puebla and Cholula brought new interest and capital to Guadalajara and the tequila-producing region.

Guadalajara's "provincial" yet "variegated, expansive, and prosperous" economic base distinguished it from other cities throughout the country.[109] Compared to its modest size in 1600, by 1800 the city had transformed into a "handsome urban center" complete with a university, new marketplaces, and the architecturally innovative Cabañas orphanage.[110] Income from the lucrative Bolaños silver mine, the region's grain and cattle markets, and its "role as western Mexico's premier administrative and ecclesiastical center" contributed significantly to Guadalajara's flourishing local economy;[111] it also became home to one of the New World's only *consulados*, or royal merchant guilds.[112] Venture-seeking elites' interests peaked as news of new investment possibilities made its way to Mexico City. The working classes were also attentive to the changes happening in Guadalajara, especially the need for skilled labor instigated by the city's prosperity. By 1822, one-third of the city's population was comprised of migrants from other regions.[113]

Despite the growing diverse populations moving into Guadalajara, the city was residentially differentiated by race. Class and occupation likewise played a part in the structure of separation. Although the Spanish, indigenous ethnic populations, creoles, mulattos, and mestizos intermingled in public spaces, in their private lives the native peoples retreated to their quarters in the suburbs, the artisans went to their boardinghouse lodging, and more affluent residents retired to their well-appointed abodes situated in close proximity to city plazas.[114] Topographically, along the northern and eastern areas of Guadalajara ran the San Juan de Dios River, which created a deep ravine in the city's geography. This ravine further contributed to the organization of housing across racial and class lines because "from the earliest times Indians and mestizos settled across the ravine to the east, thus forming an 'across the tracks' area."[115]

Northeast of Guadalajara, the Los Altos region (which includes the towns of Arandas and Lagos de Moreno) also played an important role in Jalisco's economic and political development. Los Altos was strategically located on one of two routes that the Spanish established to facilitate commercial and military transport. In the sixteenth century, this network of roads became even more significant when it was used to deliver newly discovered silver from Zacatecas to Mexico City. Once the network of roads in Los Altos became integrated into the circuits of colonial commerce, the Spanish began to settle the region's interior.[116] The racial makeup of the population, like that of neighboring Guadalajara, was greatly affected by colonial warfare. From 1540 to 1542 native tribes, including the Téules, Caxcanes, and Cuexes (collectively called Chichimecas), fought but were eventually defeated by the Spanish in the Mixtón War.[117] Under the command of Viceroy Antonio de Mendoza, Spanish forces carried out "exemplary punishment,"[118] killing or selling into slavery the conquered indigenous ethnic combatants. The outcome of the war and the subsequent retribution that followed enabled "Spanish colonization in Los Altos *sans* miscegenation."[119] In the 1930s, historians and other intellectuals would begin to mythologize the racial purity and whiteness of Alteños (residents of Los Altos) in an attempt to create an ideal citizenry that would help modernize the nation after the revolution.

In contrast, Mexico City was necessarily more racially mixed. Before the arrival of the Spanish, it was the site of the Aztec capital Tenochtitlan and had a population of several hundred thousand. During the early years of colonization, the Spanish relied heavily on the local labor force that lived in close proximity to the city. Therefore, the sheer size of Mexico City, in combination with the colonizers' dependence on indigenous workers, impeded total division based on race.[120] When the Indian population decreased as a result of disease, Spanish officials in Mexico City were more resigned to the city's racial diversity as "the desired division of labor—Spanish merchants and property owners, Indian laborers, black slaves and domestic servants—rapidly eroded."[121] By the beginning of the nineteenth century, Guadalajara and its neighboring regions differed from Mexico City with regard to its wealth, industry, design, and structure of racial separation.

Differences in the history and organization of the two cities manifested symbolically in cultural associations. For example, unlike the pulque produced in and around Mexico City, mezcal from the Guadalajara area emerged amid a period marked by new capital investment, growth in local industry, and the increased importance of Guadalajara as a thriving metropolitan center. Whereas pulque symbolized the widespread complications and chaos associated with daily life in the colonial period,[122] mezcal signified the stability of hacienda life as it unfolded parallel to the growing prominence of the city. In other words, for elites, pulque signaled a failure on their part to control the native populations and manage urban expansion on their terms. Conversely, mezcal reflected their ability to contain the indigenous population (through their elimination, via the exploitation of their labor on ranches or by way of their isolation on haciendas) while enjoying urban conditions that were similar to European standards. Furthermore, the Spanish considered the consumption of more "modern" drinks (such as distilled spirits) as evidence of the superiority of "Western and bourgeois morality."[123] Thus, mezcal from the Tequila region not only represented a relatively successful balance of country and city life but materially embodied the characteristics of progress that allowed elites to preserve old social boundaries and construct new ones within the context of the evolving colonial economy.

The Development of the Mezcal Market

Mezcal production under the hacienda system thrived because of the availability of land and labor to grow and harvest agave. Even though haciendas were typically characterized by maize and animal production, shifting dietary demands of the growing urban consumer class prompted the cultivation and manufacture of higher-priced products such as wheat, sugar, and liquor.[124] In comparison to many agricultural crops, agave is durable and requires minimal upkeep, despite its seven- to ten-year maturation period. Jalisco's semiarid climate and wide variety of indigenous agave (*agave silvestre*), in combination with the low cost of harvesting and distillation, provided incentive to produce mezcal.[125] Because agave was plentiful, easy to maintain, and profitable, small ranch owners were also able to participate in its cultivation. Mexican independence from Spain in 1821 spawned even greater industry growth as Spanish liquor imports were suspended.[126] The inaccessibility of Spanish goods provided new opportunities for the commercial expansion of the mezcal market.

Independence severely affected how Mexicans understood themselves collectively in light of their new identity as a country. In 1825, the first formal observance of Independence Day (September 16) took place in Mexico City. A number of symbolic gestures played a crucial part in the festivities, including dances, processions, and speeches.[127] A new set of uniquely Mexican customs was beginning to emerge. Conservative Mexicans, however, spoke highly of the "civilizing" aspects of Spanish laws and culture, which they claimed help prepare Mexico for independence.[128] Elites continued to make judgments based on what people consumed. For example, in the decades following independence, upper-middle- and middle-class women in Mexico City were fascinated by European cuisine and prepared dishes such as veal blanquette and beef à la mode.[129]

Cookbooks of the period reflected the trend toward European recipes but often included alternative methods of preparation that aligned with Mexican culinary cultural styles and flavors. On one end of the spectrum, elites continued to pursue "the delicacies of continental cuisine,"[130] while, further down the scale, the middle classes were more open to experimenting with hybrid dishes. On the other end, the poor and working classes spent little time obsessing over European recipes and instead worried about how to feed their families. Those who could not afford to buy meat drank pulque for nourishment[131]—a practice that led the Mexico City council to raise taxes on alcohol and lower them on meat so as to encourage the poor to eat more and drink less.[132] Indeed, in the nascent stages of imagining a new national identity, what people consumed continued to index racial and class distinctions.

Growth in commerce also affected how people started to collectively understand themselves as Mexican. The closure of the port of Acapulco in the state of Guerrero led to an increase of commercial traffic in and out of the port of San Blas in Nayarit.[133] Travelers and merchants who passed though the western route from Guadalajara came in contact with mezcal and the agave countryside. For foreigners seeking exotic and extraordinary situations, encountering fields of agave was a visually stunning and noteworthy experience.[134] For example, in 1850, American writer Bayard Taylor dramatically described approaching the town of Tequila:

> After riding two hours in the hot afternoon sun . . . a sudden turn disclosed to me a startling change of scenery. From the depth of the scorched hills, I came at once upon the edge of a bluff . . . Below and before me extended a plain of twenty miles in length, entirely covered with fields of the maguey [agave]. At my feet lay the city of Tequila . . .[135]

In 1830 there were nine documented distilleries operating in Tequila, some of which were owned by members of the Cuervo, Orendain, and Sauza families. In that same year, the taxes generated by production equaled 24 percent of the total rent collected by the state government.[136] Several decades later in 1897, there were forty-five haciendas in Jalisco producing mezcal.[137] The state of Jalisco and the city of Guadalajara benefited substantially from the revenues garnered from the tax on mezcal. By 1918, more than a thousand pesos a day were being collected, despite protest from manufacturers that the tax burden endangered the future of the industry.[138] The tax earnings are credited with the construction of the era's most elaborate buildings, including the Government Palace and the Bethlehem Hospital.[139] Subsequently, the production of mezcal from Tequila played a significant role in establishing Guadalajara's infrastructure and securing its place as one of the most vibrant cities in Mexico.

Mezcal production in the Tequila region emerged within an economic and politically distinct context from the mezcal production that was taking place in other parts of the county. The area's close proximity to and relationship with Guadalajara ensured a steady flow of interest and investment into Jalisco, especially in comparison to the primary mezcal-producing locale of Oaxaca.[140] Labor arrangements, ethnic diversity, and land ownership were among the few characteristics that distinguished the two states. In marked contrast to the authority exercised by haciendas in states like Jalisco, native populations in Oaxaca were more self-sustaining and economically independent and held enough land "to escape the paternalism of hacienda life."[141] At the beginning of the nineteenth century, the indigenous population (88 percent) managed most of the region's resources. Indigenous towns not only owned and maintained the majority of Oaxaca's acreage, but they often controlled and regulated significant sectors of the internal market.[142] Communal land rights made them less susceptible to privatization and allowed them to retain a high level of autonomy. Because indigenous residents were seen as unlikely to embrace the idea of private property, Oaxaca was a less attractive alternative to investors, both local and foreign. The state's policy on communal land was interpreted by elites as antithetical to expansion and progress.[143] According to their perspective, the values of private property would "civilize" the *indios*, stimulate development, eliminate their crude customs, and "transform them into virtuous and hardworking citizens of the Mexican Republic."[144]

As the manufacture of mezcal in Jalisco started to modernize and become more efficient, the production of mezcal in Oaxaca remained characterized by dated procedures and equipment.[145] One historian observes that, during the mid- to late 1890s,

> We see the introduction of technical advances in the state of Jalisco, and in particular . . . Tequila, namely the implementation of a modern system that made use of optimal, high-usage distillation equipment that crushed agave and extracted juice using mechanical machines and high power presses. Unlike this situation, in the state of Oaxaca, no new technologies were introduced, and as a result, they continued making mezcal using artisanal methods.[146]

Modernization, and the economic benefits that it prompted, varied substantively from one region to another. In a period when Mexican politicians, elites, and intellectuals sought out cultural examples and practices that not only embraced but illustrated the nation's commitment to modernity, mezcal from the state of Jalisco and *not* from Oaxaca better embodied the progressive attributes valued by those in power.

The reciprocal relationship between the region of Tequila (as a supplier of tax revenue) and the city of Guadalajara (with its thriving local economy and its flourishing reputation for industry) caught the attention of investors eager to capitalize on the area's profitable momentum. Within this context, mezcal from Tequila began to emerge as a product with its own unique status. Guadalajara's distinctive standing as a city separated along racial lines, one whose image was seen as more Spanish and creole than Indian or mestizo, also strengthened tequila's rising reputation, as elites and government officials continued to embrace the racial philosophies of the colonial period by favoring European products over indigenous ones. Despite these evolving distinctions, poor and working-class Indians and mestizos carried on with their lives, preserving those daily practices and rituals that were important to them. Families kept on producing pulque and other mezcal drinks for their households or for the local market.[147]

At the same time that the production and consumption of mezcal began to increase, in Mexico City pulque drinking slowly began to decrease. Although pulque consumption initially rose significantly in the period following the conquest, average individual intake declined—or more likely leveled out—in the years leading up to Mexico's independence from Spain. Indigenous drinks were being displaced by other so-called modern drinks, including beer that was manufactured by European brewers in northern Mexico.[148] Another possible explanation for the decline is that daily alcohol consumption became a more marginalized practice in everyday city life. Contemporary ideas regarding the evils of alcohol once reserved for subordinate groups started to become applicable to the broader population in the nineteenth century as the medical establishment began to pathologize habitual drinking. Yet, pulque sales remained steady. For instance, after independence, the number of legal *pulquerías* increased, suggesting that many illegal shops became authorized during this period. Regardless, pulque's reputation as a commoner's drink would become even more tied to negative connotations as Mexican elites began, in a more persistent fashion than before, to force a European cultural framework on the entire nation.

Distinction and Discord

In 1862, prompted by President Benito Juárez's suspension of interest payments on foreign loans, French forces landed in Veracruz with the intention of conquering Mexico. While the United States was embroiled in civil war (1861–1865), France, with the support of local Mexican elites, appointed Emperor Maximilian I to Mexico. Although suffering an initial defeat in Puebla on May 5, 1862 (now celebrated as *Cinco de Mayo*), the French successfully established a limited monarchy. Once the American Civil War ended in 1865, the United States sent supplies to help the republican army and ordered the French to remove their forces from Mexico. By the end of 1867, the French withdrew their troops, the republic was restored, and President Juárez returned to power. Following this period of political crisis, commercial *hacendados*, agro-exporters, and manufacturers continued to hold the vast majority of power in Mexico. Together, these industrial-focused groups sought to associate themselves with trade and foreign capital.

Infrastructural improvements such as the 1873 expansion of the *Ferrocarril Mexicano* (the Mexican railroad) provided greater access to different products—goods like pulque totaled 30 percent of all cargo on the new line that connected Mexico City to Veracruz.[149] Between 1880 and 1892, the continued construction of railroads, including the *Ferrocarril Interoceánico* and the *Ferrocarril de Hidalgo y Nordeste*, likewise made distribution more efficient. However, because pulque spoiled quickly, its transport was limited to distances within a few hours from where it was produced. Due to this material constraint, pulque could not withstand the journey to the United States, consequently preventing its entrance into the international export market. The development of the railroad system increased demand for distilled drinks, and hacienda owners happily acquiesced and planted more agave.[150] By 1898, a western railroad line ran through several villages, including Cocula (the birthplace of mariachi music)[151] and Tequila, with a direct line back to Guadalajara. Although much of the country enjoyed the economic benefits of transportation networks, the state of Oaxaca still relied on one stagecoach service route (from Oaxaca to Puebla), which itself was inaugurated only in 1875 and took three days to complete.[152]

Railroads facilitated the distribution of *mezcal de Tequila* (mezcal from Tequila), but they also helped transport European spirits such as cognac and whiskey, which enjoyed a steady increase in popularity during this period.[153] Mexican elites were especially fond of European alcoholic beverages.[154] Historian José Maria Muriá explains that upper-class Mexicans had a penchant for all things French. Francophilia among the wealthy was so rampant that they were called *los afrancesados*, or "the Frenchified," because of their espousal of French customs.[155] Even though less than three decades had passed since the French invasion, widespread anti-French sentiment did *not* develop. For example, the overthrown Emperor Maximilian was not considered a villain but instead was seen as a "misguided hero."[156]

Although members of the upper class were among the few who enjoyed the privilege of consuming French products, the admiration of French cultural ethics was more broadly rooted in the desire to leave behind the antiquated lifestyle associated with the colonial period.[157] Noted Mexican philosopher Samuel Ramos writes that Mexicans wanted "to make a *tabula rasa* of the past and begin a new life . . . The most intelligent and active group in Mexican society proposed to use French ideology as a weapon for the destruction of old institutions."[158] The revolutionary spirit of France offered the educated classes the basic principles for combating the political oppression that took place under Spanish rule. For Mexican elites, the consumption of French products, including cognac and champagne, symbolized devotion to the principles of progress and order. In contrast, pulque, mezcal, and mezcal from Tequila were domestic drinks (that is, less distinctive and less expensive), and consuming them was evidence of one's limited purchasing power and social class. It is important to note that social class in Mexico represented more than just material wealth and cultural capital; it carried racialized connotations that stifled residential mobility and limited economic opportunities.[159] The racialized social order closely mirrored that of the colonial period: At the top were individuals of European descent, then mestizos, and finally, at the very bottom, were mulattos, blacks, and indigenous groups. Even though it was acquiring a reputation for being a modern and uniquely Mexican spirit, mezcal from Tequila still communicated one's class and racial identity and conveyed one's social values (for example, less committed to economic improvement).

Despite the conspicuous consumption promoted by Mexican elites, the production of mezcal from Tequila continued to increase. For instance, in 1900 there were sixty distilleries; in 1910 there were eighty-seven.[160] By the late nineteenth century, mezcal from Tequila's status within Mexico (as a drink special to the state of Jalisco) was becoming solidified. Although it is difficult to determine exactly when "mezcal from" (*mezcal de*) was dropped from its name, it is likely that sometime during the early part of the twentieth century it was known as "tequila" in the domestic market. Another possibility is that, when distribution increased in the United States, importers and marketers shortened its name to make pronunciation easier.

Mezcal from Tequila's reputation was also evolving within Mexican and Latin American communities in the United States, yet with implications that went beyond its regional association. For example, advertisements in the Los Angeles, California, Spanish-language newspaper, *Dos Repúblicas*, described shops' assortment of imported wines, liquors, and "the famous mezcal from Tequila."[161] In 1915, one Kansas City, Missouri, business—in addition to listing its large selection of alcohol—informed readers that "because of the closing of distilleries in Mexico, we have the only stocks of Mexican liquor because we bought up a large amount before the revolution." The two beverages advertised under this headline were mezcal and mezcal from Tequila.[162]

In contrast to their domestic (and hence, commonplace) reputation in Mexico, in the United States mezcal and tequila were advertised as "famous," suggesting that they were valued in ethnic Mexican markets. Far from exhibiting the consumer's antipathy toward economic improvement, purchasing tequila or mezcal while living in the United States served as a means of preserving and honoring cultural identity. In addition to providing news and facilitating immigrants' adjustment to a new society, early-twentieth-century Spanish-language newspapers promoted nationalism and nostalgia for their readers' country of origin.[163] Read primarily by members of the middle class, these newspapers, and the advertisements for tequila within them, enabled financially resourceful Mexicans, Mexican Americans, and other Spanish-speaking populations to learn *how* certain products illustrated affection for Mexico.

Newspapers were not the only sites where Mexican immigrants (and other Spanish-speaking individuals) living in the United States became acquainted with tequila during this time period—efforts were also made by the Mexican government. In particular, tequila was one of several products touted internationally as symbolizing the country's technical savvy and commercial potential. The promotion of Mexican products reached new heights during the reign of Porfirio Díaz (1876–1910). With the goal of attracting foreign investment, Díaz took special interest in developing the perception that Mexico was a modern, rational, and stable economic environment. Operating under the auspices that progress could be achieved by the creation of foreign markets for Mexican goods, the Díaz government participated in numerous international expositions and world's fairs. Officials wanted to sharpen Mexico's global image and, at the same time, incite productivity on the local level. Bureaucrats anticipated that participation in these shows would "awake a latent industriousness in the Mexican people."[164] As Mexican products received medals and gained international exposure, it was thought that the Mexican people would "raise their standards of craftsmanship and productivity."[165]

Branding Mexico internationally trumped domestic elites' actual drinking preferences. Regardless, new tequila-manufacturing elite families were emerging and beginning to wield their own influence in light of prevailing beliefs of the superiority of European products.[166] Making appearances at expositions in places such as Madrid, Paris, and San Antonio, Texas, mezcal from Tequila was one of a number of goods endorsed by the Mexican government. In the international market, it was referred to as mezcal from Tequila; however, the Sauza company took a different route and called their products "Mexican Whiskey" or "Tequila Brandy." Although there is no official explanation about why Sauza used these names, it is possible that associating their product with other well-known European and American drinks (whiskey and brandy) helped them appear less mysterious to new markets. Such a tactic follows the assumption and politics put forth by the Díaz administration—that Mexico could succeed if it adhered to European and American cultural principles and ways of doing business.

Breakthroughs in glass technology, especially the invention of bottling automation, enabled alcohol entrepreneurs to cut costs and increase output.[167] The new mechanized packaging added to tequila's modern cachet. The ability to purchase, hold, and pour machine-manufactured bottles not only represented a cutting-edge process, one that consumers could experience for themselves, but from a commercial perspective it also created new opportunities for companies to visually reinforce their commitment to industrialization. For example, the label for Floras Tequila (a Jose Cuervo product) features an image of the impressive machinery used in its factory (see Figure 3). The massive copper pot stills indicate that the company is distilling large amounts of tequila and is doing so efficiently and innovatively, giving the impression that this is no ordinary manufacturing plant. The factory floor is clean and orderly; technology has replaced the need for employees and the risk of human error. Flanking both sides of the machine are the numerous gold medal awards that the company has received at international expositions in recognition of its supreme taste and quality. To be sure, the label exemplifies brand pride and commercial confidence.

Porfirio Díaz's effort to revamp Mexico and its international image came at the expense of political reform and social welfare.[168] Embracing an ideology that shunned the masses and looked to Europe as a model of modernity, Porfirian attempts to stylize Mexican cultural values and tastes within a European framework gained little support outside elite circles. However, the *Porfiriatos'* backing of the tequila industry suggests that the schism created in the pursuit of modernity was not always a predictable, all-or-nothing enterprise. In the years previous to the revolution, tequila was promoted sometimes as a product that was similar to American and European distilled drinks (whiskey

FIGURE 3. Tequila label illustrating the modern production process.
Source: Enrique F. Martínez Limon (1999), *Tequila: The Spirit of Mexico.* Bath, England: Absolute Press.

and brandy) and other times as a product that reflected a unique blend of Mexican tradition and ingenuity. Regardless of Díaz's alleged preference for cognac over tequila,[169] in his regime's pursuit of modernity, tequila was one of the few goods that withstood the dense and often problematic relations associated with advancing an authentically Mexican style of enlightenment.

Conclusion

By the beginning of the twentieth century, tequila was steadily becoming associated with Mexican identity inside and outside of the nation. Although pulque was the earliest agave-based alcoholic beverage, and, by all standards, distinctively indigenous, by the early twentieth century its reputation was exactly that: too *indio*. Indicative of the chaos and difficulties of the early colonial period, for the Spanish, pulque represented their failure to gain full control over the indigenous population. As the number of pulque consumers grew, its negative connotations diminished but never fully disappeared.

Indigenous ethnic populations and mestizos, who constituted most of the urban poor, continued to favor pulque over other fermented drinks, such as beer. Up until the revolution, pulque was the most widely consumed alcoholic drink in the country. Yet, its deep-seated ties to an antiquated version of Mexico—one that was imprinted with racial and class markings—in combination with its perishability, could not endure the drive for modernity.

The production of mezcal outside of the Tequila region continued to spread during this period. However, despite its growth, mezcal manufacturers—in regions such as Oaxaca—encountered barriers that included an insufficient transportation infrastructure, which limited its distribution. Further, because it lacked strong ties to a thriving metropolitan city center such as Guadalajara, the region was unable to establish and, hence, capitalize from a confident commercial climate. Compared to the pulque of Mexico City and the mezcal produced in family-run operations, the mezcal of Tequila, Jalisco, was the least linked to indigenous culture, the lower classes, and the backwardness associated with local and small-scale production (for example, manufacturing and distribution). The rise of Guadalajara as a colonial success story, one in which Spanish elites established a thriving economic base, also contributed to tequila's rising reputation. Therefore, in the period preceding the Mexican Revolution, tequila had already acquired the momentum needed to emerge as a symbol of the nation's renewed identity—a sentiment that would take on new meaning throughout the twentieth century. As I discuss in the next chapter, enlightened narratives of Mexican nationalism, although on the surface appearing to embrace cultural diversity, remained closely linked to the principles of progress, ideals that were incompatible with indigenous values. Tequila best embodied the virtues of growth, efficiency, and unity. This association became more pronounced during the postrevolutionary period, when tequila's status would become indelibly associated with Mexico's own unique identity as a modern nation-state.

INTOXICATING ICONS

Pancho Villa, Masculinity, and U.S.–Mexican Relations

In *The New American Bartender's Guide*, mixologist John Poister describes the "original" way to order tequila: "Walk into any Mexican cantina, belly up to the bar and say, '*Tequila, estilo Pancho Villa por favor*,' Tequila Pancho Villa style."[1] Poister is not alone in making the association between Pancho Villa and tequila. Indeed, there are dozens of Pancho Villa–themed tequila brands. Besides Tequila Pancho Villa and La Leyenda Tequila 30–30 (The Legend Tequila 30-30), which refers to the 30–30 rifle used by Villa and his army, there is Viva Villa Tequila; Pancho Villa Viejo Tequila (Old Pancho Villa); Hijos de Villa Tequila (Children or Sons of Villa); 7 Leguas (7 Leagues), which is the name of Pancho Villa's horse; and Tequila Los Arango, which is a reference to Doroteo Arango, Pancho Villa's given name. There are even several tequila-based cocktails that draw on Villa's namesake (the Pancho Villa, the Pancho Villa shooter, and the Pancho Villa #2). Simply put, no other figure is as closely coupled with the culture of tequila. However, there is a large disconnect between this popular perception and historical evidence. Pancho Villa was a teetotaler who spearheaded alcohol prohibition in Mexico. So why is Pancho Villa strongly associated with tequila? (See Figures 4 and 5.)

The answer to this question requires analyzing tequila's symbolic ties to the Mexican Revolution and exploring its curious connection to the U.S. media. By the early part of the twentieth century, tequila was well positioned to become Mexico's national spirit. Unlike pulque or other types of mezcal

FIGURE 4. Tequila bottle in the image of
Pancho Villa. Photo by Gwyn Fisher.

that were deemed inferior or backward, tequila was allied with Jalisco's
reputation as economically successful, politically stable, and racially homogeneous. The impending upheaval would alter myriad aspects of Mexican
society, including how people related to one another as conationals. Amid
competing ideas about the nation's path toward modernity and a revitalized
sense of patriotism, new expressions of nationalism were established, among
them tequila as a populist symbol of *lo mexicano* (Mexicanness). The rise of
Villa as a tequila-drinking national icon is the result of a factious interplay of
clashing political ideologies, racial stereotypes, notions of masculinity, and
media representations.

FIGURE 5. Pancho Villa tequila. Photo by Gwyn
Fisher.

Revolutionary Identities and Ideologies

Early twentieth-century Mexico was marked by widespread concern about
the progress of the nation. While the vast majority of the populace continued
to suffer at the hands of Porfirio Díaz's administration, politicians sought
innovative measures to support his regime and promote fiscal development.
Central to these discussions were the ideas of positivist writers such as Her-
bert Spencer and Charles Darwin. Relying on the strict application of scientific method, positivists maintained that societies, like animal species, were
subject to the laws of evolution. When applied to the context of governance,
progress was seen as possible when societies adapted to their historical circumstances, embraced science, and valued education.[2] *Científicos* (positivist

public intellectuals), such as the prominent journalist and politician Justo Sierra, published works that praised Díaz's route toward modernization and called for the continued incorporation of scientific principles and models of economic expansion. A technocratic reformer, Sierra held that what Mexico needed, and had found in Díaz, was the resilient and objective ruler that was "necessary for the true realization of liberty."[3] The concept of race was central to the administration's quest for prosperity. Specifically, the mestizo, "the product of two races, two cultures, and two histories," was promoted as unifying a range of class and ideological contradictions.[4] Positioning himself as representing the interests of all Mexicans, Díaz heralded the mestizo as the prototype of Mexican progress. In reality, however, indigenous people and the rural masses were treated as obstacles to modernization. During a period when elites focused on developing a capitalist economy, indigenous populations, many of whom spoke only their native dialect, lived as agrarian peasants and were considered burdens by the Díaz regime.

In the years following the revolution, public intellectuals such as José Vasconcelos and artists such as Diego Rivera sought to break free from the domination of European standards that characterized life under the *Porfiriato*. Among the various intellectuals who contributed to the development of a more inclusive collective conscience was noted anthropologist Manuel Gamio (known as the father of Mexican anthropology). Interested in fashioning a Mexican nation based on a model of cultural integration, Gamio, like many anthropologists of that era, supported social policies that would assimilate indigenous cultures into mainstream Mexican society. The state-sponsored *indigenismo*[5] movement endorsed by Gamio set out to create a more inclusive national identity. This controversial approach was criticized and praised— criticized because of its assimilative focus, which promoted mestizo identity over indigenous identity, and praised because it recognized and extolled native arts, crafts, and architecture. In the end, Gamio's effort to produce "a powerful *patria* and a coherent, defined nationality" neglected to incorporate modern indigenous social, political, or economic contributions.[6] For Gamio, that contemporary native populations preserved and maintained characteristics central to pre-Hispanic life was hardly a cause for national acclaim. Instead, he saw them as obstacles.[7] Although Gamio's approach had elements of equality, it failed to break free from the traditional stance that ethnic indigenous people personified cultural stagnation and obstructed efforts to forge a modern and homogenous Mexican identity.

Manuel Gamio's attempt to establish a collective conscience that commemorated Mexico's indigenous past, although entangled in inconsistencies pertaining to the indigenous present, reflected a major shift in Mexican nationalist thought. Where once the upper and middle classes looked down on native populations, excluding them from narratives of national unity, they now started to adopt a more paternalistic philosophy that incorporated certain aspects of indigenous heritage. The concepts of *mestizaje* and *indigenismo* were commonly used by government officials to encourage a new Mexican nationalism rooted in the idea of spiritual and racial homogeneity—a *raza cósmica* (cosmic race)[8] that would allow mestizos to build a society based on the refined culture of Latin civilizations.[9] The phrase *lo mexicano*, a notion of self-awareness in which beliefs about racial equality were built into the foundation of nationalism, became equally popular during the postrevolutionary period. More broadly, *lo mexicano* was seen as an "authentic" expression of Mexican character that reflected the rise of a shared understanding that transcended the rivalry and conflict of the nation's past.[10] Novelists were among the many intellectuals who aligned themselves with new literary forms that highlighted Mexico's revitalized nationalism. Often, their storylines featured peasants and indigenous people as protagonists and emphasized their newly valued place in the nation.

Such is the case with Jalisco-born writer Mariano Azuela's (1915) famous novel about the revolutionary movement, *Los de abajo* (*The Underdogs*). Considered the "quasi-official text of the revolution" and credited as the first "novel of the masses," *Los de abajo* is loosely based on Azuela's combat experiences during war.[11] Starting off with honorable intentions, protagonist Demetrio Macías, together with a small band of revolutionaries, becomes disillusioned and corrupted by the war. Standing in contrast to the literary norms of the Porfiriato, the story unromantically illustrates the brutal and self-serving conduct of the army. Described as "the organic intellectual of the revolutionary struggle," Macías is portrayed as having a preference for Mexican products during a time when foreign goods were considered status symbols.[12] For instance, in one scene the narrator notes, "To champagne that sparkles and foams as the beaded bubbles burst at the brim of the glass, Demetrio preferred the native tequila, limpid and fiery."[13] In the pages that follow, Macías's troops boast of the cruelty they inflict as they make their way through the houses and haciendas of the rich. Commenting on their plunder, Azuela writes, "Bottles of tequila, dishes of cut glass, bowls, porcelains, and vases lay scattered."[14]

Littering the home of a wealthy family with tequila bottles suggests a figurative and literal assault against the upper classes, who favored cut glass, porcelains, and vases—affluent furnishings that were most likely imported. More significantly, however, it demonstrates how, as an emergent cultural symbol, tequila, as a Mexican product (that is, not foreign), enabled the lower classes to convey their allegiance to the nation and express their sentiments about pervasive class inequalities. Therefore, tequila metaphorically provided a means through which members of the lower classes could assert new national identities, marking their transition from disrespected citizens to acknowledged citizens.

Even with the emergence of figures, symbols, and expressions that were seen as embodying Mexican values and the new national identity, no one political faction single-handedly controlled the arena of public perception. For example, while the *indigenismo* movement gained steady momentum, it never achieved total domination. *Hispanistas*, comprised of middle- and upper-class intellectuals and politicians, maintained that Spanish attributes (for example, Catholic doctrines and the colonial system), were the "authentic genesis of the national spirit."[15] *Hispanismo* relied on the view that the Spanish had developed a superior culture, lifestyle, and political system that made them distinct. In particular, *hispanistas* held that the population that best represented these ideals came from the tequila-producing region of Los Altos, located in the state of Jalisco.[16]

Rooted in the conviction that the Los Altos region was divinely inspired because of its spatial segregation from indigenous populations and supposed European genetic purity (a result of the effects of the Mixtón War [1540–1542]), the myth of Alteño exceptionalism affirmed the region's symbolism as "a source of national redemption" amid the "racial dilemma" of postrevolutionary efforts to construct a homogeneous national identity.[17] From this perspective, Los Altos served as an idealized location from where to cultivate a national narrative that exalted Spanish customs initiated during the colonial era. According to the historian José Orozco, *hispanista* claims that the Los Altos region represented an appropriate Mexican identity ultimately failed to garner widespread popular acceptance in the period immediately following the revolution. He maintains that is was not until the advent of the Mexican movie and music industries (1930s) that Alteño exceptionalism, uniquely embodied in the image of the *charro* (Mexican cowboy), became fully integrated in the Mexican popular imaginary. Although the Mexican media of this era contributed considerably to the production and diffusion of this image, anthropologist Olga Nájera-Ramírez proposes that it was during the *Porfiriato* (1876–1911) that the *charro* emerged as a national hero and became integrated with notions of manhood, nationality, and power.[18] This suggests that elements of *hispanismo* in general, and Alteño exceptionalism in particular, were not only in circulation before the revolution but were also among the discourses that survived and flourished in spite of it. In other words, although *indigenismo* did indeed become a popular force, the ongoing influence of *hispanismo* should not be dismissed in the formation of Mexican nationalism during this time period.

The idealization of the Alteño region is rooted in a larger narrative regarding Mexican identity: Jalisco as the quintessential home of *lo mexicano*. Far from natural, Jalisco's patriotic association was formally initiated by President Plutarco Elías Calles (1924–1928). In particular, he sought to cultivate a cohesive national identity that brought together diverse segments of Mexican society (for example, those who supported, opposed, or were ambivalent about the revolution).[19] Unlike northern states such as Coahuila and Chihuahua, Jalisco played a relatively minor role in the revolution. Prompted by Calles's efforts to establish nationwide unity, and later crystallized by its religious loyalties during the Cristero War (1926–1929), within Mexico, Jalisco became widely known as a socially and politically conservative state. Less than a decade later, Mexican Golden Age films would rely heavily on Jalisco as a cinematic backdrop, further strengthening the state's prominence as an emblem of tradition.

Jalisco's reputation was also emboldened by myths regarding its racial exceptionalism. For example, the renowned public intellectual José Vasconcelos described Jalisco as the most culturally pure, prosperous, and attractive Mexican state. In his words, "The men are tall and striking . . . the women have black eyes, flexible waists, clear complexion, full of softness, they seduce by the refinement of their characteristics and their fluid and graceful walk."[20] So taken with the state's artistic attributes, in 1924 he declared the *jarabe tapatío*, a Jaliscan dance, Mexico's national dance.[21] Other scholars of the time noted that Jaliscans, especially those from the tequila-producing town of Arandas (located in the Los Altos region), "retained a high degree of their Spanish heritage" and mingled "very little with the large numbers of *indígenas* (indigenous) who inhabit adjoining regions."[22] Indeed, Jalisco played an important role in the postrevolutionary imagined community as a location where aesthetically European figures and culturally colonial symbols could be incorporated into a reconstructed collective image and national psyche.

Although Mexico had a long history of expressing its early history through female symbols (for example, the Virgin of Guadalupe), after the revolution this phenomenon shifted, and male figures became more visible in order to accommodate the patriarchal impulses of modernization.[23] The momentum of modernity operated within the scope of a masculine agenda, or "national fantasy" in which male icons mapped the country's "glorious" past onto its "coherent" present.[24] Specifically, the *charro* became a prototype used for marketing "Mexican culture for public consumption both inside and outside of Mexico."[25] What is more, representations of the *charro* aligned with the postrevolutionary romantic nationalist effort to identify customs that were seen as uniquely Mexican in order to foster a sense of national unity that appeared to promote democratic principles.[26] Despite intentions to nurture uniquely Mexican traditions and personas, the *charro* had more in common with Spanish attributes than indigenous ones.

Predating the professionalization of American rodeo, *charros* performed regularly on both sides of the border.[27] The establishment of *charro* associations (in Mexico and the American Southwest) and the promotion of *charrería* (the sport of horsemanship) in American rodeo shows helped standardize public perceptions of an idealized Mexican manhood. *Charro* associations outlined strict principles of behavior through an institutionalized code of ethics stipulating that members were barred from partaking in disorderly conduct while in costume. Drinking and fighting were expressly prohibited because carrying a real gun was part of the *charro* regalia. With the intention of encouraging responsibility and safety, the code of ethics protected the status of the *charro* as a positive representative of the nation.[28] Images of *lo mexicano* associated with the *charro* were also closely linked to romantic portrayals of hacienda life that emphasized traditional social roles (for example, class, gender, and race).[29] Although the *charro* was one example of a particular version of Mexican manliness and a symbol of "good" citizenship that was promoted locally and internationally, another icon also started to emerge during this period—one that stood in opposition to the state's representation of respectable Mexican manhood: the legendary rebel General Francisco "Pancho" Villa.

Pancho Villa and the U.S. Media

Pancho Villa exemplifies the legacy, imagery, and mystique associated with the Mexican Revolution. Described as "Mexico's *macho* hero *par excellence*,"[30] and the "Mexican Robin Hood,"[31] Pancho Villa simultaneously represents the embodiment of machismo and a symbol of national pride. Rising from poverty to fight the wealthy while advocating peasants' and workers' rights, Villa's commitment to social change evolved from a number of life experiences and crystallized during his participation in the revolution. In the years that followed the end of the *Porfiriato*, Mexico, marked by a military coup, military regime, and presidential assassination, remained politically unstable. Dismayed by the lack of social progress and the amount of continued government corruption, Villa was concerned that the country's leaders were losing sight of the revolution's goals. Specifically, he blamed President Venustiano Carranza for the turmoil within Mexico.

Although initially maintaining friendly business relations with the American government, Villa was troubled by their increasing support of Carranza's probusiness reforms. Unease turned to anger when U.S. officials reneged on an arms deal and abruptly stopped selling weapons to him and his army. In response, on March 9, 1916, Villa led 1,500 troops across the U.S. border, killing seventeen Americans in Columbus, New Mexico. Villa and his army instigated the attack with the intention of severing U.S.–Mexican relations and bringing Carranza down.[32] However, the plan failed; the United States and Mexico did not break off relations, and Carranza remained in power. President Woodrow Wilson responded to the assault by sending 10,000 troops under the command of General John Pershing to locate Villa and his army. President Carranza also sent troops. Pursued by two different and well-equipped armies, Villa evaded arrest from both. In 1920, after two U.S. Army expeditions failed to capture Villa, the Mexican government accepted his surrender and retired him on a general's salary. In 1923 he was assassinated in Parral, Chihuahua.

By challenging the authority of the U.S. government and the Mexican establishment, Villa embodied resistance to exploitation and injustice on both sides of the border. The image of Pancho Villa contributed to a revitalized Mexican nationalism, one that was distrustful of foreigners, especially Americans.[33] Immortalized in music and film, Pancho Villa became an emblem of

Mexican national identity in Mexico and the United States. Mexican *corridos* (folk ballads) sung in northern Mexico and in the American Southwest commemorated his determination and ability to outsmart both armies. Hundreds of *corridos* were written about Villa, glorifying him as a hero of the common people of Mexico.[34] One characteristic of these songs was the depiction of Pancho Villa in relation to alcohol. For example, in Miguel Lira's "Corrido de la muerte de Pancho Villa" (Ballad of the Death of Pancho Villa),[35] Villa is described as having visited a cantina on the day of his assassination:

¡Pobre Pancho Villa . . . !	Poor Pancho Villa!
Iba dejando Parral	As he was leaving Parral
Saliendo de una cantina,	Walking out of a cantina,
El valiente general	The brave general
Autor de La Valentina	Composer of "La Valentina"[36]
"Si porque me ves borracho,	"If I look drunk to you it's because
Mañana ya no me ves;	Tomorrow you won't see me again;
Si me han de matar mañana,	If they're going to kill me tomorrow . . .
Que me maten de una vez . . ."	Let them kill me now once and for all . . ."
¡Pobre Pancho Villa . . . !	Poor Pancho Villa!

In this *corrido*, Villa has a premonition of his death as he walks out of a cantina. In a confrontational tone, he proclaims, perhaps in earshot of his would-be assassins, or perhaps just to himself, "Let them kill me now once and for all." At the end of the stanza, the lyrics remind listeners to lament the revolutionary leader's inevitable demise.

According to the eminent border scholar Américo Paredes, *corridos* are folk performances that communicate collective ideas and illustrate sentiments of resistance. *Corridos*, he maintains, are dialogical responses to the conflict and tension of Anglo–Mexican border relations during the early part of the twentieth century. Many *corridos* of this time period contested dominant representations, among these the consistent depiction of Mexican revolutionaries as bandits by the U.S. press.[37] *Corridos*, therefore, often inverted U.S.-based meanings of Mexicans as "lazy, dirty, thieving, devious, conspiratorial, sexually hyperactive, and overly fond of alcohol" such that, depending on the listener, mentioning Pancho Villa's cavalier language and presence at a cantina could be interpreted as a lampooning of American stereotypes.[38]

Movies in the United States and Mexico also documented Villa's rise as a symbol of Mexico's revolution and elevated the public status of army generals, populist figures, and reform-minded groups who participated in the revolutionary movement. Mexican films captured the tumultuous postrevolutionary period and popularized Mexican folklore, actors, and singers throughout Latin America.[39] In the United States, Villa's revolutionary reputation spread when a film presented recordings of Villa in battle and sympathetically told the story of the hardships he faced in his youth. Depicting the rebellion as a popular protest by poor and upright Mexicans fighting for justice, the footage showed Villa distributing food and clothes to the poor and promising land to his troops.[40] The American press was fascinated by Villa's image and ran numerous stories both condemning and defending his pursuits. For example, the *Fortnightly Review* described Villa's actions as "a recital of cold-blooded murders, thefts, torturings [sic], and atrocities of an even worse description," while the *Nation* magazine described him as "very different from the purely selfish and utterly ignorant cutthroat and robber."[41]

Villa worked closely with American movie producer Harry Aitken to film his battles and screen the newsreels in the United States, Mexico, and Canada. However, filming real-life attacks proved to be difficult, and the scenes turned out to be a disappointment. In February 1914, Villa (or his bodyguard) killed a British rancher seeking reimbursement for lost cattle. Almost immediately, once-sympathetic publishers began to portray Villa as "a bandit born."[42] These representations were further embellished after Villa's attack on Columbus, New Mexico. However, even before his U.S. incursion, Villa's actions provided the American press with an excuse to describe Mexicans as warring tribes and outlaws. For example, one journalist observed, "Mexico is not, in fact, a nation, but a country peopled by many tribes of Indians . . . none reaching what we would call civilization."[43] Often, newspaper articles and cartoons depicted Mexican statesmen and revolutionaries as violent bandits and insatiable drunks. For example, as Figures 6 and 7 illustrate, representations of male drunkenness not only underscored Mexican irreverence to social order but also fed into and gained momentum from U.S. domestic racism toward blacks, immigrants, and Native Americans prevalent during this period. Drawing on exaggerated racialized images and using labels such as "ignorant" or "savage" enabled the press to easily communicate the ineptitude of Mexicans to the American public by relying on an already established language of racial and ethnic inferiority that was used to disempower other communities of color.

FIGURE 6. Editorial cartoon from 1914: "How
long will it continue?"
Source: Los Angeles Times, March 30, 1914.

Mexican men in general, and Pancho Villa in particular, were prime tar-
gets of the U.S. media.[44] Yet, Pancho Villa's image was manipulated to communicate both American and Mexican views of the revolution. For poor and
lower-class Mexicans, Villa symbolized the promise of equality and a future
in which the "underdogs" could prevail. For wealthy, land-owning Mexicans,
Villa and his revolutionary counterparts were viewed as threats to the status quo. At first celebrated by the United States and then later denigrated,
Villa's image caught the attention of the American public, whose knowledge

FIGURE 7. Editorial cartoon from 1914:
"A substitute for pulque."
Source: Los Angeles Times, May 9, 1914.

of Mexico was limited to "picture postcards, newsreels, silent movies—pictures for excitement, not explanation."[45] To be sure, media depictions of Villa "visually reinforced the radical otherness of Mexicans to U.S. whites."[46] In one glaring attempt to further accentuate this "radical otherness," the *Los Angeles Times* went so far as to claim that Pancho Villa was actually "a negro native of Maryland," who, after getting into trouble with the law in Texas, fled across the border, became a bandit under the name of "Rondolz," and joined the Mexican army.[47] Pancho Villa was reduced to a villain and bandit capable only of destruction—a specter against which American innocence, morality, and masculinity was defined.

In Mexico and the United States, Villa was depicted as the epitome of machismo, an exaggerated stereotype of manliness that appealed to conservative gender, familial, and cultural categories; a type of "symbolic capital" that sustained national and individual identity.[48] Portrayals of Villa's "macho" attributes were framed differently and served separate purposes in both countries.

Instead of having purely negative connotations in Mexico, Villa's macho characteristics stressed codes of courage, honor, and respect. In his analysis of the perceptions of machismo within Mexican and Latino culture, Alfredo Mirandé maintains that there are at least two models of machismo. The first, known as the "compensatory view," is a pejorative conception that emphasizes violence, irresponsibility, and male dominance over women as fundamental to the essence of Mexican male character. The second, described as the "ethical view," directs attention away from outward qualities of physical strength and virility and focuses on "inner ones such as personal integrity, commitment, loyalty, and most importantly, strength of character."[49] Challenging both the Mexican establishment and the U.S. government, Villa was respected by "common" people and feared by elites. Therefore, similar to the multiple and often-contradictory conceptions of machismo, Villa likewise became associated with characteristics of Mexican manhood that differed within Mexican culture and varied across national borders. These depictions also had similarities, especially with regard to how they represented Villa in association with alcohol.

In cultural accounts as wide ranging as *corridos*, American newspaper articles, and Mexican and Hollywood films, Pancho Villa is portrayed in relation to alcohol. The consistent representation of Pancho Villa with alcohol is curious for several reasons. First and foremost, contrary to the popular portrayal, Villa abstained from alcohol. In fact, because of his concern about alcoholism in Mexico, he outlawed alcohol in his home state of Chihuahua and ordered the death penalty not only for the individuals who violated the ban but also for their horses, dogs, and goats.[50] Before his relationship with the U.S. government deteriorated, Villa publicly expressed his admiration for President Wilson in the form of a toast, but not before adding the following disclaimer: "For the first time in my life I am going to propose a toast, and for the first time in my life I am going to drink a toast, and it will be the first time that I ever willingly let liquor pass my lips."[51] In the famous 1914 meeting of Villa's army with Emiliano Zapata's army in Mexico City, Villa purportedly gagged on a sip of brandy when the two generals shared a toast.[52] A nondrinker and nonsmoker, the highly self-disciplined Villa, in statements made to American newspapers, often described his enemies as "drunks"—in essence, labeling them as despicable. In an article published in the *San Francisco Examiner*, Villa exclaimed, "I will go back to work as soon as I drive out that drunkard, Huerta. I am only a poor man. I wish only to see my country-men freed from tyranny. I am a patriot. Yet I am the man they call the Bandit Villa."[53] Ironically, it was Villa, and not Huerta, whose image would be forever associated with alcohol.

Although Pancho Villa abstained from alcohol, his image became and remained intimately linked to tequila on both sides of the border. U.S. news-papers played a role in forging this association. For example, when British rancher William Benton was assassinated in 1914, the front page headline of the *Los Angeles Times* declared, "Blame Tequila for Execution: Benton Victim of Villa's Lust for Liquor, It Is Said."[54] The article continued by stating, "Gen. Francisco Villa, with four of his cronies, were crazed with marijuana and tequila at the time Villa gave the order to shoot William S. Benton, a British subject and wealthy ranchman."[55] The newspaper reported that Villa and his "so-called advisors" were "more or less under the influence of the native tequila" when the events unfolded.[56] A similar image was circulated through other forms of media. In his research on the early-twentieth-century U.S. drug war against Mexican immigrants, Curtis Marez analyzes how American film depicted Villa and his army. Well received in the United States and in Europe, the 1934 motion picture *Viva Villa!*, starring Wallace Beery as Pancho Villa and Fay Wray as his love interest, famously portrayed Villa as hostile, drunk, and misogynistic. Describing a particularly vivid scene, Marez observes that, while in a drunken stupor, Villa's "sexual sadism" is released. Threatening to rape Teresa, the owner of the hacienda that his army has taken over, he aggressively tells her, "I only know how to make love one way. If I see an angel I got to make love that way, I got to grab hard."[57] In addition to depicting Mexican men as Neanderthal, criminal, and perverse, the script characterized Villa as immoral and unintelligent. American moviegoers were presented with distorted images that portrayed Pancho Villa and revolutionary Mexicans as consistently inebriated and out of control.

The American media's use of tequila as a metaphor for Mexican deviance emerged from and became structured within a range of material and symbolic registers related to the changing logic of U.S. national expansion. Heightened tensions regarding the U.S.–Mexican border as an ambiguous territory required a new language to explain the enforcement of stricter regulatory controls between the two countries. Further, new rationalizations were needed to justify the increased U.S. intervention in Mexican domestic affairs. In her work on the American quest for power in foreign countries, Amy Kaplan argues that the logic of Manifest Destiny extended internationally and hinged on the racial othering of foreign people and places.[58] The force of American empire instigated various conflicts at the same time that it established a context in which U.S. entrepreneurs could justify their efforts to economically and politically control Mexico.

American and European investors sought to broaden their enterprises and develop business ventures throughout northern Mexico. However, not everything panned out as planned. When work in mining and railroads slowed down in the early years of the twentieth century, Mexican laborers started to migrate to the United States in sizable numbers. Thus, large-scale corporate enterprises, which operated under the protection of the U.S. foreign policy, created a set of structural conditions that gave rise to an increase in Mexican immigration to the United States.[59] These unexpected circumstances, or what Kaplan refers to as "the anarchy of empire," signaled the breakdown "of the system of order that empire aspires to impose on the world."[60] Regardless of the instability associated with the U.S. pursuit of Mexican territory, the American government was often not held accountable for their actions. Instead, the U.S. press decried the rise in immigration, called for tighter border regulations, and blamed Mexicans for engaging in the criminal act of entering the country "illegally."

Compounding matters, the American temperance movement, with its deep ties to nativism, was gaining political traction. The growing overlap between prohibition philosophy and anti-immigrant sentiment operated as a "symbolic crusade" that invoked the language of morality, which denigrated "one group in opposition to others within the society."[61] Fundamental to this binary were notions of cultural and racial superiority. Moral Americans (that is, white, Protestant) did not drink at all, while immigrants (that is, nonwhite, Catholic) drank too much. From the perspective of outspoken temperance proponents, in choosing to drink alcohol, immigrants from different backgrounds demonstrated their tendency toward depravity and rejection of American values. Amid these circumstances, tequila was frequently cited as evidence of Mexican inferiority in nineteenth- and twentieth-century newspapers, magazines, and journals. For example, one article described "the native drink" in the following manner:

The very cheapness of this vile stuff, which brings it within the reach of all, is a calamity. American whisky is bad, but this is infinitely worse in the physical and moral degeneracy wrought, especially among the best families. Unless the [Mexican] nation awakes to this awful curse, it will become a nation of decadent manhood.[62]

Much like the linkages among cheapness, vileness, and decadent Mexican manhood, tequila served as a metonym for Mexican irresponsibility and unpredictability. Writing specifically about tequila and mezcal, the scientifically based *American Journal of Pharmacy* declared that the drinks were "very powerful in their effects. A Mexican Indian, addicted to their use, can drink a glass of any one . . . without effect; two or three glasses will set him demonically crazy."[63] Subsequently, journalists, travel writers, and newspaper columnists *produced* images of Mexico and Mexicans for Americans and other English-language readers by symbolically locating Mexican deviance within a Mexican product.

Projecting negative meanings about Mexicans onto material objects at a time when Americans were more likely to read about other cultures than interact with them illustrates how symbolic and material aspects of consumption were used to extend the reach of U.S. imperialism. Elaborating on how justification processes operate in specific historical periods, Mary Louise Pratt contends that the collective works of European travel writers legitimized colonial intervention and economic expansion to the general public. For Pratt, struggles over power and control were and continue to be played out in what she calls "contact zones."[64] A contact zone is an allegorical battleground where cultures interact, with one group asserting dominance over the other within a sphere of contentious engagement.[65] The imagining of Mexico through narratives regarding tequila and alcohol operates as a type of contact zone in which ideologies, such as Manifest Destiny, are rationalized through the authoritative accounts of journalists, travel writers, and newspaper columnists.

Described as overindulgent and subject to demonic lunacy when consuming their "native" drink, the only solution left for Mexicans and Mexico, it seems, is the aid and intercession of the United States. Produced and reinforced through the media, the racialized connection between tequila and deviant Mexican behavior helped justify the aspirations of U.S. expansionism. In Mexico, however, imagery and rhetoric about Pancho Villa and tequila were being mobilized to contest the portrayal of Mexicans as degenerate.

Branding Pancho Villa

The U.S. media portrayal of Pancho Villa as a macho, tequila-drinking bandit established a stable analogy in which notions of masculinity and alcohol consumption were fused together within the broader framework of Mexican national identity. In spite of the constancy of this formulation, national identity, as sociologist Stuart Hall explains, comprises unstable signifiers that appear to represent the nation's "true" character. Far from fixed, national identity:

> . . . has its histories—and histories have their real material, and symbolic effects. The past continues to speak to us . . . It is always constructed through memory, fantasy, narrative and myth. Cultural identities are the points of identification, the unstable points of identification or suture, which are made through the discourse of history and culture. Not an essence but a *positioning*.[66]

The dominant positioning of Pancho Villa and Mexicans in relation to alcohol and tequila operated on multiple levels. First, it reflected the logic of empire that promoted U.S. political and economic expansion within Mexico. Second, the portrayal of Mexicans as intemperate and dangerous to the U.S. national well-being (through the metaphor of tequila) reproduced the image that alcohol abuse was inherent to Mexican masculinity. The U.S. positioning of Pancho Villa simultaneously affirmed long-standing preconceptions of Mexican inferiority and served as the very basis from which a set of new influential stereotypes were established. Finally, it erected boundaries that stabilized meanings of "foreign" and "domestic"—concepts that upheld the purity and integrity of U.S. national identity.[67]

While tequila was becoming closely associated with negative stereotypes of Mexicanness in the mainstream U.S. media, in Mexico it was slowly becoming associated with aspects of populism, nationalism, and, to a certain degree, modernization.[68] New technologies in production, such as the replacement of the in-ground stone oven with the above-ground brick oven, and advancements in the distillation and bottling process, improved efficiency and output.[69] Greater demand, both locally and internationally, led to an increase in the amount of distilleries and the establishment of new tequila-producing zones outside the Tequila region in areas of Jalisco such as Autlán and Ciudad Guzmán. Overall, the decades leading up to the revolution saw the accumulation of land and the founding of hacienda estates by local tequila industrialists. With greater wealth, already well-do-do families expanded their businesses.[70] Infrastructural improvements facilitated tequila's transport within the country and into the United States. Thus, the period before the revolution was marked by relative prosperity in the state of Jalisco, which, while not affecting everyone equally, became crystallized in the Mexican imaginary as an era that symbolized steady economic growth in the backdrop of the idyllic countryside.

Caught in a continuum of competing philosophies regarding national identity, tequila's reputation was subject to the fluid nature of consumer culture. Indeed, tequila's shifting connotations were consistently shaped and re-shaped not just by consumers but also by the state and by capital interests.[71] Within this matrix of meanings, aspects of tequila's masculine and national-ist attributes fused with the image of Pancho Villa. Not the image promoted by *hispanistas* or *indigenistas*, Pancho Villa emerged from the revolution-ary milieu as an icon of *lo mexicano*—a symbol that was as subversive as it was problematic, fitting into neither prevailing identity nor master narrative completely. Instead, meanings and representations of Pancho Villa were ne-gotiated within and in response to the dominating beliefs of *hispanismo* and *indigenismo* that pervaded the postrevolutionary period. On one hand, the rise of Villa's reputation and association with *lo mexicano* was bolstered by the widespread disillusionment in the capabilities of Mexican leaders to gov-ern the nation in a manner that prioritized local development and the rights of ordinary people. On the other, Villa's representation as an icon of *lo mexi-cano* served as a response to the distorted portrayals of Villa and Mexicans by members of the American media. Different from the sober and polished image of the *charro*, Pancho Villa stood as an alternative formulation of na-tional belonging. Hence, Pancho Villa's status materialized as a symbol of re-sistance to the official discourse of the Mexican state and as a rejection of the debased images of Mexicans circulated in U.S. popular culture.

In Mexico, Pancho Villa's image as a gunslinging, tequila-drinking bandit-hero is a source of romance and independence—qualities easily incorporated into different expressions of social positioning. For instance, as a cultural icon, Pancho Villa evoked sentiments of a particular account of national pride in which expressions of bravery and loyalty were constructed as indelible to the country's character. Although certain negative traits (for example, drink-ing, womanizing, and fighting) were promoted and mythologized in Mexi-can *corridos*, Pancho Villa, a national hero who died a violent death much like the estimated 2,000,000 Mexicans killed during the revolution, became more known for his martyrlike qualities and less associated with the abusive traits embellished by the U.S. media. With justifiable goals, honorable intentions, and the ability to relate to the experiences of less privileged Mexicans, Pancho Villa's complicated life and brutal death tempered his disreputable attributes. The relationship between tequila and Pancho Villa was inevitable because their representations were shaped by and emerged within similar historical situations rooted in cross-border conflicts—struggles in which their images were mobilized to racialize Mexicans as foreign "others" dangerous to the well-being of American virtue and Anglo manhood.

Conclusion

The period during and following the revolution was pivotal in bolstering tequila's reputation as Mexico's national spirit. In the midst of widespread social transformation, new symbols were mobilized by the state to promote a united national identity. Struggles between conflicting groups (liberals and conservatives) and their ideologies (*indigenismo* and *hispanismo*) regarding how to modernize Mexico followed the prevailing European philosophy that a state should embody a united populace, all of whom speak the same language, share the same history, and embrace a common culture.[72] With an emphasis on unity and no true commitment to equality, both *indigenistas* and *hispanistas* sought to establish a homogeneous national identity whose past traditions would serve as a base from which to stimulate modern development. The new Mexican revolutionary state was eager to disseminate notions of *lo mexicano* that were "rooted in an 'authentic' mestizo rural culture of which it was the legitimate custodian and beneficiary."[73]

The embodiment of machismo, Pancho Villa emerged as a symbol of the revolution on both sides of the U.S.–Mexican border. Challenging the Mexican establishment and the American government, Pancho Villa was simultaneously depicted as a villain and hero whose attributes became incorporated into divergent conceptions of Mexican masculinity. Despite his abstinence from alcohol, Pancho Villa's characteristics were narrated through alcohol in general and tequila in particular. In the United States, Pancho Villa's macho, tequila-drinking image established a racialized metaphor that fused notions of Mexican manhood and alcohol consumption onto dysfunctional notions of Mexican national identity that justified U.S. expansionism and validated the increased policing of the border. In Mexico, Villa's portrayal in popular culture emphasized laudable aspects of machismo that elevated his status as an icon of resistance who stood up to the Mexican and American governments. The negative associations among Villa, Mexican identity, and tequila produced by the U.S. media, however, bolstered Pancho Villa and tequila's symbolism as subversive expressions of *lo mexicano*.

The 1919 passage of the Volstead Act in the United States, which outlawed the sale and production of alcohol at the federal level by way of a constitutional amendment, further enhanced the belief that alcohol consumption (and alcohol consumers) stood in opposition to American values. With legitimate political power, prohibition proponents enacted legislation to restrict travel to Mexico for the purpose of purchasing alcohol.[74] Together, these circumstances nurtured the notion that crossing the border into Mexico signified one's predilection for taboo activities that included not just alcohol, but drugs, gambling, and prostitution. As a site of vice that contrasted with the virtuous laws of the United States, Mexico was portrayed as risky, unruly, and immoral—a location where forbidden behavior was seen as customary and, perhaps, even expected. Although Mexico also passed prohibition measures during this period, enforcement was uneven as revenue from alcohol tax provided much-needed funds following the revolution. As the push for progress became more important for Mexican elites once the revolution ended, pulque's reputation as an indigenous and urban-poor product continued to clash with the image of a modern nation. Consequently, *pulquerías* throughout Mexico City were forced to shut down while the production and consumption of beer from European-owned companies was actively encouraged.[75] Such practices illustrated the continuing deference to foreign products, consumers, and capital. Tequila, however, had an advantage that beer companies did not: It originated in Mexico *and* it was closely associated with an emergent, mestizo, and nonelitist ethos of patriotism. In the decades that followed, this detail would prove vital to the evolution of *lo mexicano* throughout Mexican popular culture. Tequila, a uniquely Mexican spirit that provided a language of coherence amid the triumph and turmoil of the revolution, would become intimately woven into idealized narratives of *mexicanidad* on a national and international level.

GENDERING *MEXICANIDAD* AND COMMERCIALIZING CONSUMPTION

Tequila and the *Comedia Ranchera*

The 1941 box-office hit, *¡Ay Jalisco no te rajes!* (Oh Jalisco, Don't Back Down!), is regarded as one of the most successful Mexican Golden Age cinematic achievements and is frequently credited with elevating the status of director Joselito Rodríguez and composer Manuel Esperón. The film was heralded as actor Jorge Negrete's "first great triumph" that established him as Mexico's "quintessential" *charro*.[1] The dashing leading man, Negrete, was tall, handsome, romantic, and proud, swiftly singing his "sorrows as readily as his joys."[2] The film's success likewise advanced the careers of actors including Carlos López, Victor Manuel Mendoza, and actress Gloria Marín. Making a brief appearance in the film was singer Lucha Reyes, whose resounding version of the title song became an instant classic. Embodying the characteristics of *lo mexicano*, *¡Ay Jalisco no te rajes!* was one of many films of the period that featured cantinas, ranchos, and haciendas set in a nostalgic, rural past that was unharmed by the deep class conflict that accompanied the revolution. *Comedias rancheras* (Western melodramas) promoted a visually striking spectrum of national imagery and elevated the rising reputation of products such as tequila by depicting it as the "drink of choice" for *charro* protagonists.

Mexican film specialists have addressed how the Mexican media have historically been mobilized to support state and elite agendas.[3] Specifically, they hold that Mexican cinema effectively championed government propaganda and that, much like Hollywood, it was used to endorse certain "appropriate" standards of life.[4] However, scholars also propose that aspects of film can challenge administrative agendas and contest cultural imperialism. Cinema scholar Teresa de Lauretis argues that, along with conformist performances in film, progressive representations are also present but that they tend to operate at a more subtle, or local, level of resistance. In particular, she calls for a more critical analysis of the intersections of gender and sexuality that move beyond identifying expressions of difference.

Building on previous studies of Mexican cinema and Mexican popular culture, I contend that the presence, imagery, and consumption of tequila functions as a site—or, in the words of de Lauretis, a technology—that registers both conventional and alternative approaches to understanding the attributes of Mexican identity within the *ranchera* genre. On first glance, *comedias rancheras, canciones rancheras* (country or rural songs), and the printed materials they inspired appear to promote classic notions of a bygone period in Mexican history in which ideas about femininity and masculinity are central to the celebrated essence of *mexicanidad*. In what follows, I consider how, taken together, performances, stylistics, lyrics, representations, and interactions with tequila illuminate new tensions that sometimes contradict, but also sometimes uphold, a range of gendered national subjectivities.

Drinking Nostalgia

Tequila's rising presence on film and in music coincided with a range of shifting market circumstances and international relations. Tequila exports benefitted greatly from the effects of World War II (1939–1945), when the availability of U.S. whiskey and European distilled spirits declined significantly. For example, in 1940, 21,621 liters of tequila were exported, and by 1944 that number had risen to 4,500,000 liters.[5] According to popular lore, U.S. demand was so great that tequila was watered down by distributors in the trains that transported it across the border.[6] Once the war ended in 1945, foreign consumption waned, and by 1948, only 8,800 liters were exported.[7] While international sales decreased, domestic production and consumption steadily increased as roads within the region were paved, facilitating accessibility to other parts of the country. In the ten-year period from 1945 to 1955, the manufacture of tequila rose from 6,000,000 liters to 10,643,570 liters.[8]

Within Mexico, tequila's reputation continued to evolve as it acquired a new prominent role in cinema, especially in the *comedia ranchera*. Carlos Monsiváis explained tequila's shifting significance in this way:

> Cinema was in urgent need of new institutional icons to inspire both comedy and drama. Directors and scriptwriters alike turned to images of the mariachi, the betrayed man, the community in search of festivity, the agonized outpouring of secrets, the metamorphosis of the peaceful man into a hurricane of fury, the fierce macho dissolving in tears. To carry the imagination along such rough yet delectable roads, a strong drink was called for.[9]

From Monsiváis' perspective, tequila was the logical choice to accompany new cinematic icons: a robust drink for robust movie stars—or, more aptly, a "macho" drink for "macho" actors. Thus, Mexican cinema became an important channel for amplifying tequila's notoriety and linking tequila to the glorified intensity of *mexicanidad*.

Tequila's presence in film promoted—and in many respects idealized—representations of Mexican manhood. Featuring actors like Luis Aguilar, Pedro Infante, José Alfredo Jiménez, and Jorge Negrete, *comedias rancheras*, more than any other artistic genre, bolstered tequila's image as a natural element of a bygone era. Mexican directors—in concert with the dominant political trend of the period—made films with patriotic subjects set in idyllic and unchanging countryside settings.[10] Plots centered on *charros'* romanticized lives in rural Mexico. Because *charros* were already widely recognized as symbols of Mexican identity, they were cast to depict "common" Mexicans on the big screen. The *charro* came to represent the "true Mexican"—not only did he defend his family and country, but he also sang songs, danced *jarabes*, and took part in *charreadas* and local festivals.[11] *Charro* protagonists fought for the rights of the less fortunate and extolled the virtues of honesty and courage; they embodied an array of idealized nationalistic attributes that were central to the storylines of *comedias rancheras*. However, unlike the sober image enforced by real-life *charro* associations, on the big screen they commonly participated in excessive barroom drinking, offensive behavior, and the mistreatment of women.

Despite his unruly demeanor, the *charro*'s upstanding character was always reestablished by the end of the film. Notably, he was able to connect with audiences by conveying his innermost feelings through the *canción ranchera*. The performance of *ranchera* songs, with their emotional, romantic, and valiant themes, absolved the *charro* of his unflattering antics. In the presence of other *charros*, or sometimes by himself, singing released his sentimentality, humanized him, and tempered his distasteful conduct, which was often directed at a female love interest. By publicly reflecting on his actions while drinking tequila—his truth serum of choice—the *charro* symbolically spills his soul, and as a result his faults are always forgiven by both audiences and by those he hurt or disrespected. Gender studies scholar Palomar Varea maintains that the *charro*'s unique ability to redeem himself is intimately tied to the racial/ethnic dimensions of Mexican nationalism. Specifically, she argues that the *charro*'s character was often infused with references to particular political and class sectors whose values were synonymous with conservative ideas of *lo mexicano*.

Central to the *charro*'s genuine mystique are his ethnic and regional origins: Because he is from Jalisco, he is steeped in European associations that reinforce and reflect a specific notion of authentic Mexican identity.[12] While Jalisco's European reputation has a legacy that extends to colonialism, it was recycled during the period of postrevolutionary recovery when officials sought to distance the national character from the image of the war and instead promote new and idealized archetypes of Mexicanness. In *comedias rancheras*, Jalisco was portrayed as a fantastic and mythic setting where venerated notions of what it meant to be Mexican were scripted into reality. This representation was also reinforced through the songs sung by *charro* protagonists. "*Tequila con limón*" (Tequila with lime), the famous track from Miguel Zacaría's 1944 film, *Me he de comer esa tuna* (I Will Have That Woman) that exemplifies the stability of these associations:

Traigo música en el alma	I have music in my soul,
Y un cantar aquí en el pecho	And a song here in my chest;
un cantar que me desgarra	A song that tears me apart
cuando lo hecho por amor.	When I sing it with love;
lo aprendí por esos cantos	I learned it in these fields,
con heridas de barbecho	With wounds from fallow land;
con tajadas de mayetes	With slices from machetes;
y el vibrar del guitarrón.	And vibrations from the *guitarrón*.
Lo sentí por el palenque	I learned it in the *palenque*
apostando un gallo fino	Betting on a fine cockerel
y me siento suficiente	And I feel up to the task

pa' cantarlo por allí.	Of singing it around here;
Al orgullo de Jalisco	The pride of Jalisco,
lo nombraron mi padrino	Is what they called my godfather,
y no tiene más ahijados	And he has no other godchildren,
porque ya me tiene a mí.	Because he's already got me.
Sangre brava y colorada	Brave, red blood,
pretadora como filo de puñal	As challenging as the edge of a dagger,
es la sangre de mi raza	Such is the blood of my *raza* [people],
soñadora y cancionera	That dreams and sings,
sangre brava y peleonera	Brave and troublemaking blood,
calentona y pretendiera	Valiant and quarrelsome
como penca de nopal.	Like the nopal cactus leaf
A las patas de un caballo	On the hooves of a horse,
juego siempre mi dinero	I always bet my money
y si unas veces fallo	And if I lose sometimes
me desquito en un albur.	I get even with a bet
traigo siempre flor de boca	I always carry like a flower in my mouth
la tonada que más quiero	The ballad I love the most
para ver a quien le toca	And to see whose turn it is,
y pa' hecharla a su salúd.	And to sing it to their health
Y sentir hervir la sangre	And feel your blood boil
Por todito el cuerpo entero	Throughout your entire body
pa' gritar "¡Viva Jalisco!"	So to scream, "*Viva Jalisco!*"
con el alma y corazón.	With all of your heart and soul
Que bonito y que bonito	How beautiful and how nice
el llegar a un merendero	To arrive at a picnic
y beber en un jarrito	And drink a jug
Un tequila con limón.	A tequila with lime
Sangre brava y colorada . . .	Brave, red blood . . .

Set in a cantina, this musical scene portrays the handsome lead (Jorge Negrete) surrounded by fellow *charros* who chime in with *gritos* (cries), which, in a call-and-response fashion, acknowledge the shared passion and earnestness of the performance. In the background, female attendants, dressed in traditional *china poblana* outfits, are also present—serving tequila to surrounding

tables of all-male groups of patrons. The setting accentuates traditional notions of gender-appropriate duties, the lyrics naturalize the bonds between
the singer (Negrete) and pride of ancestry—one linked to Jalisco, its music,
and its drink, tequila. Dozens of other popular *canciones rancheras* of this
era, including classics like *"Ella"* and *"El charro Mexicano"* helped forge the
connection among Jalisco, tequila, and *lo mexicano*. Within the space of the
cantina, a locale that bridged rural and urban *mexicanidad, charros* could express an authentic sense of self and convey their enthusiasm for heteronormative romance.

Cantina scenes were ubiquitous in *comedias rancheras* and other Golden
Age films. In real life and on the big screen, cantinas were important gathering places—working-class saloons, "manly environments"—locales that were
implicitly (and at times explicitly) reserved for male patrons.[13] Within these
highly gendered-segregated spaces, where women on occasion worked as
servers, sold snacks, or sang songs, tequila is almost always the drink of choice
for male characters. In cantinas, both protagonists and antagonists reckoned
with their comical, complicated, or tragic circumstances. Repetition—of settings, objects, story lines, and even the recurrence of certain actors—played a
critical cinematic role in this era. Because of the historical ties (and tensions)
that coupled Mexican masculinity with alcohol, cantinas and the consumption of tequila were incorporated into this recurring narrative strategy. As
the most "transportable medium" of the time, film quickly and widely dis-
seminated visual messages about the key sequences of Mexican men's lives to
Mexican and international viewers.[14]

Spanning across film genres, working men of varying degrees of social
respectability were depicted as imbibing tequila to liberate themselves from
the turmoil of heartbreak or the constraints of daily life. The much-loved
Cantinflas, Mexico's most famous comic actor, was another character who
appeared on screen drinking his share of tequila.[15] Initially disregarded by
the Mexican elite and embraced by the masses, Cantinflas was "a lumpen,
streetwise irritant, the master of *mal gusto* (bad taste)."[16] According to legend,
Cantinflas's meteoric rise to fame occurred after filling in for a friend as master of ceremonies at a *carpa*, a type of traveling show frequented by members
of lower socioeconomic classes. The nervous Mario Moreno Reyes, as he was
then known, took the stage, wet his pants, and began explaining his actions
in an incoherent fashion. The crowd went wild for his over-the-top antics, and
someone yelled, "En la cantina, tú inflas!"—literally, "You've been tanking up

FIGURE 8. Cantinflas and Manuel Medel, *Águila o sol* (Heads or Tails) (1937).
Source: Filmoteca, UNAM. Reprinted with permission.

in the cantina."[17] These words melded together for Moreno, and Cantinflas
was born (see Figure 8).

Whether the protagonist was a *charro*, gunslinger, underdog, streetwise
irritant, or Casanova, during the Golden Age of Mexican cinema, tequila
emerged as the on-screen drink of choice. Much like images of Pedro Infante
and Jorge Negrete (Figure 9), who personified various enduring expressions
of masculinity (for example, noble, loyal), tequila straddled the boundaries
of tradition and modernity that symbolized national coherence in a period
of continuing postrevolutionary recovery and shifting social norms. Importantly, the Mexican public of this era not only trusted their on-screen idols
to guide them through the unsteady waters of modernization but mimicked
actors' gestures, humor, and ways of speaking—hence copying a range of expressions and ways of being.[18] An emblem of *lo mexicano*, tequila's presence in
Golden Age film ensured that it would eventually become a coded and spir-
ited metaphor for resilience in the face of societal change, providing assurance
on the one hand and yet leaving space for improvisation and subversion, on
the other (Figure 10).

FIGURE 9. Luis Aguilar and Jorge Negrete, *Tal para cual* (Tit for Tat) (1953).
Source: Filmoteca, UNAM. Reprinted with permission.

FIGURE 10. Pedro Armendáriz, *Juan Charrasqueado* (Juan Charrasqueado) (1948).
Source: Filmoteca, UNAM. Reprinted with permission.

The *China Poblana*

Gender and race play a central role in securing ideas of a collective notion of Mexicanness in which the *charro*, as a dashingly handsome and humble macho, kindles the sympathy of viewers by confronting his vulnerabilities and commiserating with his *cuates* (buddies) over tequila. His female counterpart, known as the *china poblana*, likewise played an important role in bolstering the *charro*'s enduring reputation. Unlike the *escaramusa* who rode horses in *charreadas*, the *china poblana*'s role was far more limited—she was often depicted as the silent and respectful companion of *charros*. The name, *china poblana*, originally referred to a style of dress worn by women from the state of Puebla,[19] though in the 1940s the costume began to acquire new meanings in relation to Mexican womanhood.[20] While the term *china* is now commonly used as a generic term for "servant" or "country girl," during viceregal times, the word referred to a woman of Asian background (for example, Filipina, Chinese, or Japanese).[21] On the big screen, however, she was implicitly of a respectable class background, was mestiza, and was characterized by what she wore—an embroidered white, green, or red blouse and a castor skirt decorated with colorful sequins and beads. By the end of the first half of the twentieth century, the *china poblana* was "a quintessential nationalist type"[22] that exemplified the ideals of Mexican femininity.[23]

The *china poblana* costume was ubiquitous in films, festivals, and cultural events—public places where nationalism and commercialism were becoming increasingly connected to one another. Because it resembled the clothes worn by European peasants, it was culturally, politically, and racially neutral, and therefore nonthreatening. In other words, the use of the *china poblana* costume over all other indigenous outfits (for example, those worn by less affluent women in Oaxaca) as emblematic of Mexican femininity effectively shaped a style of *lo mexicano* that gestured toward European sensibilities and excluded aesthetic contributions from African and Asian influences, despite the etymological aspect of its name. With an emphasis on simplicity, representations on film and in print ads simultaneously reflected and idealized aspects of Mexican daily life and native customs. Advertisements, including magazine and newspaper illustrations, postcards, and calendars, helped communicate and standardize essentializing characteristics. The advertising industry played a prominent role in exalting a united image of Mexico through the marketplace.²⁴ By the twentieth century, the *china poblana* figure was a customary feature in beer ads, on tavern serving trays, and on cigar and cigarette wrappers. She also appeared in tequila calendars for companies such as Jose Cuervo and Sauza, accompanying handsome *charros* in festive and patriotic settings (see Figures 11 and 12). A pervasive form of advertising in cities, towns, and villages, these calendars were seen daily by thousands of people as they walked by shops, cantinas, and other businesses. The calendars launched images of tequila (in relation to the *charro* and the *china poblana*) "into the very center of social existence," incorporating the racialized, nationalistic scenes into the domestic and public sphere.²⁵

Calendars often portrayed the consumption of tequila in relation to cockfighting, breaking a horse, or wooing a suitor. In Figures 11 and 12, attractive women accompany male companions at a *charreada* and a card game. In contrast to the robust and macho men featured in the pictures, the women, dressed in *china poblana* outfits, appear playful and flirtatious. In Figure 11, four light-skinned women (signaling that they are from Los Altos, Jalisco's most "European" region) greet a *charro* who carries a bottle of tequila after finishing (and presumably winning) a *charreada* competition. While three of the women gaze longingly at the *charro*, a fourth holds a colorful bouquet. Directing her smile at the viewer, she leans in to deliver the flowers as the *charro* (perhaps her paramour) rides toward her in the arena stands. Unlike his beaming romantic interest, and the other women who express dreamy gratification, the *charro*'s expression is measured as he pulls the reins of his horse with one hand and raises a bottle of tequila with the other. In contrast to the women's whiteness, the *charro*'s just-dark-enough complexion indicates, without a doubt, that he is mestizo.

Figure 12 depicts a *charro* playing cards with a group of men and who is accompanied by his *china poblana* companion. The *charro*'s emotive reaction and body language suggests that he has just won the game (and the money accruing on the table)—he is laughing and is about to take off his hat in jubilation as a fellow player laments, with mouth agape, his own loss. In stark relief to the mestizo appearance of the *charro* and the other card player, the woman, dressed in a light-blue, scoop-neck *china poblana* dress, is fair skinned. She too is happy about the results of the card game; however, her expression is, above all, coquettish. With her hands placed on her hips, her torso raised upright, and her head tilted back in the direction of the *charro*, she smiles at the

FIGURE 11 AND FIGURE 12. Calendar images, Jose Cuervo Tequila. Photos by Gwyn Fisher.

game's outcome. Although the bottle of tequila sits on the card table, she is not the intended consumer; she is there to accompany and support her *charro* suitor but will not partake in the festivities.

The calendars mirrored the population's optimism about modernization at the same time that they helped support efforts to redefine Mexico according to a very specific set of cultural traditions. Depicting modest women and vigorous men, tequila calendar art reflected and reinforced gender roles that emphasized female submissiveness and male dominance in the context of an increasingly commodified national image. Further, they standardized racial archetypes, whereby traditional figures (that is, both light-skinned women and just-dark-enough men) were portrayed as implicitly originating from the state of Jalisco. The essence of Mexican femininity, the *china poblana* and her light complexion fashioned popular conceptions and expectations of Mexican womanhood as gender representations became more visually prominent in the public sphere and intersected at a greater pace with commercial culture.

Machorra Femininity

More than any other actress of the time, Sara García, "Mexico's Mother," embodied the epitome of maternal attributes central to the *comedia ranchera*.[26] Born in 1895 to Spanish immigrants, García's career began in 1917 with the silent film *En defense propia* (In Self-Defense). One year later, at the age of twenty-three, she played her first role as a much older woman. García enjoyed on-screen success and worked with some of the most famous directors of the time. Even with these accomplishments, in 1934, she had fourteen teeth pulled so that her gums could look naturally aged in the hope of landing her first lead in the theatrical production, *Mi abuelita la pobre*.[27] These drastic measures paid off, and when she transitioned to working in sound films she had little trouble finding work as an elderly mother or grandmother. García's matronly characters were often described as self-sacrificing women who were "passive, resilient, resourceful, and asexual with no visible limits to either her goodness or self-denial."[28] Yet not every role represented her in this stereotypical manner.

By the late 1930s, Sara García's career was flourishing; however, she would enjoy even greater stardom in the 1940s when she began acting in *comedias rancheras*. In the widely celebrated films *Los tres garcia* (1947) and *¡Vuelven los Garcia!* (1947), she played the rambunctious Grandma Luisa, the widowed family matriarch of the Garcia family. Both films track her attempt to call a truce between the three feuding Garcia cousins (played by Pedro Infante, Abel Salazar, and Victor Manuel Mendoza), each a son of one of her three fallen sons. Donning large, wide-rimmed black glasses and smoking a cigar in nearly every scene, the feisty Luisa curses liberally as she belts out orders to the help and chastises her grandsons. When not trying to resolve familial issues, she is depicted as attending mass or offering advice to the fair-skinned female actress (played by Marga López) who wins the affection of the three cousins. Family is first for Luisa, and she is not afraid to take her cane and smack anyone who stands in her way.

In contrast to her other female costars, Grandma Luisa's no-nonsense style strikes a unique balance of providing feminine comedic relief that adheres to traditional notions of Mexican womanhood at the same time that it challenges strict definitional boundaries. Diana Bracho offers insight into this paradox by maintaining that what might initially seem like a contradiction is actually a by-product of patriarchal conventions. Based on her own experiences as a Mexican actress, she writes that directors in the Golden Age era were far from sympathetic when it came to the cinematic representation of women. When writers did create a strong feminine character, they often gave her male characteristics. As Bracho explains, "The Mexican woman became an omnipresent matriarch, a substitute for the masculine figure who holds his own with everything and everyone."[29] Specifically, these characters were assigned hypermasculine traits that depicted them as "*machorras*," the slang for tomboy or a female macho.

Grandma Luisa's *machorra* femininity provides an opportunity to more deeply understand how Mexican masculinity is tied to national identity and amplified through nonnormative masculinities. In Mexico, the word *machorra* has derogatory connotations—it is widely assumed that *machorras* reject men and are attracted to women.[30] Women who appear too masculine are often the target of innuendo that insinuates that they are maladjusted or are not "real women." The *machorra* is generally seen as pathological or, in the case of Bracho's analysis, as affirming the superiority of dominant masculinity. Much like Judith Halberstam's description of female masculinity, I argue that García's *machorra* femininity both coincides with and challenges "the excesses of male supremacy."[31] García's adaptation of Grandma Luisa's *machorra* character places unconventional femininity within the story line of the *comedia ranchera*, destabilizes the traditional gender roles associated with *lo mexicano*, and exposes the workings of dominant masculinities within Mexican film.

Sara García starred in hundreds of movies and was an acclaimed actress in her own right. Her on-screen interactions with Pedro Infante—throughout the course of the seven films they made together—helped secure her cinematic reputation. Infante's roles, which embodied the stereotype of the philandering but light-hearted, tequila-drinking *charro*, sharpened ideas about macho Mexican masculinity, and Sara García's characters played a part in cementing this association. Nowhere is this more evident than in the *comedia ranchera* film, *Dicen que soy mujeriego* (1949), (They Say I'm a Womanizer). As

Doña Rosa, a wealthy hacienda *patrona* (boss), García attempts to change her grandson's (played by Infante) over-the-top womanizing ways. Much like her earlier roles, she smokes a cigar, whistles, and curses. When riding her horse on a day out hunting with a group of male hacienda workers, rather than sitting sidesaddle, she sits astride like a man. Later, in the same scene, she shoots and kills a rabbit on her first try, unlike the parish priest who accompanies her. While the rabbit lies motionless on the ground, she shouts, "Am I good or what?!"

Doña Rosa is responsible for the family and the home; however, her primary emotional role is taking close care of Pedro, her orphaned grandson. Different from the stereotype of the pious and self-sacrificing mother, she crosses the customary lines often associated with maternal or grandmotherly comportment. Doña Rosa's *machorra* femininity enhances Pedro's sentimentality and facilitates his ability to reflect on his indiscretions. In one such scene, while drinking tequila with the cantina bartender, Pedro drunkenly and remorsefully exclaims that he is the "black sheep" of the family. When he returns to the hacienda, singing alongside mariachis in the direction of Doña Rosa's upstairs window, he sobbingly acknowledges the pain he has caused her and Tucita, his illegitimate daughter. In the following scene, the pair is in a cantina, seated at a table with two empty tequila bottles. Leaning inward, Pedro asks his grandmother if they should drink another. "Yes," she says, with her voice noticeably slurred. After extinguishing her cigar and letting out a loud hiccup, Doña Rosa lifts her glass and together they down a shot of tequila (see Figure 13).

Sitting at a different table is the family servant, Bartolo, who is quickly summoned by Doña Rosa. Together they approach the bar where two wine glasses are arranged next to each other. Covering one eye, she raises a pistol and shoots one glass, lets out a cackle, and then shoots the other glass. In the background, Pedro laughs uncontrollably as she makes Bartolo hold a glass of wine on his head as he tremblingly tells her he does not want to die. After she fires the successful shot and the glass explodes, he faints. Doña Rosa laughs out loud, returns to the table, and tells Pedro the he too will have to prove his marksmanship skills and shoot a playing card from her hand. Pedro refuses, but Doña Rosa pours him another shot of tequila, "Here, drink this." Still reluctant, she yells, "Shoot or you're not my grandson!" Pedro takes the rifle, proclaims that he is not a coward, shoots the gun, and accidentally misses, grazing his grandmother's shoulder.

FIGURE 13. Sara García and Pedro Infante in *Dicen que soy mujeriego* (They Say I'm a Womanizer), 1949.
Source: Pascual Espinosa Collection.

In an era when cantinas were considered improper places for "good" women, Doña Rosa is depicted as comfortable and commanding in a location reserved for men—she is the one who insists that she will accompany her grandson to the cantina. Amplifying the scenic backdrop are empty bottles of tequila—an elixir that soothes sadness and enables an outpouring of unmistakably masculine emotion. Representations like these are emblematic of what film scholar Sergio De La Mora calls "cinemachismo," the repertoire of cultural cues that reinforce the centrality of male heterosexuality in Mexican cinema.[32] Places like cantinas and products like tequila assist in the stabilization and standardization of notions of Mexican manhood. The cultural assumptions built into cinemachismo, and its heightened emphasis on a certain (but limited) account of masculinity, symbolically allows for actuations of *machorra* femininity as yet another element through which notions of normative masculinity are sustained.

There are, however, limits to the recognition and incorporation of *machorra* subjectivity in *comedias rancheras*. Under the influence of tequila, Pedro takes Doña Rosa's target-shooting challenge, and he injures her. By unintentionally missing the target (the playing card), he puts an end to her teasing, reasserting his superiority as his actions make clear that *machorra* femininity can never truly threaten it or take the place of authentic masculinity. A complicated and undertheorized aspect of the Mexican Golden Age era, *machorra* femininity is but one of many expressions of womanhood in *comedias rancheras*. Coming of age in the postrevolution period, actress and singer Lucha Reyes shifted the terms of Mexican iconicity by further challenging the representation of Mexicanas in sonic and cinematic culture.

La Tequilera

The revolution prompted significant changes in women's roles in Mexican society. *Soldaderas* (female soldiers) fought alongside men, smuggled ammunition, and worked as journalists and activists.[33] Their contributions to the war effort prompted (albeit slowly) new attitudes toward women's place in the nation and resulted in an increased demand for their labor once the fighting ceased. Their military involvement encouraged dialogue regarding women's suffrage and brought new attention to the unjust effects of gender inequality. Formal combat records dedicated sections to women's efforts, praised female participation, and acknowledged their efforts to defend their country. The recognition of women in the revolutionary movement (however limited) sparked new momentum for the acceptance of women's civic participation in other aspects of everyday life.[34]

Women's organizations began to assert themselves in larger numbers by the end of the first decade of the twentieth century, and in 1922 women won the right to vote in local elections. Three years later, in 1925, the state of Chiapas granted women equal political rights to men. These successes were largely due to the actions of progressive state leaders; indeed, clergy and conservatives (both men and women) challenged these efforts.[35] The implementation of these changes was sluggish despite the organizing efforts of women's groups throughout the 1920s.[36] (Women finally won the right to vote in municipal elections in 1946; in 1953, women were granted the right to vote in national elections.)[37] In 1932 civil codes were passed that granted women more rights within marriage. Although women began to formally participate in greater numbers in work outside of the home, economic equality was slow in coming. Poor and working-class women, such as those who worked in *pulquerías*, were no doubt very familiar with having their labor devalued. Change was gradual and difficult to achieve, but by the end of the 1930s, women were granted the ability to sign legal documents that enabled them to enter into binding contracts.[38]

In 1938, new legislative measures were enacted that established copyright protections for authors, editors, and translators. The updated codes also reflected a new interest on the part of the government to support bureaucratic structures that promoted the growth of an emerging consumer culture oriented toward public spectatorship, including the development of radio studios and broadcasting.[39] Performers from Mexico's urban musical theater became increasingly popular as radio started to emerge as a vibrant entertainment medium. Radio broadcasting was also closely connected to film as both media promoted the same popular music and performing artists.[40] The symbiotic exchange between the two entertainment formats, together with the growing demand for singers and songwriters after the Mexican Revolution, provided new opportunities for women to enter several musical genres.

As the revolution came to a close by the early 1920s, the country experienced significant changes in its self-image and sense of national identity. In particular, the recovery period instigated a new admiration for the cultural contributions of peasants and the urban proletariat. Before and during the *Porfiriato*, the *canción ranchera* genre featured French titles and sentimental themes and was sung in bel canto, a popular European style of singing. After the *Porfiriato*, however, the genre's themes and orchestration changed substantively, with refrains focusing on peasant life on haciendas.[41] No longer limited to songs heard in cantinas or *pulquerías*, professional (that is, reputable) singers also began performing its songs on stage.[42] The increased popularity of the genre translated to *canción ranchera* artists who were closely linked to the songs they sang. Performers were seen as popular heroes, revered for their talent to intuit and articulate what people experienced in their everyday lives.[43] A powerful musical expression that was rooted in oral tradition, the *canción ranchera* allowed listeners to sing along with musical refrains and, at the same time, convey through melodies the shared joys and hardships of navigating the postrevolution period. These complex aesthetic qualities served as a sonic site where community values were not only presented, but transmitted, replicated, and contested.[44]

During the 1930s, the popularity of the *canción ranchera* continued to spread due to the growing number of radio stations and rising interest in radio listening. Altering local social relations by connecting rural communities to both national and international spheres of cultural exchange and radio broadcasting, together with the nascent medium of sound film, instigated new musical dialogues and accompaniments, including folk ensembles that included female entertainers. One such artist, Lucha Reyes, profoundly influenced the genre and performance of mariachi music. Born on May 23, 1906, in Guadalajara, Mexico, María de la Luz Flores Aceves—or Lucha Reyes—is referred to as "the queen of mariachi,"[45] "the greatest practitioner of Mexican music," and "the most authentic performer of Mexican music."[46]

When Reyes was six months old, her father died, and, when she was seven, her mother moved the family to Mexico City.[47] From birth, Reyes faced a range of challenges. She was plagued by health issues, and at the age of four she contracted typhus, rendering her mute for a year. One legend holds that her voice returned in reaction to an argument between her mother and brother when, upset by what she was witnessing, Reyes began to scream in frustration.[48] By the age of thirteen she was performing in the *carpas* and *revistas* (theatrical revue shows) of Mexico City to support her family.[49] Reyes won a local talent contest and voice lessons that taught her how to sing *zarzuelas*, traditional songs popular among European royalty that enabled her to perform and gain respect among middle- and upper-class audiences.[50] To be sure, she was appealing to an array of musical tastes and garnering the interest of a broad spectrum of listeners.

In 1920, Reyes moved to Los Angeles, California, to develop her skills as a soprano. Accompanied by fellow *carpa* performer Nancy Torres, also known as "*la Potranquita*" (the young mare), Reyes toured the country, sometimes singing in duets. At the age of seventeen, Reyes married Gabriel Navarro, who would later publish several books and become a writer for *La Opinión*, the oldest Spanish-language newspaper in the United States. In her highly original work on the careers of Mexican female singers, Antonia Garcia-Orozco suggests that Torres and Reyes were lovers, a detail that her then-husband Navarro had no knowledge of until they were married.[51] Describing a claim made by one of her interviewees, Garcia Orozco explains that, around the time when Reyes discovered she was pregnant, Navarro learned of her relationship with Torres and beat her; she miscarried. After her miscarriage, Reyes reportedly began to drink heavily.[52]

On returning to Mexico in 1929, Reyes signed a contract with the radio station XEW. In Mexico City, she performed with Trío Reyes-Ascensio and then later joined El Cuarteto Anáhuac, with whom she toured Europe. While on tour, Reyes endured throat infections and respiratory problems. Complicating matters, the boat trip across the Atlantic further aggravated her symptoms, and when she arrived in Mexico she was very ill. Mute for a year,[53] she suffered permanent vocal cord damage and lost an octave of her range.[54] Other accounts suggest that the damage to her throat was related to excessive drinking.[55] Despite conflicting explanations, one thing was clear: Reyes's new husky voice complemented the *canción ranchera* style of music performed by mariachis.

During this period, it was unheard of for women to sing with mariachis because of the myriad taboos associated with transgressing gender boundaries.[56] These negative connotations did not stop Reyes from embracing a vocal style known as the *estilo bravío* (bold style) and performing with mariachis.[57] Reyes's decision to sing with mariachis was not initially embraced by all sectors of society. Upper-class listeners likely interpreted this decision as betraying the aesthetic musical sensibilities associated with conservative values.[58] Upper-class audiences were also likely taken aback by her appearance—Reyes often wore the *china poblana* outfit when she sang.[59] Unlike other actresses who donned such regalia—and who rarely spoke, let alone called attention to themselves—Reyes's robust voice, full figure, wide-armed gestures, and bobbed hair embodied a less-than-conventional femininity. Far from demure, her visual appearance and singing style signaled a violation of the rigid gender conventions that supported traditional notions of Mexican womanliness. Together, Reyes's subversive stylistics, that is, her queer presence and commanding performances, presents a more complicated and purposeful notion of Mexicana sensuality.[60]

By 1930, Lucha Reyes was a regular performer on the program, *La voz de América desde México* (The Voice of America from Mexico). She sang live on the radio, established a record contract with RCA, and became a household name. Between 1935 and 1943, Lucha Reyes recorded numerous radio hits, sang in theatrical productions,[61] and appeared in nine films with some of the most noted actors of the era. Although never actually headlining as the female lead,[62] it was Reyes's vocal range and manner of singing that entranced industry insiders and audiences alike. She "gave lavishly of her voice, tearing it apart, whining, crying, laughing and cursing."[63] Listeners were enthralled by her mixing of singing techniques and dismissal of unwritten conventions. She even challenged fashion norms by occasionally wearing *charro* trousers on stage.[64] Reyes's style was avant-garde because she unabashedly mocked male privilege and claimed male bravura for herself.

Eccentric performances by female artists that bucked traditional codes of femininity were the exception to the norm during this era. Like Reyes, the beloved singer Chavela Vargas, pushed the boundaries of "appropriate" feminine comportment. "La Chabela," as she was known, moved from her native Costa Rica to Mexico in the 1950s and, like Reyes, suffered hardships at an early age, including polio and blindness. Often blacklisted because of her "obscene" behavior, which included openly flirting with female members of the audience, her idiosyncratic style and vocal technique placed lesbian subjectivity into the patriarchal world of Mexican music.[65] The intensity of Lucha Reyes's unusual voice and performance style, like that of Chavela Vargas, made her highly sought after by Mexican film directors, club owners, and composers. One such composer, Alfredo D'Orsay, wrote a song that would become one of her biggest hits, "*La Tequilera*" (the female tequila drinker, 1941):[66]

Borrachita de tequila	My soul is always
llevo siempre el alma mía	drunk with tequila
para ver si mejora	to see if it can heal
de esta cruel melancolía	from this cruel melancholy.
Ay! Por ese querer	Ay, because of that love
Pos' qué le he de hacer,	so what can I do,
si el destino me lo dio	if destiny gave it to me
para siempre padecer.	to always suffer.
Como buena Mexicana	Like a good Mexican woman
sufriré el dolor tranquila	I will suffer the pain tranquilly
al fin y a cabo mañana	since after all tomorrow
tendré un trago de tequila.	I'll have a drink of tequila.
Ay! Por ese querer	Ay! Because of that love
Pos' qué le he de hacer,	so what can I do,
aunque me haya traicionado	even if he betrayed me
no lo puedo aborrecer	I cannot hate him.
Ay! ya me voy mejor	Ay! It's better I leave
por qué aguardo aquí;	what am I doing here;
dizque por la borrachera,	they say I lost it all,
dicen todo lo perdí	because of being drunk.

The name "*La Tequilera*" signals a gendered play on language, as "tequila" in Spanish is always preceded with the masculine pronoun *el*. Using the feminine pronoun *la* in combination with a word that is grammatically masculine underscores the writer's insistence on calling attention to both *who* is singing and *what* it is that person is singing about, thus leaving little room for misinterpretation: The singer is a woman, and she is describing her experiences with tequila. Although the moniker "*La Tequilera*" suggests a lighthearted subject, the name, when placed in context with the lyrics, actually conjures themes of anguish, betrayal, and inebriation—issues that resonated with women who, for fear of public judgment, often did not openly address them. By drinking too much tequila, the interpreter violates gender-appropriate and middle-class norms. Punctuated by Reyes's raspy voice and the complex orchestration of the mariachi arrangement, the melancholy lyrics are skillfully transformed through the ironic and playful recognition of her nickname. At a time when it was largely taboo for women to consume alcohol (especially liquor like tequila) or publicly express their desire to drink or get drunk, the song challenged a number of societal conventions. Her actions therefore likely resonated with the experiences of poor and working-class women who were often assumed to lack cultural refinement.[67]

The lyrics of "*La Tequilera*" clearly depart from traditional feminine expectations; however, equally important is Lucha Reyes's performance of the song because it highlights how tequila operated as a site where dominant ideologies could be unsettled through consumption. The resounding first verse, where Reyes professes that her soul "is always drunk with tequila," evokes both wit and sadness, depending on how she performed the song, reconfiguring its energy on her own terms. Reyes's inflection is vital for punctuating the subversive tone of the forthcoming lyrics. Acknowledging that destiny will bring her suffering after the betrayal of her lover, like a "good Mexican woman," it appears as if she will willingly accept her impending fate and sorrow. Having established an air of inevitability, the lyrics then, out of form, declare that she will drink some tequila. Despite her lover's disloyalty, she admits that she cannot hate him, and then returns to provide more autobiographical details that may or may not have contributed to her unavoidable situation: "They call me the tequila drinker, as it was from my baptism, because they baptized me with a shot of tequila." The reference to baptism, a Catholic ritual and the first of the holy sacraments, alludes to the lifelong expectations of the church, especially with regard to women's comportment. Finally, the last stanza again gestures to the inevitable; however, this time it is with a sense of marked irreverence conveyed by the interjection, "Ay!" The only thing left for Reyes to do, she sings, is to "leave what I'm doing here" and acknowledge the persistent judgment of others, who "say I lost it all because of being drunk."

The closing lines of the song leave room for several interpretations. On the one hand, they could signify demise or the realization of self-destruction. On the other, they might signal a moment of self-reflection that nods to a future where change is possible. For example, when Reyes states that she has decided to leave her toxic environment or lover, such exact and abrupt lyrics might very well provide some women with the confidence they need to move on from or alter their current circumstances.[68] Although having no concrete or singular meaning, the lyrics to "*La Tequilera*" communicated a range of accounts that undoubtedly spoke to the experiences of Mexican women by creatively acknowledging the challenges associated with the societal norms regarding femininity. Indeed, the situated performance and use of "*La Tequilera*" as a classic *canción ranchera* provided a culturally appropriate means for women to confront and expand what was deemed culturally appropriate behavior for women (see Figure 14).

By making reference to the consumption of tequila—a drink popularly associated with "macho" attributes—women, within the genres of Mexican music and film, similarly invoked the imagery of tequila for their own uses, "sometimes highlighting their subordination, sometimes talking back to that subordination, but always calling attention to their concerns, desires, experiences and needs."[69] Paradoxically, the static association of tequila with expressions of a masculinized national identity enabled an amplified inversion of its revered meaning, creating new opportunities for women to transgress traditional gender norms. Further, just as *ranchera* songs provide an opportunity for women to express anger and convey disappointment, tequila likewise functioned as an ambiguous space where women could assert a range of emotions and destabilize the gendered dimensions of consumption. Tequila, in spite of its close alignment with masculine *mexicanidad*, should not be dismissed as a one-dimensional trope that maintains social categories or enforces conservative political culture. Instead, as explained by Teresa de Lauretis, it operates as a type of technology that exists within the margins of dominant discourse, that, although less evident, serves as a site where local levels of resistance and self-representation unsettle traditional expectations.

Lucha Reyes's rumored abuse of alcohol would ultimately shape her notoriety. Tragically, Lucha Reyes's life would end too soon: On June 25, 1944,

FIGURE 14. Lucha Reyes, date unknown.
Source: Filmoteca, UNAM. Reprinted with
permission.

she died at age 38, after consuming twenty-two Nembutal capsules (a type
of barbiturate), reportedly with tequila. Guadalajara newspaper *El Informador* wrote that friends of the singer attributed her suicide to Reyes's reaction
to the death of Concepción Martinez, her former mother-in-law, who had
passed away four days earlier.[70] The newspaper also noted that Reyes had sent
her adopted daughter to purchase the pills and that a police captain tried to

remove the pills from her mouth and injured his hand in the process. Deliberate and exceptional in life and in death, Lucha Reyes's suicide, much like that of Mexican actress Lupe Vélez (also in 1944), is perhaps better understood through a structural explanation rather than a moralistic one. Extending the insight of Chicana studies scholar Rosa-Linda Fregoso, Reyes, like Vélez, was ahead of the times, finding it difficult to manage the strictly enforced and often-intertwined norms that shaped family, religion (Catholicism), and gender within Mexico. Reyes's complex life and troubling death broke with social conventions and moral standards of the time period. Bold and brilliant, Lucha Reyes was and remains one of Mexico's most extraordinary musical performers ever to interpret the *canción ranchera* and challenge attitudes about tequila's heteronormative ties to masculinity.

Conclusion

Technological advances in cinema, print media, and radio introduced the Mexican public to the *comedia ranchera* and its *canciones rancheras*, two cultural forms that shaped how audiences interpreted and related to tequila as a symbol of national identity. Initially celebrated as an expression of *lo mexicano* synonymous with the trials and tribulations of *charros*, tequila became closely associated with hacienda life that heightened the drink's connection to customary notions of gender, sexuality, class, and race—conventions that closely aligned with patriarchal dimensions of power. Fashioned "between the lines" of mainstream discourse, various connotations "co-exist concurrently and in contradiction" to each other in the practice of Mexican popular culture.[71] Thus, commodities—like the subtext of performances, such as those by Lucha Reyes—likewise operate as sites where meanings are contested and alternative identities are legitimized.

Tequila's close cinematic ties to the *comedia ranchera* solidified its relationship to a certain time and place, one that remained embedded in the nation's past. Off-screen, there was increased interest among the growing urban and upwardly mobile classes in acquiring cosmopolitan material goods, foreign products that could allow them to experience and participate in modernization. Accompanied by technological advancements and the spread of consumerism, consumption—not just in Mexico, but around the world—signaled the emergence of new practices of distinction and self-identification.[72] It is important to note that not everyone supported these changing norms, especially those who did not have the economic means to participate in market-based displays of difference, while others may have not wanted to link themselves to changing trends. Regardless of one's social standing or taste preference, the coupling of tequila with the images and sounds of a bygone era became a salient feature of the gendered, raced, and classed terms that were defining *lo mexicano* during this period. By the mid-1950s, tequila was emblematic of a certain account of masculinized national identity whose appeal was gradually waning. This association would change as tequila's international reputation continued to grow in unexpected and unintended ways in the decades that followed.

TOURING TEQUILA AND HARVESTING HERITAGE

The Past's Enduring Presence

In 2003, Jose Cuervo, the world's leading producer of tequila, opened Mundo Cuervo (Cuervo World), an expansive, multiacre complex on their hacienda and factory, La Rojeña, in Tequila. Daily tours offer visitors the opportunity to learn about tequila's history and "drink in the surrealistic landscape of blue fields and the mountain backdrops of Jalisco."[1] Located just off the town's main square, Mundo Cuervo is a site where tourists, especially middle-class Mexican tourists, are called on to participate in the affirmation of Mexican identity. As one advertisement invitingly puts it, "Come and see how we have created, out of the rich history of our national drink, a world of . . . traditions that bring a story of hope and life to the people of Tequila . . . A magnificent setting and a mandatory destination for all Mexicans who are proud of their roots."[2] According to Jose Cuervo, Mundo Cuervo's grounds are more than just a place to drink Mexico's spirit; they offer visitors the opportunity to "meaningfully experience" Mexican tradition.[3]

Although Mundo Cuervo is the largest and most extravagant of Tequila's attractions, it is not the only one vying for tourist pesos and dollars. Notably, in 2004, Cofradía Tequila launched Turístico 360, an all-inclusive "totally 100% Mexican" experience that, in addition to providing guests with five-star boutique accommodations in private bungalows, promises "fun, entertainment, relaxation, adventure, and culture" that includes a folkloric music recital, gourmet food, and a night tour of their manufacturing plant.[4] The region is undergoing a boom in tourism-based development as both large and medium-sized tequila companies pursue new revenue streams. Tapping into this potentially lucrative industry allows companies to market their products to a broader set of customers. Although each tour touts the unique attributes of its products, they also share an overarching characteristic: They depict Tequila and tequila—the place and the product—as vital components of *lo mexicano.*

The equation of tequila as a heritage destination and an iconic object has led to the conception of new and recycled myths, including the *jimador* (agave farmer) and Mayahuel (the Aztec goddess). These figures have emerged within what I call "hacienda fantasy heritage"—a manifestation of the contradictions taking place in the Tequila region: Contrary to the patriotic image promoted by tequila companies, the industry is increasingly controlled by transnational—and not Mexican-owned—corporations. By invoking the nostalgic ambiance of Spanish colonial order and the imagery of hacienda life made famous in *comedias rancheras*, tequila industrialists endorse "a cultural salve of equal parts dissonance and romance" to obscure these changes.[5] The *jimador* and Mayahuel play a starring role in highlighting tequila's long-standing and otherworldly attributes. At the same time, they effectively bridge tequila's legendary past with its modern present. These phenomena are indicative of what Daniel Chávez refers to as "multiple temporality,"[6] the balancing of tequila's new global appeal without compromising its traditional characteristics. This chapter explores Tequila's evolution into a "mandatory destination for all Mexicans" and analyzes how meanings of *lo mexicano* are produced in the process.

Tequila: The Essence of Mexico

Tequila is a forty-five-minute drive from the state capital, Guadalajara, and four hours from the popular beach resort of Puerto Vallarta. Organized bus tours from these cities capitalize on the region's rustic reputation by promoting trips that offer a nostalgic journey to the Jaliscan countryside. For instance, one well-known company offers an excursion that begins at Sauza Tequila's factory, El Indio (The Indian), "where you can see the agave cultivating fields" and experience the grounds' "authentic Mexican ranch style."[7] Starting the day at El Indio allows tour guides to connect aspects of tequila's "natural" (agave) attributes to its ethnically "authentic" characteristics (indigenous or mestizo). Advertisements for Mundo Cuervo likewise invoke notions of an essential Mexican identity—one rooted in a history that Jose Cuervo claims they created. In their words:

> We cannot speak of the history of Mexico itself without considering the history of Jose Cuervo. They walk together in time, legends which gave birth to our identity . . . Visitors today can walk the quiet venerable streets of the town of Tequila and rest their eyes upon the blue carpet of fields of agave. [Visitors can] accompany the *jimadores*, the agave harvesters, on their arduous journeys to the fields and share the secrets of Jose Cuervo for the creation of our spirits.[8]

The promotion of Tequila as a uniquely Mexican location allows tequila companies to market their brands as naturally embodied in a collective past and physically rooted in a particular place.

Implicit in this place-based association is Jalisco's significance in historic and contemporary depictions of Mexican tradition. Widely regarded as the nation's "most Mexican" state, Jalisco promotes iconic imagery, such as *charros* and mariachis, that is frequently represented in domestic and international media.[9] These nostalgic connections coalesce in the train tour, Tequila Express la Leyenda (Tequila Express: The Legend), also known as the Tequila Express. Established in 1998 by the Guadalajara Chamber of Commerce, the goal of the Tequila Express is "to revive the magic of the passenger train while showing fellow countrymen and visitors alike Jalisco's most deeply rooted traditions: tequila, mariachi music, and *charrería*."[10] The train, which has hosted more than 175,000 tourists from seventy-five different countries, has as its destination the town of Amatitán, home to Herradura Tequila's hacienda and distillery.

During the early stages of my research in Guadalajara, nearly everyone I talked to about my project mentioned the Tequila Express. I initially thought that it would cater to foreign tourists eager to participate in a nine-hour tequila "excursion." Arriving early to the train station, I was pleasantly surprised (and relieved) by what I saw: The lobby was filled with Mexican families: grandmothers, grandfathers, aunts, uncles, mothers, fathers, and children. Armed with digital video cameras and designer handbags, passengers arrived well dressed for the occasion. As I later learned from the sign-in sheet, international tourists, who numbered roughly thirty of the 210 passengers, were mainly from the United States, but also Canada, Panama, and France. Mexican tourists came from as far south as Chiapas and as far north as Chihuahua.

On entering the station, passengers were directed to one of several lines, named *blanco* (white), *reposado* (rested), *añejo* (aged), and *extra añejo* (extra aged), after the four categories of tequila. The large wall behind the counter was set up as the façade of an old-fashioned hacienda entrance, replete with distressed terra-cotta stucco, red-tile roof shingles, and black wrought-iron lamps, reminiscent of Spanish colonial aesthetics. Even before the tour began, it was clear that we were being prepared for a journey back in time. At the check-in counter we were given boarding badges that read, "Tequila is the perfect complement to travel the world; the culture of tequila, its agave landscape, mixed with mariachi music. This is the genuine expression of our country."

As the final passengers checked in, a fifteen-man mariachi ensemble made its way to the front of the station with their instruments in tow. Dressed in black *charro* attire decorated with ornate white embroidery, they organized themselves into a single line and faced the crowd. Without introduction, they raised their instruments and began to play. Those seated in the lobby stood up and started to gather around in a crescent-shaped crowd, six to seven people deep, many capturing the energetic performance on their cell phones. As the mariachis performed classic songs, including *"Guadalajara"* and *"El son de la negra"* (The Song of the Black Woman), parents nudged their children to pose next to the performers as they snapped pictures while instructing them to smile. Fashionable older women approached the mariachis in groups of two and three, posing for husbands and friends. Excitement permeated the station as some sang along and others chimed in with *gritos* (cries), signaling the release of the crowd's anticipation.

Once the mariachis finished their welcome serenade, passengers were ushered into two gender-specific lines for a security inspection that included a metal detector and an individual bag check. A dapperly dressed porter escorted individuals to their assigned carriage. While people took their seats, an audio recording in both Spanish and English welcomed visitors aboard "Mexico's most modern passenger train." As the train started moving forward, three attendants introduced themselves, gave a brief overview of the day's itinerary, and began serving Herradura tequila, mixed drinks (for example, *palomas* and *charro negros*), and an array of beer and soda. The last distinctively urban structure we passed was the sprawling Guadalajara Technology Park, a 400-acre (170-hectare) compound, described by locals as "Mexico's Silicon Valley." As the train slowly made its way past chemical, pharmaceutical, and software companies, the landscape gave way to green pastures, dirt roads, tin-roofed houses, and grazing cattle, oxen, and goats.

Eight air-conditioned buses awaited our arrival in Amatitán and shuttled us to the grounds of Herradura's hacienda. Once off the bus, we began a walking tour of the manufacturing plant and were shown the company's custom-made autoclave ovens used for cooking agave. Samples of the baked agave were passed around as the tour guide assured the crowd that it was safe to eat: "At Herradura, quality and safety are our top priorities." Herradura's success (it is the third-largest tequila manufacturer in the world), he explained, was related to their use of state-of-the-art equipment and adherence to traditional artisanal methods—a contradiction that went unnoticed by those in our group. From there, we were taken to the original production facility, built in 1870. Walking through the aged wooden doors, fellow tourists oohed and ahhed as we made our way into the dark and dramatically lit cellar. Inside were dozens of wells made of brick and stone, where the late-nineteenth-century fermentation process took place. "Here," our tour guide enthusiastically exclaimed, "is where the legend of Herradura tequila was born."

After touring the facility, we were escorted to a small movie theater and shown a fifteen-minute video that included a romantic dramatization of what daily life was like in the early years of the hacienda. We learned of the company's history, the founding De La Peña family's devotion to Catholicism, and the "mystical enthusiasm" of their workforce. The video ended with a montage of dreamlike images that included hacienda workers and agave fields as the narrator's voice declared, "This is what we call authenticity!" After the presentation we were taken to a spacious covered patio for a buffet. While drinking tequila and eating our fill of *sopes, tortas ahogadas*, and *mole*, the entertainment segment commenced with performances by "the world's youngest *charro*" and a Mexican comedian. For the final two hours, a DJ spun classic and contemporary Spanish-language music as both young and old took to the dance floor. In the late afternoon, the festivities came to a close, and the buses once again appeared to deliver us back to the train station.

As a cultural journey, the Tequila Express enables collective participation in portrayals—or performances situated in a bygone era—that mirror popular representations of Mexico. Studying Africa in the context of global consumer culture, anthropologist Paulla Ebron describes how ideas about Africa are brought to life through structured sightseeing events. Much as in Ebron's observations, Mexico is made meaningful through the staged interactions of individuals who intentionally define it for tourists.[11] The images of tradition that are promoted in spectacular experiences are manufactured to produce specific effects. On the Tequila Express, performances not only generate notions of Mexicanness but solidify ideas regarding company loyalty to the nation. By participating in these encounters, tourists validate corporate ties to Mexican heritage. Tourist performances are therefore both responses to power at the same time that they confer power to those who orchestrate events. Partaking in the Tequila Express "frame[s] the nation as an object" and generates cultural meanings that collectively shape how people interpret certain places.[12]

On this and the dozens of other tours I took, a very specific form of commercialized nationalism served as the base on which tequila's narrative in general, and company stories of origin in particular, were framed. Central to the touristic repertoire were ideas regarding family, religion, and loyalty to the idea of a shared Mexican identity. Companies effectively fused together aspects of commercialism and patriotism. Within this context, Mexican visitors were consistently positioned as cultural insiders and treated as if they were embarking on a sacred pilgrimage to a location that embodied the ideals of what it meant to be Mexican. In her work on tourism, nationalism, and consumer practices, Marita Sturken explains that the traditional meaning of pilgrimage refers to a religious journey and implies a sense of personal transformation.[13] Much like American visitors to emotionally charged sites such as the Oklahoma City National Memorial, tourists to Tequila are encouraged to absorb the sensation of an intimate, authentic, and demystified experience.[14] Mexican visitors are not just curious travellers; they are dedicated consumers and active patriots.

Tourism in Tequila focused on nourishing a sense of collective belonging situated in a noble and glorious past. Ironically, however, on the Tequila Express Mexican tradition was also portrayed in tandem with dialogues that emphasized modern innovation. For example, on the one hand, tour guides always discussed the cutting-edge technology used by companies to promote product quality. On the other, guides also reassured tourists that each company followed time-honored traditions. This, and the many other paradoxes like it, reflects the calculated lengths through which tequila manufacturers seek to purposefully synchronize their reputations as simultaneously reverent of Mexico's past and present. In the Tequila region, these strategies encompass a patchwork of reincarnated landscapes and fictitious figures that manage the illusion of authenticity—processes that obscure the realities of modernization and the economic struggle endemic to the region.

Hacienda Fantasy Heritage

In the sixteenth century, colonizers settled in the town of Tequila and exploited the resources and labor of indigenous people. Under Spanish rule, native people became wards of the state, were ordered to pay tribute to the crown, and were forced to move to the outskirts of the town center.[15] Many tribes lived in the region, including Tequilatos, Tequihua, Texcuexes, Chimaluacanos, Guadrana, and Nahuatlacas.[16] The Spanish considered these individuals dangerous and subsequently sold them as slaves. Colonizers distanced themselves from the various indigenous communities, as they frequently revolted against Spanish rule. Particularly, in 1620 members of the Guadrana took over the main plaza in Tequila in protest over the regime.[17] Reports of collective violence left leaders in New Spain and those across the Atlantic "horrified and extremely nervous."[18] The upheaval also reinforced the Spanish worldview that indigenous populations were barbaric and prone to brutality. Those colonial settlers who withstood the tumult of the period were rewarded with haciendas, large landed estates that operated much like plantations in the southern United States. Native people were integrated (often forcibly, but also voluntarily)[19] into the caste system as servants to the *hacendado* (landowner) or *patrón* (boss).

Well-to-do families grew agave on their haciendas because it was easy to maintain and profitable. Local residents, with the know-how to grow and harvest local flora, played a crucial, but behind-the-scenes, role in the early development of blue agave specialization in the region and later its evolution into a commercial enterprise. African slaves were also brought to western Mexico, although few details of their lives survive.[20] What can be said with certainty, however, is that in order to cultivate large tracts of agave, haciendas required a substantial amount of workers to extract, cut, and transport the 80- to 200-pound plants. While men toiled in the fields, women's work focused on domestic duties that included cooking, cleaning, retrieving water, gathering firewood, and taking care of the family.[21] Increased demand for mezcal and an accessible labor force facilitated the transition to commercial agriculture.

Tracts of agave soon filled the fields and hills of the countryside. Ironically, although the escalating presence of agave was initiated by the momentum of modernity (that is, the shifting sociocultural and economic effects of colonialism), it continues to be depicted as a timeless phenomenon. Contemporary travel writers, such as American author Lance Cutler, when describing their arrival to Tequila, rely on a common narrative structure that highlights their experience exiting the city and entering the countryside where agave is grown:

> We leave the city [Guadalajara] and drive across a dusty volcanic plateau. Wide bands of iridescent blue agave shimmer in the heat, occasionally broken by small bands of vibrant green sugar cane fields. The fields stretch out in colorful rectangles. Agaves are planted everywhere, spreading across the wide expanse of plateau to the base of the surrounding hills, and crowding between the road and the low stone walls surrounding private property.[22]

Cutler's passage to the Tequila region is eventfully portrayed as a departure from modernity and an arrival to an environment where nature defines the terrain. Mexican author Margarita de Orellana writes, "Tequila reminds us of a particular world, a world that was born of a shared imagination—a wild, rural landscape of robust men on horseback . . . the terrain of hard beauty is as hypnotizing to contemporary travelers as it was in centuries past."[23] Accounts such as these are reminiscent of the documents produced by nineteenth-century travel writers at the same time that they highlight the role that the Tequila landscape plays in the contemporary national consciousness.[24]

Signaling the transition from an urban to a rural setting that is unblemished by the passage of time, Tequila's "shared imagination" relies on gender as a means of narrating the past—a past that is romanticized through masculinized imagery. The portrayal of idyllic scenery inhabited by "robust men" is not unique to Mexico. Sociologist R. W. Connell illustrates how "frontier masculinity" is embedded throughout American history.[25] Frontier masculinity is a fictional narrative based on notions of the wilderness, individualism, ingenuity, and strength; it is an idealized form of patriotic masculinity. In addition to embodying the principles of nationalism, frontier masculinity plays an important role in representations of those who live in the Tequila region and work in the tequila industry. Specifically, romanticized images of Tequila as a rural place feature people who never complain about the conditions of their employment. For example, one tourism brochure describes workers as "people whose skin is tanned by the sun offer their hands to the field, their soul to the roots, their hearts to the agave, and a smile for you." In this bucolic scenario, "tanned" (read: mestizo) workers are portrayed as living in close harmony with the land while exhibiting the pride of their labor. Residents of the region are represented as enthusiastic about sharing their adoration of the agave countryside and eager to welcome outsiders.

Encouraging visitors to their hacienda, Herradura Tequila emphasizes the delightful qualities of their factory:

> As evidence of centuries and of the hard work within the hacienda, the factory still stands, surrounded by mysticism. Time stopped there, and being quiet, the sound of the workers can still be heard as well as the squeaking of the old *tahona* (agave press), taking out the precious juices from the boiled agave in the ovens. The original factory, a magical place, is one of the most charming touristic destinations in the vicinity.[26]

Often portrayed as "pure, vigorous and ennobled by their contact with the soil," employees are described as dedicated to the hacienda.[27] What is more, the factory is recast as mystic and magical, a move that not only masks the realities of manual labor but underscores the company's connections to artisanal methods of production that they no longer use. By highlighting the "charming" qualities of their factory, companies like Herradura fuel fanciful tales that arouse "touristic passions."[28] This widely promoted fictitious history is an example of the logic associated with hacienda fantasy heritage.

Hacienda fantasy heritage builds on the notion of "Spanish fantasy heritage," terminology that refers to the early twentieth-century fascination with Spanish missions and colonial stylistics in the state of California.[29] In their ambition to develop Southern California as a premier sightseeing destination, Anglo tourism boosters worked diligently to fashion a romantic revival of the state's Spanish ancestry. Race also influenced their pursuit; the celebration of a sublime Californian past helped dispel modern anxieties about the Mexicans and Mexican Americans who shared their surroundings. In seeking to regain control over the environment, Anglos turned to a comforting vision of a long-gone era, embracing the Spanish culture's "apparent romantic chivalry, preindustrial innocence, and harmonious hierarchy as a respite from the ugliness of modern times."[30] By imagining a sublime past—one based on their own terms—Anglo Americans found psychic consolation in their effort to redefine local identity by remodeling the cultural landscape.

Like its forerunner, hacienda fantasy heritage reflects an active reshaping of public memory based on preindustrial principles. The swift adoption of a fantasy-based hacienda aesthetic by private industry and public programs—visible in the architectural framing of distilleries, offices, buildings, and the agave landscape—is indicative of how the region is presently being incorporated in a project of national imagining that endorses all aspects of tequila's organizational structure. As a result, in the twenty-first century, tequila is being memorialized as indelible to the idea of Mexican heritage itself, one rooted in a romantic, innocent, and above all invented past. In the following pages, I discuss two figures who have emerged within the realm of this new nostalgic reality, the loyal *jimador* and the Aztec goddess Mayahuel.

The *Jimador*

In the Tequila region, the image of a provincial workforce provides a human connection to the landscape; workers "have intrinsic appeal" and nourish a sense of "touristic interpersonal solidarity" as they demonstrate their intimate ties to the hacienda.[31] Unlike *charros* who are portrayed in Mexican popular culture as tequila consumers, the *jimador*, or the agave harvester, is a regional figure who is affiliated with its production. With his *coa* (a long tool with a rounded flat blade at the end, similar to a hoe), the *jimador* uproots agave from the ground and slices off its spiny leaves (*pencas*), leaving only the heart of the agave (*piña*) ready for transport to oven autoclaves. Mature *piñas* (between seven and ten years old) can weigh up to 200 pounds and have roughly 200 *pencas*. On average, a *jimador* can harvest up to 100 *piñas* a day. Despite an array of technological improvements that facilitate the transfer of agave from the field to the factory, the physical extraction of agave can only be done manually. Hence, the *jimador* plays a necessary role in the manufacture of tequila.

There are dozens of types of highly skilled jobs on haciendas and in distilleries; however, the *jimador* is the only worker introduced to tourists. As part of the walking segment of the Tequila Express, we were brought to the edge of an agave field where a *jimador* silently dug up an agave from the ground and chipped away at its *pencas* while a guide narrated the process and fielded questions. The middle-aged *jimador* arrived dressed in white cotton trousers and a buttonless top, straw hat, and *huaraches* (open-toed sandals). The peasant-style uniform, in combination with the bright bleached color of his clothes, played into the hacienda's old-world mystique. The *jimador*'s silence, coupled with his quaint regalia, likewise reinforced the impression of the company's venerable qualities, respect for tradition, and connection to a noble past. Unlike the touristic representation, real-life *jimadores* are often young men ranging in age from sixteen to thirty, who work in groups of three to five as they harvest agave and load the heavy *piñas* onto a large truck. In the fields, *jimadores* are dressed in jeans, t-shirts, baseball caps, and closed-toe shoes or boots—a sharp contrast to the middle-aged, spotless, white-costumed, sandal-wearing lone *jimador* performing for visitors.

In nearly every tour, guides referred to the physical intensity of the *jimador's* job and described *jimando* (agave harvesting) as a craft that has been handed down from one generation to the next. As a means of illustrating the skill involved in the process, Tequila Express tourists were given the opportunity to slice off a *penca* using the *jimador's coa*. Lining up eagerly, they approached the large agave and clumsily hacked away at its *piña*. One after another, volunteers commented on the degree of difficulty that harvesting agave entailed. By offering tourists the chance to participate in the act of *jimando*, tour guides instigate several symbolically powerful performances. On an immediate level, visitors are taught to value the otherworldly dimensions of the countryside—a landscape in need of knowledgeable and honorable custodians.

Tourists are also reminded of the region's primitiveness and distance from modern industrial demands. Unlike the daily grind of urban living, on the hacienda, craftsmanship is valued over mechanization, and the contemporary burdens of mass production are rendered obsolete. On a more subtle level, *jimando* affirms the attributes of obedient mestizo masculinity and confers admiration on noble *patrones*, tempering the history of hacienda caste relations. By partaking in the physical dimensions of *jimando*—a vital aspect of tequila production—tourists affirm companies' authority as protectors of "authentic" Mexico (see Figures 15 and 16).

Although theirs is a job that has existed for centuries, *jimadores* have only recently materialized as cultural icons. The first reference I could locate documenting the role of *jimadores* was in a 1983 Sauza Tequila coffee table book titled *Tequila: Lo nuestro* (Tequila: Our Heritage).[32] A decade later, in 1994, the *jimador* entered the public sphere on a grander scale, when Herradura Tequila introduced their brand El Jimador. Currently the best-selling tequila in Mexico, El Jimador's label brandishes the image of a *jimador* working in an agave field. Herradura marketing materials sentimentally associate their brand with the venerable characteristics of real-life *jimadores*:

> Tequila is only as good as the men who make it, the *Jimadores* . . . These proud workers, whose skills have been passed down for generations, are the heart of El Jimador Tequila. It is their hard work and their proud dedication to crafts-

FIGURE 15. *Jimador*, Herradura Tequila. Photo by Gwyn
Fisher.

manship—knowing precisely the right time when the agave is ready to be harvested—that is the inspiration. And, it's to them that every glass of El Jimador
Tequila is toasted.[33]

The emergence of the *jimador* helps define the Tequila region of Jalisco as an
idealized site with workers whose ancestral lineage not only ties them to the
land but also to the product.

The *jimador* embodies the attributes of frontier masculinity and is racialized through the imagery of *mestizaje*. Implied in the *jimador*'s representation
is his indigenous background, and it is his mestizo identity that signals his

FIGURE 16. *Jimador* working in an agave field, Amatitán. Photo by Gwyn Fisher.

desire to please his *patrón*. In contrast to indigenous and African slaves who were prone to uprising and rebellion, the *jimador* is dedicated, compliant, and humble. In essence, he *is* of the soil, able to toil for hours under the hot sun. He works independently in the fields and takes pride in his role in the production of tequila.

Historian Jeane Delaney's research on the gauchos of Argentina provides a valuable perspective from which to consider the materialization of the *jimador* as the embodiment of tequila's authentic Mexican heritage. As she explains, the glorification of the gaucho as a symbol of Argentinean identity emerged at a time when real gauchos were disappearing from the pampas as a result of changes in rural production. Early work by historians suggested that the elevation of the gaucho, and the simultaneous devaluation of newly arriving European immigrants, was a result of efforts by Argentinean elites who were concerned with the growing numbers of immigrants participating in the labor movement. Delaney's account broadens this analysis by considering the intersecting effects of mounting class anxieties and the increasing emotional costs of modernity that became more apparent as Argentineans started to experience societal change.[34]

Like the veneration of the gaucho, the celebration of the *jimador* is a modern occurrence; both are revered as diligent figures whose noble characteristics illustrate the genuine qualities of a bygone era. Yet differences also exist. In the case of Argentina, the gaucho's admirable virtues stood in contrast to European immigrants, who were depicted as calculating and unethical. Unlike urban immigrants who sought new ways of making money through speculative investments, gauchos were represented as indifferent to the pursuit of wealth; they were "real men" who worked with livestock, maintained a close connection to the land, and accepted their lot, respecting and even admiring their *patrones*.[35] Rather than embodying a stand against corrupt immigrants, the figure of the *jimador* is employed to deflect threats associated with industrialization, including challenges to the paternalistic organization of hacienda life and labor relations.

The *jimador*'s popularity has gained considerable traction because of tequila's increasing presence in the international marketplace and as a result of various media tie-ins that perpetuate the fascination with the processes and people of Tequila.[36] Witnessing the backstage work of *jimadores* allows middle-class tourists to interact with the romantic tableau of an antiquated era reminiscent of themes lifted from Mexico's cinematic Golden Age, recycled on present-day television programming.[37] A recent media-related boost to tourism came as a result of *Destilando Amor* (Distilling Love), a tequila-themed soap opera that aired in 2007 and continues to screen in syndication in the United States and throughout Latin America. Winning that year's "Telenovela of the Year Award," the widely watched program was partially set and occasionally filmed in Tequila. Against the backdrop of the picturesque (and fictional) Montalveña Hacienda and its endless fields of blue agave, protagonists Gaviota and Rodrigo consummated their forbidden love.[38]

Experiencing Tequila's countryside setting, and perhaps tasting tequila while in it, recalls an imaginary time when *charros* on horseback roamed the landscape, drowned their sorrows, and toasted their triumphs in local cantinas. However, inconsistences abound. Despite their famous depictions on the big screen as overseers and defenders of the traditional order of hacienda life, *charros* are not present on the grounds of tequila distilleries. Instead, the *jimador* effectively fulfills the *charro*'s role as the noble caretaker of the nation's customs and natural resources—in this case, the blue agave, tequila's raw material. Taking the *charro*'s place within the organization of the hacienda fantasy heritage, the relatively recent recognition of the *jimador* as an esteemed guardian of tequila assists in depicting tequila companies as loyal to Mexican legacy. In other words, the *jimador*'s entrée into tequila's cultural narrative has enabled companies to latch onto a "real" idyllic figure in their branding, in their tours, and in their stories of origin. In doing so, companies portray themselves as forthright *patrones* who preserve the *jimador*'s honorable role as the embodiment of the nation's traditional identity.

Timing is also relevant when contextualizing the circumstances surrounding the rise of the jimador. It is far from coincidental that the *jimador*'s remodeled reputation was mobilized by tequila companies just as the tequila industry started to shift from a primarily nationally run enterprise into one controlled by large, multinational corporations with headquarters in cities like London and Chicago. Lacking the proper financial resources to acquire land and the equipment necessary to meet the demands of the changing market at the end of the twentieth century, small-scale distillers and agave growers were often excluded from many of the gains associated with the industry growth.[39] In comparison, by 2002, industry leaders like Herradura and Jose Cuervo had already acquired roughly 45,000 acres of land, further securing their stronghold.[40] During this period, these and other large companies also began to grow their own agave, compromising the livelihood of independent farmers who traditionally supplied agave to these organizations.[41]

Today the tequila industry is run primarily by transnational liquor conglomerates. Most of the top-producing firms are foreign owned. For example, Sauza Tequila is owned by Allied Domecq, Viuda de Romero Tequila is owned by Pernod Ricard, Cazadores Tequila is owned by Bacardi, and Herradura Tequila is owned by Osborne. Many Mexican-owned, medium-sized distilleries are engaged in strategic alliances with multinational corporations.[42] Companies wasted little time in deflecting images of faceless foreign CEOs as brand representatives by recasting them and their organizations as committed to Mexican culture and, at times, portraying them as critical contributors to *lo mexicano*. To be sure, the virtuous *jimador* stands in contrast to images of the modern, profit-driven corporate executive who has little interest in the process, the land, or the people involved in the manufacture of tequila.[43] In an effort to avoid any association with the foreign incursion into a "national" industry, transnational corporations foster romantic linkages that deflect attention from the shifting relations of production. The *jimador* is a seamless figure through which corporations can illustrate their respect for Mexican identity, maintain forms of race- and class-based control reminiscent of colonial arrangements, and in some cases nourish the impression that they are Mexican companies.

Finally, "economic reconversion," or the shifting organization of the industry from small- to large-scale production and ownership, has also affected the conditions of local employment.[44] Greater mechanization of the manufacturing process has led to a decrease in the number of well-paying jobs in the region, contributing to greater migration to urban areas or to the United States.[45] Consequently, and in contradiction to company tours describing their *jimadores* as local craftsmen whose skills are passed from one generation to the next, distilleries are hiring manual laborers from Chiapas, Mexico's poorest state.[46] In fact, some employers prefer to hire Chiapan men because they are seen as accustomed to earning low wages.[47] One personnel director of an agave-growers association described his preference for Chiapan workers:

> What's the problem? We're being left without people. People go from Los Altos [Jalisco] to the United States, they go to Canada, and they go other places to work, and we are left without a strong supply of labor, right? . . . They're accustomed to live in very poor conditions . . . so it's not hard for them to adapt here.[48]

Many of the new migrants are certainly accustomed to living in "very poor conditions." In Chiapas, indigenous people, 83 percent of whom work in agriculture, earn a per capita income equivalent to 32 percent of that of nonindigenous individuals in the state,[49] while 71.6 percent of the indigenous population reportedly suffers from malnutrition.[50] The image of the loyal, diligent, and mestizo *jimador* conceals the harsh effects of economic reconversion—including the incorporation of a disposable (and exploitable) labor force—all while increased profits benefit foreign investors at the expense of Mexican indigenous *campesinos* and the local community.

Mayahuel

Traditional Mexican mores hold that drinking alcohol in public is a pastime reserved for men. Indeed, up until the 1980s, cantinas could prohibit women from entering their establishments.[51] Although still an ideal embraced by some, today this gendered standard is commonly considered outdated. Nearly every tequila representative and brand owner I talked to mentioned the evolution of the once-popular principle that "good" (that is, chaste) women did not drink alcohol. As evidence of these changes in attitude, they explained that today women comprise over half all tequila drinkers in Mexico. In addition, they also mentioned the Aztec goddess Mayahuel and her role in tequila's story of origin. Most distilleries sport elaborate murals or striking statues of Mayahuel, and company tours often begin in front of these artistic renderings. Much as with the *jimador*, the promotion of Mayahuel's connection to tequila is also a recent phenomenon. Who is Mayahuel? And why is she so central to stories about tequila's history?

Mayahuel is the Aztec goddess of agave and fertility; she is also closely associated with the ancient indigenous drink, pulque. Mayahuel appears in various pre-Columbian texts, such as the Fejérváry-Mayer Codex, which depicts her as an agave plant and as nursing a child.[52] Other texts, such as the Laud Codex, picture her sitting on a turtle with her legs extended, "invoking her amplified fertility."[53] Symbolically fusing aspects of nature, spiritualism, and human ingenuity, Mayahuel is both divine and earthly. The beliefs surrounding her origin likewise reflect this duality. Indigenous folklore holds that one night Ehécatl-Quetzalcóatl, the cosmic wind, traveled to the heavens to visit the young virgin Mayahuel. While Mayahuel slept next to her sisters and grandmother (a Tzitzimime, or star demon), Quetzalcoatl whispered into her ear and convinced her to descend to earth and join him in the shape of a tree made of two branches. When Mayahuel's grandmother awoke and discovered her missing, she traveled to earth with a group of star demons to find her granddaughter. Locating the tree in which the couple had united, Mayahuel's grandmother broke the branches apart and gave her granddaughter to the star demons for them to eat. After they left, Quetzalcoatl rescued a few remains of Mayahuel's body and buried them. From these pieces grew the first agave plant.[54]

A lunar deity, Mayahuel is depicted as having 400 breasts from which she nourishes humans with her white, milklike liquid, pulque. Her children, or

FIGURE 17. Mayahuel, from the Fejérváry-Mayer
Codex.

her agave offshoots, are known as *hijuelos* (sucklings). A beloved, sacred, and
sacrificial figure, Mayahuel is heralded as the goddess of tequila. On tequila
tours and in coffee table tequila books, Mayahuel is portrayed as the link that
bonds tequila to an indigenous and feminine heritage. As one author writes,
"Since Mayahuel's death, the nectar [of agave] became a ritual beverage and a
ceremonial offer to the Gods and Deities. Thus, without an indigenous Goddess's strength, sacrifice, and suffering, the world would not have tequila!"[55]
According to this and numerous other accounts, Mayahuel is *the* matriarch of
tequila (see Figures 17 and 18).

Mayahuel's native, mystical, and matriarchal association suggests a
timeless connection to tequila and Mexican culture. Yet, as I explained in

FIGURE 18. Mayahuel with *jimador*, Mundo Cuervo. Author photo.

Chapter 1, ancient indigenous communities did not drink tequila.[56] For centuries, pulque was the only alcoholic product with which Mayahuel had any connection. Mayahuel's diminished linkages to pulque and her adoption into contemporary tequila lore parallels another matriarchal transformation and transference in Mexico: the worship of the Virgin of Guadalupe over Tonantzin, the Aztec fertility goddess.

According to legend, in 1531, Juan Diego, a poor indigenous boy, reported that the Virgin Mary had appeared to him on a hill at Tepayac (near modern-day Mexico City), where locals worshipped the deity Tonantzin. When the area bishop asked for proof, Juan Diego returned with a folded *ayate* or *tilma* (a woven cape made from agave fibers) filled with rose petals. When he opened the cape, inside was an image of the Virgin. Believing a miracle had taken place, the bishop ordered the construction of a church on the site of the apparition. Because she had addressed Juan Diego in Náhuatl, and was described as having dark-skinned features, the story of the Virgin of Guadalupe (as she became known) greatly appealed to native populations, assuring them of their place in colonial society.[57]

Scholars maintain that Guadalupe's apparition at Tepeyac was a tall tale intended to evangelize indigenous groups by superimposing Catholic shrines

on pre-Hispanic places of pilgrimage.[58] Despite determined efforts, the absolute elimination of Tonantzin from local heritage was unsuccessful; for many
people, the Virgin of Guadalupe and Tonantzin were and are the same icons
of Mexican spirituality.[59] Guadalupe's malleability resonates with aspects of
tequila's contemporary culture; several of her sacred attributes evolved in a
parallel fashion to those associated with the Aztec goddess Mayahuel. For
example, the eminent Mexican author Octavio Paz wrote, "Mother of gods
and men, of stars and ants, of maize and agave, Tonantzin-Guadalupe was the
imaginary compensation of the Indians for the state of orphanage to which
the conquest had reduced them."[60] According to this observation, Tonantzin-
Guadalupe, and not Mayahuel, was the "mother" of agave.

Mexican historian Fernando Benítez explains that Mayahuel's significance
dissipated as she was "substituted by the Virgin of Guadalupe, the new lady of
the magueys [agaves]"[61] In describing a Tolucan village's dedication to Guadalupe, Eric Wolf wrote, "There, the image of the Virgin is addressed in passion-
ate terms as a source of warmth and love, and the pulque or century plant beer
drunk on ceremonial occasions is identified with her milk."[62] William Taylor
recounted that not only were there fields of agave named after the Virgin but
that in the eighteenth century the Virgin of Guadalupe was sometimes called
the "Mother of Maguey" [agave].[63] Worshippers drank pulque on the anniver-
sary of her sighting, while a 1772 report described the rays of light surrounding the Guadalupe image as agave spines.[64]

Where indigenous communities once revered Mayahuel as the "lady of the
magueys" and the maternal provider of pulque, over time Guadalupe's symbolic resonance became more renowned as the foremost feminine icon and
mother of the land. Thus, just as reverence for Tonanztin was diminished by
the appearance of the Virgin of Guadalupe, it seemed that Mayahuel might
yield the same fate. Instead, however, they both became associated with agave,
pulque, and later tequila. Mayahuel and Guadalupe were, and remain today,
compatible mythic figures that incorporate attributes central to the traditional ideals of *lo mexicano*: They are mothers, they are spiritual, and they
embody epic tales through which Mexico can be "imagined as eternal."[65] As a
pious and privileged icon, by the twenty-first century, Mayahuel's status took
on new meanings as the goddess who birthed the spirit of the nation.

Mayahuel's ubiquity in contemporary tequila lore is related, in part, to
pulque's undesirable status and qualities. During colonial times, state officials
considered pulque an "uncivilized" indigenous product, and its consumers

were deemed obstacles to development. Even without its racially imbued reputation, pulque went sour after three days and therefore lacked the basic physical properties needed to enter international markets. Taken together, pulque was incapable of representing Mexican modernity. As a result of these symbolic and material circumstances, pulque never attracted sufficient large-scale corporate interest, never benefited from government-sponsored protective measures, and never fostered a viable tourism industry. Put simply, pulque never required "proof" of its indigenous heritage; it was already *too indio*. In contrast, the tequila industry enjoyed support from the Mexican government and was one of the first products to represent the nation at international expositions and world's fairs in the late nineteenth century.

Regardless of the efforts of tequila industrialists and the Mexican government, tequila was not embraced as an enlightened or industrious product in important markets like the United States. In the early decades of the twentieth century, tequila's reputation had more to do with danger, excess, and hangovers than productivity and craftsmanship. Despite, or perhaps because of, this notoriety, the tequila market continued to grow during the period from the 1940s through the 1960s, attracting the interest of transnational alcohol conglomerates who initiated partnerships with large and medium-size tequila distilleries. In the 1970s, the implementation of government-backed legislation, including tequila's recognition as a Denomination of Origin (DO)—in which it acquired state protection and internationally acknowledged property rights—created an air of professionalism and accountability that likewise marked a shift in the product's reputation. Tequila's status was further consolidated in 1994 with the institutionalization of NAFTA and in 1997 through a trade agreement with the European Union. In both of these measures, nations agreed to recognize tequila's DO status and allow the Mexican government to prosecute individuals in those regions who manufactured illegal tequila-like products.

Much like the circumstances that prompted the evolving significance of the *jimador*, Mayahuel's connection to the industry came at a time when large tequila companies needed to appear loyal to Mexico and Mexicanness: Mayahuel was an authentic icon whose indigenous qualities inexorably linked tequila to the origins of *lo mexicano*. Tourism industrialists and government officials have long relied on indigenous symbolism in the marketing of Mexico's ancient appeal as a vacation destination.[66] For example, archaeological sites, including Chichén Itzá and Teotihuacán, two of the country's major attractions, not only bolster the nation's image but also portray Mexico as simultaneously modern, unified, and prestigiously prehistoric.[67] Fostering the perception of a nostalgic indigenous past is crucial for appearing to unite the population under a single—and easily commodified—Mexican identity.[68]

Not all indigenous groups are exalted equally—special emphasis is placed on the contributions of the Aztecs as the nation's preeminent culture. This practice continues today in the tequila industry with the elevation of the Aztec goddess, Mayahuel. At first glance, the integration of Mayahuel could be seen as a measure of inclusivity, as it couples tequila with an indigenous heritage. Yet, at the same time, the repeated use of Mayahuel loosens Aztec ties to pulque and obscures the centuries-long involvement of various native peoples in the manufacture of artisanal distilled agave-based drinks.[69] Although the Aztecs controlled much of Mexico, they never wielded significant power in the tequila-producing regions of Jalisco. Mayahuel is therefore an anachronistic figure, salvaged to provide a timely sense of ancient prestige for the increasingly foreign-owned industry.

Mayahuel's feminine qualities also explain her popular connection to tequila. In particular, she embodies pre-Hispanic evidence that women played an important and historic role in tequila's culture. The murals and statues found at nearly every distillery attest to her symbolic significance in the present—painted and sculpted into being, her ubiquitous representation allows companies to show the public that they recognize the venerable contributions of women. Additionally, Mayahuel's maternal and pious qualities provide a "cultural salve" for the many years that tequila was exclusively associated with traditional Mexican masculinity.[70] Her presence serves as a reminder that "good" women *can* drink tequila. Mayahuel's myth flourishes as tequila companies actively search for new ways to attract potential female consumers, a vital demographic that has often been overlooked by tequila marketers.[71]

Conclusion

Tequila captures the imagination of middle-class Mexican tourists by appealing to long-established and newly formulated repertoires of national identity. Combining well-recognized aspects of Mexico's symbolic economy of identity (cuisine, dance, and music), tours like those offered by Mundo Cuervo and the Tequila Express allow travelers the opportunity to insert themselves into the Jaliscan countryside and relish in the nostalgic sentimentality of preindustrial

Mexico. Snapping photos in agave fields, walking the grounds of haciendas, and chiming in with mariachi *gritos* mimics familiar images and actions from *comedias rancheras* that "enhance the personal intensity of experience."[72] Within the controlled setting of distilleries, and the attendant hacienda fantasy heritage through which the visitor experience is structured, companies portray themselves as dedicated to the past, present, and future. In the words of anthropologist Claudio Lomnitz, widely recognized cultural symbols (such as tequila) "cannot reside principally in the world called 'traditional': the modern must be granted a privileged place in the national utopia."[73] In the booming tequila tourism industry, this equilibrium is maintained through a discursive balancing act: Tequila is both deeply traditional and exceptionally contemporary.

Foreign-owned tequila companies sustain the impression that they are genuinely concerned about the customs and craftsmanship associated with tequila's manufacture. By relying on such strategies, these companies nourish the impression that they are defenders of tequila's authenticity and guardians of Mexico. The *jimador* and Mayahuel provide a sense of "moral stability" within the collective consciousness of middle-class Mexican tourists.[74] Tourism is but one arena where patriotic structures of feeling are forged.[75] In the next chapter, I explore how all Mexicans are called on to defend tequila as a national symbol through legislation that promotes, guards, and enforces tequila's patrimony.

PURSUING PRESTIGE

Regulation, Resistance, and the Limits of
Mexican Authenticity

"Our values are based on the values of the Mexican nation, its laws, and its statutes,"[1] reads the first line of the organizational philosophy of the Mexican Academy of Tequila Tasters. Founded in 2000 by *"maestro tequilero"* (tequila master) Francisco Hajnal Alfaro, the academy is the sole taste-rating association recognized by the Tequila Regulatory Council (TRC) and the National Chamber of the Tequila Industry (NCTI), the two primary governing bodies of the industry. In addition to conducting blind ratings of tequilas by category (*blanco, reposado, añejo, extra añejo*), the academy, comprised of seventy "selected" members, defends "the traditions that have shaped our country and will support them in the name of tequila because it deserves the respect of friends and strangers."[2]

Protection is also a goal of the *Distintivo T* (Distinctive T) certification program designed for hotels, restaurants, and bars. Operated by the TRC and the NCTI in conjunction with the Mexican government, *Distintivo T* promotes tequila awareness, upholds "the authentic culture of tequila," and "protect[s] the denomination of origin of this drink that is a national patrimony."[3] According to program organizers, certification benefits not only those participating businesses, but also their personnel, clientele, and the tequila industry. To maintain accreditation, establishments with *Distintivo T*-trained employees must, among other things that I discuss later in the chapter, display tequilas by their different categories and regions. By following this protocol, each locale effectively publicizes its distinct product assortment and educates customers more broadly on the diversity of tequila. Intended to preserve "the prestige earned by our national drink for its excellence,"[4] *Distintivo T* and the Mexican Academy of Tequila Tasters tap into the patriotic intensity associated with tequila while they confer authoritative criteria through which powerful social actors tout tequila's connections to certain aspects of *lo mexicano.*

These are just two of the organizations and programs, sponsored by government officials and private organizations, whose stated goals are to guard and advance the tequila industry. This chapter illustrates how the acquisition and implementation of formal measures (including place-based designations, regulatory councils, tourism initiatives, and certification criteria) often benefit influential tequila industrialists at the expense of small-scale tequila businesses, local residents, and the artisanal knowledge long associated with the manufacture of tequila. Beyond legitimizing the authority of large multinational enterprises, the proliferation of protective standards demonstrates the multipronged process through which consumers are called on as citizens— and citizens are called on as consumers[5]—to participate in the elevation of tequila as one of the nation's "common symbolic denominator[s]."[6]

In the pursuit of prestige, state officials and industry elites acquire legitimacy and craft a repertoire of consent through the adoption of statutes that focus on tequila's role in contemporary Mexico. Presented as serving the public good, these defensive initiatives promote private investment. By following a market-oriented path of development, one that advocates government intervention in support of the interests of multinational companies, inequalities are perpetuated in the tequila-producing regions of Jalisco. A key element of this process is the mobilization of the rhetoric of national loyalty in relation to how Mexicans interact with tequila. As I show, in addition to delineating class, race, and gender statuses, consumption is also symbolically harnessed to confer the terms of citizenship; it provides "important definitional frames for the way people see themselves as public"[7] and exemplifies the nation's commitment to modernity.[8] (See Figure 19.)

Preserving Places

Spiritual referents are commonly rallied to reinforce the "sacred" links between Tequila the place and tequila the product. For instance, in describing the "land that gave its origin to the world famous tequila," one tourist

FIGURE 19. Billboard entering Tequila with the slogan *"Tu Tierra Te Llama, Vívela"* (Your Land Is Calling You, Experience It). Author photo.

brochure proclaimed it "a gift from ancestral Gods, [a] drink with a taste of history."[9] State authorities likewise embrace its divine attributes. In 2004, the secretary of tourism awarded the town the title *"Pueblo Mágico"* (Magic Town). The *Pueblo Mágico* program was established to recognize places that "have always been part of the nation's collective imaginary and that represent fresh and different alternatives for natives and foreigners."[10] Each *Pueblo Mágico* is described as "a reflection of our México, what it has done for us, of who we are, and we should feel proud . . . each pueblo, despite the passage of time and modern ways of life has known how to conserve and value its historical and cultural heritage."[11] Publicity campaigns nurture notions of a collective imagined history for "natives and foreigners" alike, one that flourishes in spite of the changes ushered in by "modern ways of life."[12]

Working on federal, state, and municipal levels, the initiative emphasizes the traditions of twenty-three communities. The goal of the *Pueblo Mágico* program is to support areas that often do not benefit from tourism in the same way as other high-profile destinations; it is also supposed to spotlight the communities' lesser-known histories. Tequila and the other towns initially awarded the designation to receive an annual grant from the state ranging between US$50,000 and US$700,000 for improvements in public services, such as the restoration of water and drainage systems and the renovation of museums. In Tequila, the program funds bilingual street signs, hotels and youth hostels, and road expansion. Although the program is promoted as a means to enhance the town's tourism potential and support its residents, not all of these goals are being met. Specifically, many of the sponsored improvements are taking place on the main boulevard into Tequila and on the roads where the largest tequila factories in the industry are located,[13] including La Rojeña, the distillery owned by Jose Cuervo Tequila. The current changes being made under the auspices of *Pueblo Mágico* are benefiting industry elites.

Other proindustry changes include the decision to rename the 110-year-old street called "24 *de enero*" (24th of January), which was dedicated to the town residents who died in the Battle of Mojonera in 1873, to Jose Cuervo Street, thereby dedicating it to the largest tequila company in the world.[14] Indeed, according to tequila scholar González Torreros,[15] it was Don Juan Beckman, the president of Jose Cuervo Tequila, who played a key role in ensuring that the town became a participating member of the *Pueblo Mágico* program. As a Jose Cuervo public relations director explained, Beckman spoke directly with Mexico's Secretary of Tourism Rodolfo Elizondo, telling him, "You can't leave Tequila out of Pueblos Mágicos."[16] Described as an initiative to benefit the public good, the government-sponsored *Pueblo Mágico* program is influenced by and subsequently works in concert with influential private actors.

Tequila's induction into the *Pueblo Mágico* program helped create the infrastructural conditions and provided momentum for its bid for World Heritage recognition. Founded in 1972, the UNESCO program identifies, protects, and preserves the "cultural and natural heritage around the world considered to be of outstanding value to humanity";[17] it also organizes management plans and reports on the conservation of its sites. Added to the list in 2006, nearly 86,000 acres of western Jalisco's tequila-producing region[18] joined the ranks of places such as the pyramids of Egypt as sites so exceptional that they "belong to all peoples of the world, irrespective of the territory on which they are located."[19] Broader protections are also included. For example, as a World Heritage site, the tequila-producing region is safeguarded by global guidelines enforced by the Geneva Convention. Under these widely recognized parameters, individuals or groups seen as endangering the region are subject to prosecution by the United Nations. World Heritage recognition carries with it international cachet at the same time that it strengthens tequila's place in the narrative of Mexican identity. In the words of NCTI president, Francisco Quijano Legorreta, "It's something that makes us proud and honors us; it is something that will increase the reputation of the drink that identifies Mexico in the world."[20]

When the list of recipients was announced, the UNESCO declaration made front-page news throughout Mexico.[21] Local officials praised the effects it would likely have on tourism, with some claiming that it could bring up to 4,000,000 visitors a year to the region.[22] World Heritage recognition bolsters local tourism at the same time that it legitimizes the tequila industry as central to the rural countryside and positions it as intrinsic to Mexican national identity. Attesting to the resonance of this relationship, one journalist affirmed, "The Tequila landscape has generated literary works, movies, music, art, and dance, all celebrating the links between Mexico, tequila, and its place of origin in Jalisco."[23] The widespread praise garnered by the designation conveys how nostalgic portrayals in the media influence the collective memory surrounding tequila and the idea of Mexico itself.

The newest of the three initiatives, *La Ruta del Tequila*, or the Tequila Trail, was formally launched in 2009 by the Tequila Regulatory Council. Much like the *Pueblo Mágico* program, the trail is described as "promoting our national drink" and "increasing competitiveness within the tourist industry and related sectors in the municipalities of El Arenal, Amatitán, Tequila, Magdalena and Teuchitlán."[24] I first heard of plans for the trail in 2007 when I attended a formal blind tasting and rating event held by the Mexican Academy of Tequila Tasters.[25] After the proceedings ended and members had cast their votes, I spoke with the group's attorney who was monitoring the ballots (gathering the formal written reviews and placing them in a locked box). He told me about the plans for the trail and explained that the route was loosely based on Napa Valley in Northern California. As he saw it, the trail was a logical "next step" because tequila was now a "legitimate" World Heritage site, "Napa Valley has a trail, and now we'll have a trail as well."

The Tequila Trail is partially underwritten by an Inter-American Development Bank grant of US$1.5 million for sustainable tourism. The funds are intended to promote public–private partnerships and corporate responsibility through cooperation between the approximately 100 small and large manufacturers. In addition, the grant is supposed to provide technical and financing assistance to micro, small, and medium-sized enterprises in the region, including hostels, restaurants, and local transportation. The Tequila Regulatory Council and the Jose Cuervo Foundation are the sole executing agencies of the endowment. Although the projected results of the initiative have yet to be realized, every time I returned to Mexico and inquired about the progress of the trail, residents and local vendors were unenthusiastic. As one owner of a small tequila company put it, "That's Cuervo's thing; no one really believes it will do what it is supposed to do [increase tourism to smaller distilleries]."[26] Despite the investment of public development funds, many of the people I talked to doubted that the trail could benefit the region.

Although the emergence and use of initiatives of distinction (*Pueblo Mágico*, UNESCO World Heritage, and the Tequila Trail) are relatively new phenomena, their implementation can be situated within a longer historical trajectory related to Mexican identity. Claudio Lomnitz explains the reason behind the Mexican government's acquisition of international accolades. In particular, he argues that Mexico's pursuit of well-recognized designations is linked to the government's adoption of Import Substitution Industrialization (ISI) policies that were carried out during the period from 1940 to 1982 but whose effects reverberate to the present day. Intended to reduce the country's dependence on foreign goods, the primary goal of ISI was to shift the conditions of trade so that Mexico could export value-added products that were less prone to price fluctuations. In broad terms, ISI was a strategy adopted by less-developed countries as a means of increasing economic growth and improving self-sufficiency. Under ISI, the Mexican government supported the establishment of production facilities that manufactured goods that were once imported. One drawback of this approach was that the types of industries created under ISI tended to be less competitive in the international arena because they were promoted in and intended for the domestic market. Ironically (and unfortunately), the implementation of ISI placed Mexico (as well as other Latin American countries) "in a new and more dangerous relationship with more advanced industrial countries than ever before."[27]

Under ISI, the Mexican state played an increasingly important role in sponsoring industrialization and shaping the institutional and symbolic "framework for citizenry."[28] During the forty-year period of ISI, corruption flourished under the one-party regime of the PRI, spawning deep distrust between the populace and the state. Politicians responded to this suspicious association by portraying themselves as unequivocally dedicated to the nation.

The eventual shift to a free-trade model in the 1990s, which expanded the availability of diverse Mexican products (such as tequila) into the global marketplace, generated a new, heightened rhetoric about the importance of national goods—rhetoric that was espoused by political and business elites. The ability of a Mexican product to gain international recognition was flaunted as the ultimate symbol of achievement. Because most Mexican investors or manufacturers could not attain this degree of international success on their own, and because they were accustomed to the terms of ISI, they sought the state's protection against the risks associated with the global market—all while both groups lauded the importance of cultural traditions and local products.[29]

Taken together, these circumstances produced a contradictory dialectic between the endorsement and rejection of globalization. For Lomnitz, this ambivalence stimulated a change in the narratives associated with Mexican nationalism. In his words:

> Whereas under ISI there was only one dominant form of nationalism, and it was predicated on the teachings of the Mexican Revolution and had the national state, personified in the president of the republic, as its ultimate locus, today there are two forms of nationalism, one that sees reaching full modernization and the rule of the international standard as the ultimate patriotic end, and another that insists on the intrinsic superiority of local products and traditions.[30]

The *Pueblo Mágico*, UNESCO World Heritage, and Tequila Trail programs can be understood in relation to this paradox. On the one hand, state officials and large multinational tequila corporations praise the heightened recognition of tequila in the domestic and international sphere. Tequila is repeatedly touted as an esteemed national product that has made it in the global marketplace. Correspondingly, Mexican citizens should take pride in its success. On the other, the acquisition of formal standards—standards that consistently emphasize tequila's quality and its need for protection—create new obstacles for small-scale agave farmers, family-run distilleries, and those people who live in the tequila-producing regions of Jalisco.

Less powerful individuals directly affected by these initiatives were very vocal about their frustration. For example, the local Tequila town administrators and members of the community I interviewed expressed concern about the ability of the new programs to have a positive impact on the region. Irma, who works closely with several public and cultural institutions in Tequila, explained that most of the residents were unaware of what the initiatives signified because "little effort was made by the state to educate or initiate dialogue with the local community . . . They only work if the current administration works and only if they are truly interested in the programs."[31] Fernando, a tourism official, echoed Irma's observation about the overall lack of knowledge about the initiatives. Specifically, he noted that when the UNESCO designation was announced some farmers feared that this meant that officials would seize their agave fields. As these examples illustrate, it was not at all clear to residents how these initiatives would make their lives better.

Like Irma and Fernando, Juan Pablo, a town council representative, estimated that only 20 percent of the residents of Tequila knew what either of the designations meant. When I asked why he thought that was the case, he suggested that the lack of knowledge was a result of inadequate communication between state and local officials. In his words, "They [state officials] come from Guadalajara and put up banners: 'We're a *Pueblo Mágico.*' They tell us to keep our houses and streets clean because tourists want to see a *Pueblo Mágico.*"[32] One of the first projects initiated by the *Pueblo Mágico* program was street resurfacing. Juan Pablo explained that workers stripped the traditional pavement and replaced it with cobblestones. Frustrated with the disruption caused by the construction, townspeople sarcastically referred to the new project as "*Pueblo Mágico* streets." To be sure, the replacement of the town's roads paralleled broader changes happening in the region: the stripping down of residents' input into development projects and the resurfacing of their new *Pueblo Mágico* identities.

Although tourism in Tequila was important to the local administrators I talked to, it was not their top priority. Specifically, they were more concerned with the town's infrastructure, unemployment rate, and education system— matters that, in their opinion, were overshadowed by the interests of tequila companies and higher-ranking government officials. As Irma put it:

> They [the state and large tequila companies] come to transform it all, to construct beautiful houses. They invent seafood restaurants even though there isn't an ocean close to us; they invent a gastronomy that has nothing to do with our identity. This affects our present-day image. They come from the United States and think their model will work here; they start to put boutiques, unisex shops, with all of their *anglicismos.* Even our language is starting to erode, our language that is so beautiful. Our identity begins to suffer.[33]

Irma's remarks call attention to the imbalance between what it means to enact new initiatives and what it means to experience their effects. Furthermore, her comments highlight the misfires that take place when efforts to preserve traditional elements of a society first cater to outside concerns rather than the well-being of the local population. In the case of Tequila, initiatives appear to compromise the very goals they are supposed to uphold.[34]

Born and raised in Tequila, Gildardo works at one of the many artisan stalls that flank the main thoroughfare leading to the town. I asked him what changes, if any, he had noticed since the *Pueblo Mágico* designation. He explained:

> The tourists are all brought directly to Jose Cuervo. They are the biggest of all the distilleries here in town, they [tour operators] go to Guadalajara and get them [tourists] and take them straight to Mundo Cuervo. People used to drive a lot more. It's bad, Cuervo and Sauza get the tourists with their all-inclusive packages. Sometimes tourists come from the United States already a part of an all-inclusive tour. It has been like this for a while, but yes, it's gotten worse since we became a *Pueblo Mágico*.[35]

Like Gildardo, the owner of a magazine stand in the center of town lamented that part of the problem is that tourists "eat, drink, buy shirts, and tequila, and do not even buy a piece of gum" beyond the walls of Mundo Cuervo.[36] Other local retailers echoed similar concern that the *Pueblo Mágico* designation was "a benefit for them [Cuervo]" while the town was "as messed up as always."[37] In Tequila, supposedly public initiatives are widely seen as benefiting private interests and not local residents.

Authenticity, Efficiency, and Protection

The Mexican government, in conjunction with powerful private corporations, elevates the tequila-producing region's status through the acquisition of domestic and international initiatives to assert its control over the political, financial, and cultural aspects of tequila. The founding of the *Pueblo Mágico* program, the creation of the Tequila Trail, and the pursuit of UNESCO World Heritage recognition comprise the newest of such undertakings. Earliest among these efforts took place in 1978 when the government formally registered tequila under the Lisbon Agreement for the Protections of Appellations of Origin (AO).[38] The AO registration system protects products from the deleterious effects of globalization and is classified under the broader category Geographic Indication (GI). Regulated by the World Trade Organization (WTO) and defined under the General Agreement on Tariffs and Trade, GIs identify a good as originating in a specific territory, region, or locality, where a given quality, "reputation or other characteristic . . . is essentially attributable to geographical origin."[39] Further, they not only protect a product based on its geography, but they also take into consideration human elements such as how specific production styles and local craftsmanship influence its quality. A label of origin, GIs are widely associated with wines and spirits but can also be applied to other foods.[40] In Mexico, tequila's GI is more commonly referred to as a Denomination of Origin (DO).[41]

Tequila's DO guards the industry from international competition and strengthens the links between Mexico's history, landscape, and products.[42] Under these guidelines, tequila's qualities are portrayed as intrinsic to the surrounding geography and its inhabitants. Tequila, as a unique place, serves as a physical location from which to imagine the evolution of tequila as a product so steeped in Mexican culture that it is literally a part of the nation's geography. However, despite the level of specificity outlined in tequila's DO, especially its implicit ties to Mexican patrimony and local knowledge, not everyone in the region has the same level of access to its advantages. With the majority of blue agave fields in Tequila owned or leased by large corporations, residents who grow agave for the purposes of producing their own liquor are unable to benefit from many of the formal designations now associated with the drink.

Locally owned, small-scale producers often avoid seeking legal recognition of their blue agave-based products because of the high costs involved in calling their drinks "tequila." When the Mexican government established the Official Mexican Norm (*Norma Oficial Mexicana*) in 1978 and required companies to conform to government-approved testing measures (and their accompanying fees), many owners, rather than follow the regulations, simply stopped using the name "tequila" on their product labels. Instead, they call their drinks "distilled agave" (*destilado de agave*) or "agave firewater" (*aguardiente de agave*). Most of these spirits are made of the same ingredients as tequila (blue agave). Yet, despite the generations of local knowledge employed by many small-scale operations, they face difficulties when it comes to exporting their products or securing distribution because they cannot use the name "tequila." Intended to deter the manufacture of illegal tequila, standardize quality, and safeguard the industry from global competition, the ramped-up measures create hurdles for less powerful local producers.

Tequila Regulatory Council campaigns that warn against the purchase of inauthentic tequila cast an air of illegitimacy over distilled agave products. Assumed to be manufacturing pirated (*pirata*) tequila or low-quality tequila (*guachicohol*, literally, "yucky alcohol"), producers not only face economic disadvantages but they are forced to deal with the drawbacks of being depicted as unlawful and substandard. For instance, when I asked a town official who worked closely with the local branch of the Tequila Regulatory Council why he thought some producers opted not to observe the regulations, he replied:

> It's because people are disorganized. You know that this is a big problem in Tequila, more so here [Tequila] than in Los Altos. Lots of people produce clandestine tequila, and it's a product that is very dangerous for your health, and what we have to do is keep telling people: Please look at the label, please don't buy it from the freeway [vendors]. Don't believe them [vendors] when they tell you 5 liters for 50 pesos [approximately US$5] because you could end up blind. Maybe you don't know because you're a foreigner, but we've always had problems in our country with *productos similares* (similar or generic products) and *productos piratas* (pirated products). The people don't comply.[43]

According to this statement, not only do distilled agave spirits pose a danger to people's health, but those who produce and sell them should not be trusted. Additionally, inexpensive tequila is described as an index of low quality, thereby supporting the notion that legitimacy must always come at a price. Health risks due to contamination or as a result of missteps in the distillation process are always present, even with regulated products. Nevertheless, the rhetoric about "pirated products" almost always depicts its producers as placing the population in peril.

Although portrayed as not wanting to observe Tequila Regulatory Council guidelines, the distilled agave manufacturers I interviewed insisted it was not a matter of choice but a matter of cost: They could not afford to pay the yearly fees associated with the council's membership and the use of the name "tequila." Paulina, whose family owns and operates a small distilled agave operation in Tequila explained:

> It affects us a lot [not being able to call our product tequila], especially with regard to sales. Because we are a small business the large companies don't allow

us to enter the market . . . what we do is the same process. In a laboratory test, our product is the same as 100 percent tequila. It's that we don't have the name. There are even tequila companies whose products don't comply with the regulations, and they have the name tequila and the denomination of origin of tequila. It is a bureaucratic hassle imposed by the Tequila Regulatory Council. They came to us and made an offer [to acquire certification], but we're talking about thousands of pesos. We can't afford it.[44]

Financial barriers are not the only drawback that Paulina's family operation faces. As she put it, "Our product cannot compete with big companies—they already have their own history like Sauza and Cuervo; they are seen as traditional. I think that every small business also has their own history, it's that our market is not very big." Paulina's comments call attention to the success achieved by large corporations who closely align themselves with narratives of tradition. Her remarks also illustrate how less-powerful manufacturers are unable to benefit—symbolically or monetarily—from tequila's ties to *lo mexicano*.

At the same time that local and international designations heighten Tequila's visibility as an "authentic" Mexican place and product, they render distilled agave spirits as "inauthentic" and depict them as opposing the principles of *lo mexicano* by implying that certain products are more genuine than others. Ironically, these family-run operations are more likely to adhere to time-honored methods of production (such as cooking agave in clay ovens) and are less likely to use chemical-intensive pesticides in their fields. Instead of using industrial machines, they frequently rely on a *tahona* (a mill powered by a mule to extract the juice from cooked agave). The priorities of the region's residents who depend on local resources, draw on centuries-old traditions, and employ alternative manufacturing approaches are marginalized locally and cast as illegitimate and unpatriotic.[45]

These examples echo the findings of Clare Hinrichs's work on the marketing of the state of Vermont as a sublime countryside retreat. During the 1980s and 1990s, wealthy families began moving to Vermont, purchasing holiday homes. One effect of these changes was a boom in area tourism. Both bureaucratic and entrepreneurial agencies lauded the state's "rural charms and virtues."[46] Although some Vermonters were able to capitalize on this reputation, most were too affected by the lack of well-paying jobs or were concerned about slipping into poverty. In a similar fashion, the case of Tequila illustrates how claims about the region's idyllic setting, or the product's patriotic significance, fall short on helping residents—those with limited resources—profit from the potentially lucrative reputation that established tequila companies are able to use to their advantage. Consequently, those stakeholders who "trade on the appeal" of Tequila as a "magical" or an "internationally recognized" place are not usually local residents, but powerful actors and agencies.[47]

Protecting National Interests

Formed in 1994, the Tequila Regulatory Council "ensure[s] the prestige of tequila by means of investigation and specialized studies, disseminating the many elements that confer value and reinforce its culture."[48] A private, non-profit organization, the council guarantees the legitimacy of tequila's Denomination of Origin, protects tequila from foreign imposters, and keeps an inventory of agave. Top among their objectives is the promotion of "the culture and quality of the drink which has earned an important place amongst the symbols of national identity."[49] As evidence of the state's support of the organization, in 2005 Mexican President Vicente Fox attended the swearing-in ceremony of the council's new president, Miguel Ángel Domínguez Morales. An article published by the Tequila Regulatory Council described the events in this way:

> The First Executive expressed his recognition of all those who take part in the agave-tequila productive chain. He also pointed out that tequila is the product with the greatest impact on Jalisco's gross domestic product, thanks to an industry that provides direct jobs to over 45 thousand Jalisco families. He also commended the eleven years of leadership of this regulatory body, in particular its work in promoting and defending our national drink.[50]

Publicizing and defending the reputation of Mexico's national drink are also goals of the National Chamber of the Tequila Industry (NCTI). Established in 1968, the chamber represents the industry at large and is comprised of individuals who "freely and voluntarily join to work together in favor of tequila, patrimony of Mexico."[51] The Chamber plays an important role in the overall regulation of the industry by promoting tequila as a "successful drink" and defending "the culture that surrounds it as a traditional value of Mexico."[52]

During my time attending classes for the University of Guadalajara's Tequila Diploma course, two NCTI representatives delivered a much-anticipated guest lecture. The representatives began with a brief overview of tequila's evolution and discussed the drink's growth in domestic and international markets. For instance, they compared tequila to other distilled drinks: In the United States, vodka represented 25 percent of the market, while tequila represented 5 percent. They explained how people in other cultures drank tequila: In Germany they drink it with a wedge of orange and cinnamon, while in the United States it is primarily consumed in margaritas, which they referred to as "the world's most popular cocktail." Internationally, distilled beverage sales were stagnant, but since 2001, tequila sales were rising at a rate of 13 percent annually. As the world's fastest-growing drink category, tequila's profitability was increasing at an impressive pace. There were, however, threats to its image and financial value: The production of counterfeit tequila.

On a PowerPoint slide titled "Tequila Industry Challenges: Combating Piracy," the speakers began to show us how to identify illegal tequila. Referencing the projected image of a large brand label, they discussed how to identify key information on a tequila bottle. Small arrows pointed to a Tequila Regulatory Council sticker, registration number, and the words *hecho en México* (made in Mexico). As they explained, illegal products tarnished the name of tequila and the idea of Mexico itself. In recent years, they had identified unregulated operations in China, the United States, and Argentina. Speaking out of turn, a fellow classmate jokingly remarked, "See, Mexico's even fashionable in China"—a nod that acknowledged tequila's global popularity but also referenced the increasing public concern over Chinese competition with Mexican labor and goods. The comment garnered a few laughs among the audience, but the speakers' tone remained somber. Further emphasizing the seriousness of the topic, the final slide of the presentation read, "In the promotion of tequila outside of Mexico, we all play an important role as its natural defenders. The heritage of tequila belongs to all of us and its image represents us and our country: We all should protect it." Describing Mexican consumers as "natural defenders" of tequila fuses acts of consumption to the responsibilities of citizenship.

Protection is also an important theme for the Tequila Regulatory Council. In a speech delivered to the council after his election, the new president publicly reiterated the organization's commitment to the drink's preservation:

> My friends, you may rest assured that in the Tequila Regulatory Council we
> will continue to work to ensure the authenticity and quality of our national
> drink, and to safeguard our first Mexican Appellation of Origin. I know that

the representatives of our three levels of government are convinced of the benefits of our initiatives and support them. In this task, undertaken in collaboration, we will succeed in strengthening and guaranteeing the prestige of our tequila, symbol of Mexico and legacy of all Mexicans.[53]

Although a private, nonprofit organization, the Tequila Regulatory Council maintains close ties with various government branches, such as the Ministry of Economy and customs officials. In an open letter to council associates, a quality assurance representative described how the effects of globalization and the regionalization of markets led to an increase in competition among services, products, and companies. In his words, it became "necessary to make use of all possible factors, such as quality, that can help improve our level of competitiveness."[54] As a means of assuring "continuous growth and keep[ing] abreast of the current demands of the agave-tequila production chain," the Ministry of Economy provided access to "tools and mechanisms" that could help the TRC enforce quality standards that included audits and certification programs.[55]

To improve their "level of competitiveness" and, at the same time, illustrate the measures that they were willing to take to ensure that all regulations were being followed, several procedures were initiated to enhance quality control. Top among these was the purchase of satellite imagery from Landsat 5. With a resolution of twenty-five meters per pixel and covering nearly 40,000 square kilometers per scene, the high-tech project was described as representing:

> . . . a basic tool in searching a methodology that allows us to have an updated inventory of Agave tequilana Weber blue variety, and to make positive and consequent decisions towards a strategic planning based on objective questions such as: How much agave is there? How old is it? Whose agave is it? What is the fenological status?[56]

Through the use of multispectral remote sensing, Landsat 5 is able to identify the location of agave crops. By overlaying the satellite images with aerial photos or topographic maps, the areas are divided into separate vectors and then individually numbered. Such technology enables the council "to know promptly where the largest quantity of agave plantations is concentrated and that it is the variety permitted."[57] This type of surveillance is intended to deter companies from buying unregistered agave that is usually harvested by small-scale farmers or local residents.

Despite its effectiveness, there were several setbacks—data from Landsat 5 were unable to determine who owned which agave or to assess the phytosanitary conditions of the crops. To make up for this shortcoming, the council developed what they call the Geographic Information System (GIS), a procedure that monitors the number of agave in sanctioned areas. Central to the GIS is the work of field verifiers or agricultural inspectors who visit farms to certify that crops are cultivated in approved land and check that growers are registered with the council's database—in effect, making blue agave a controlled substance. Complementing the efficiency of the GIS was the introduction of the TRCard, an electronic identification card (much like a microchip-implanted credit card) for agave suppliers. The TRCard maintains plant inventory through the registration of agave.[58] Protecting the quality of tequila through TRC verification is described as a vital measure in efforts to combat the manufacture and export of counterfeit tequila.

With tequila exports on the rise, the Tequila Regulatory Council joined forces with Mexican customs authorities to fight against "the producers or marketers of fake tequila as they tried to take fake tequila across our borders for sale abroad."[59] In addition to working in partnership with customs agents, they also entered formal agreements with other government bureaus, such as the Office of Tax Management. However, it was the 2002 signing of the "Collaboration Agreement on Foreign Trade Matters" that most effectively highlighted the council's ability to mobilize state cooperation. Specifically, new stipulations allowed council-trained personnel to work as "observers and representatives of the tequila sector in all customs offices and certain areas of customs [operations]."[60] By establishing a permanent training program to teach customs authorities how to identify illegal tequilas, the TRC established a pipeline of certifiers to represent their interests in forty-eight border control offices. As they see it, such alliances illustrate "the will of the Mexican authorities to cooperate to prevent damage to the Denomination of Origin and are a vehicle for the constant advancement of mutual cooperation to protect a product exclusive to Mexicans."[61]

Prestigious products deserve prestigious care. By enrolling various government offices and applying new heightened regulations in the defense of tequila, officials assert their authority as caretakers, not only of tequila but also of the nation's reputation. Although making claims about authenticity can be used as a strategy by less powerful individuals to resist commercialization,[62] it can also be used to support commercial interests and traditional definitions of national identity. The standardization and formalization of the tequila industry works at various levels in an effort to maintain the trust of the populace while also providing them with the correct tools (Landsat 5) and knowledge (how to examine bottle labels) so that they too can preserve Mexico's "spirit." Such endeavors are not limited to national boundaries: Tequila merits global protection.

Legislating Local Tradition in the International Marketplace

The Tequila Regulatory Council's alliance with customs agents has led to the detention and arrest of tequila smugglers attempting to cross Mexican state and international borders. For example, in 2003, 4,000 liters of distilled cane liquor labeled as tequila was destroyed in San Diego, California, after it was discovered by Tijuana officials. Later that same year, a tanker carrying 22,000 liters of mislabeled tequila was detected by officials in Reynoso, Tamaulipas. The manufacture, transport, and sale of illegal tequila is not just a domestic concern; there is also mounting unease over the production of tequila outside of Mexico. Prompted by the growing global popularity of tequila, noncertified producers are seeking to enter the market and cash in on the increased demand.

To combat the sale of counterfeit tequila, in 1999 the World Trade Organization publicly destroyed thousands of bottles of tequila from Russia, Spain, and Japan in a main square in Brussels, Belgium. The WTO's actions were seen as a response to mounting pressure to enforce international property regulations.[63] Because the enforcement of WTO laws applies only to fellow members, Mexican officials established supplementary legislative provisions with nonmember nations to protect tequila. One of the most fervent international disagreements about the potential for the illegal production of tequila took place in 2000, when China sought WTO membership. Every country that requests WTO affiliation must establish a bilateral trade relationship with existing members. Mexican representatives made clear their reservations about China's commitment to protecting tequila's Denomination of Origin. Specifically, they noted China's track record of failing to pay tariffs on thousands of products, remarking that, in the past, they submitted false invoices and skirted regulations by exporting their products through third countries.[64] From the perspective of government officials, China could easily do the same with tequila. Because blue agave could easily flourish in certain Chinese climates, tequila administrators expressed concern that the Chinese government might also allow the production of counterfeit tequila. Mexican diplomat Raúl Urteaga commented on the issue, saying, "The word 'tequila' is synonymous with Mexico, or more correctly, with the state of Jalisco where tequila is based . . . just like you can only produce bourbon in the United States or Cognac in France, we want to ensure that tequila will be produced nowhere else."[65]

The manufacture of counterfeit tequila was one of several matters that fuelled Mexico's apprehension to establish a bilateral agreement with China. Officials were also anxious that China might flood the marketplace not just with imitation tequilas but with a range of other inexpensive goods.[66] Although NAFTA legally prevents the United States from importing Chinese tequila or tequila from any other nation, intellectual property provisions do not safeguard the import of toys and textiles, products that China could produce and sell at a lower price than those made in Mexico. Increased competition with China, especially with regard to supplying the U.S. market with consumer goods, has severely affected the Mexican economy—in the late 1990s alone, even with NAFTA in place, Mexico lost 200,000 manufacturing jobs to China.[67] Finally, however, in late 2001, after months of negotiation, Mexico eventually signed a trade agreement with China, enabling them to officially join the WTO as its 143rd member nation.

Although supported by the Mexican government and acknowledged by various nations, protective legislation does not necessarily ensure an end to the production—or the threat of production—of counterfeit tequilas. For example, in late 2006, the Chinese news source *People's Daily Online News* reported the discovery of a fourteenth-century distillery where a tequila-like product was made. Chinese experts deduced that the archeological remains, which were traced to the Ming and Qing dynasties, proved that "China had developed mature tequila distilling technology."[68] Writers and Internet bloggers speculated that the Chinese government might attempt to challenge Mexico's claim to the intellectual property of tequila.[69] Here, the implication is that if Chinese industrialists can prove that tequila was produced there 200 years before its emergence in Mexico, then Chinese officials might have the grounds to challenge Mexico's authority over tequila.

As the example in the preceding paragraph illustrates, pursuing protective standards and making claims to authenticity have limitations, especially as tequila becomes more global. Despite these drawbacks, tequila's Denomination of Origin is consistently marshaled by Mexican officials and industry leaders to preserve intellectual property rights and stoke notions of shared collective experience. Taken together, these circumstances reinforce the notion, to Mexican consumers especially, that they should defend tequila's status in the global marketplace. Yet, even within Mexico, it is not enough to value and uphold tequila's reputation—distinctions are encouraged within the realm of consumption to further bolster tequila's legitimate ties to the nation and highlight consumers' new and important role in this process.

Defending Distinctions: *Distintivo T*

Distintivo T certification protects consumers by "attack[ing] the proliferation of adulterated drinks and pseudo tequilas that affect the prestige earned by our national drink for its excellence."[70] Initially, only Mexican-based establishments could apply for certification; however, today there are *Distintivo T*–certified locales in the United States, Colombia, and France that partake in ensuring the security of the "national drink . . . and the patrimony of all Mexicans."[71] Establishments can apply for *Distintivo T* recognition, but they are required to fulfill a range of criteria. For instance, they must:

1. Show evidence of an internal filing system that accounts for each bottle of tequila in their possession.
2. Make sure that all the tequila they sell is TRC certified.
3. Prove that they are properly storing tequila.
4. Display their tequilas by categories, types, and regions.
5. Provide customers with a tequila-based cocktail menu and offer food prepared with tequila (in the case of restaurants and hotels).
6. Show that they are properly disposing of used tequila bottles.
7. Allow for biannual inspections by the TRC (or one of its certified partners) to make sure that they are following the program's requirements.

In addition to these requisites and paying US$450, employees and managers must attend classes taught by members of the Tequila Regulatory Council or the National Mexican Academy of Tequila Tasters. The course was organized into four modules: "The Regulation of Tequila," "The History of Tequila," "The Cultivation and Harvesting of Agave," and "The Elaboration of Tequila." At the end of the coursework, each participant must take a final exam and pass with a grade of 80 percent or higher to become *Distintivo T* certified. *Distintivo T* simultaneously commodifies expertise and intellectualizes notions of authenticity (on their specific terms and by their detailed metrics), all while espousing the rhetoric of historical preservation.

According to publicity materials, defending the authenticity of tequila protects the health of consumers by eliminating the risks associated with unregistered tequilas. Indeed, employees of *Distintivo T* businesses "go the extra step to promote the true culture of tequila."[72] An online promotional video, available in Spanish, English, and German, offers further information about the program's goals. With flashing images of agave and *jimadores*, and narrated with a voiceover similar to that of a military recruitment presentation, the segment begins by posing the following questions:

> How far are you willing to go to protect what belongs to you? Where do you get the courage, the strength, the anger to fight for what is yours? Do you really believe you have the spirit needed to face a fight without a truce? Are you willing to give everything until reaching victory?[73]

The booming voice pauses and snappily affirms, "We know you are!" The speaker then explains the mission of the *Distintivo T* program as "preserv[ing] a symbol that belongs to us by right, and by tradition, a patrimony that belongs to all Mexicans by birth or by heart. To protect its manners and customs, its essence, its territory, its life, this is the work that we do every day."

Throughout the presentation, tequila is described as a symbol and product that retailers can actively participate in safeguarding. In their words, "We need your help to support the growth of tequila by preventing unfair competition practices that harm the good name of tequila through the sale of imitations or other products that mislead and deceive the consumer." From this perspective, business owners who acquire certification protect customers and support the integrity of the nation's interests. Through the language of citizenship and duty, tequila is portrayed as personally significant in the lives of those who advocate its rightful place in the narrative of Mexican identity. Such cases illustrate how loyalty to the nation increasingly involves solidarities based on the possibility of potential threats–threats that might jeopardize corporate agendas (for example, competition from imitation or misleading tequila). Identifying the characteristics of citizenship through the promotion of consumer and *not* political accountability, the Tequila Regulatory Council describes the benefits of becoming certified through the *Distintivo T* program:

> The main and most important one is that thanks to your participation tequila, symbol of our country, of our land, of our people, will be protected by hands that value it as the spirituous, unique and original beverage that it is. If we all protect it in the same manner there will not be a person or beverage that can tarnish or harm the essence of which, no doubt, is one of our greatest legacies, tequila. It is in our hands to keep it alive. Join our cause. Our country and our tequila are counting on you![74]

By participating in the *Distintivo T* program, individuals demonstrate their commitment not only to tequila but to the nation itself. The ending, with the affirmation, "It is in our hands to keep it alive. Join our cause. Our country and our tequila are counting on you!", highlights the compelling discourse through which consumer identifications are recast through appeals to patriotism. By attaching "critical national identifications"[75] to consumption, the defense of tequila is framed as vital to the preservation of *lo mexicano* in domestic and international arenas.[76]

An index of *lo mexicano*, tequila is presented as tantamount to the present-day protection of national interests—national interests that are at once traditional and in need of modern safekeeping. The Mexican government likewise participates in narratives of authenticity that go hand-in-hand with the goals of tequila industrialists who, through legislation, assert their authority in the marketplace. Attempts at total control of the linkages between tequila and national identity rely on emotional connections that draw on notions of spirituality, tradition, and commitment to the well-being of the nation. Such circumstances point to attempts to reshape the terms of participation in tequila's culture, blurring the boundary between what it means to be a consumer and a citizen. These new connections require that Mexicans conceive of themselves as willing to actively take part in tequila's defense.

Conclusion

Federal and state officials, executives of tequila companies, and representatives of the tourism industry portray tequila as a vital and vibrant symbol of the nation. Drawing on rhetoric that emphasizes the rural past and the modern present, these groups fashion notions of unified nationality, histori-cal memory, and self-understanding. By representing the Mexican polity and populace as collectively supportive of tequila's place in the national project, they affirm their role in shaping measures that defend the tequila industry against competitive threats that are real, elusive, or imaginary. As "idioms of distinction," UNESCO World Heritage and *Distintivo T* endorse tequila's worthiness of protection and concurrently transform this merit into a meta-phor of national defense.[77] The end result is a validation of the validating mea-sures, whereby tequila industry elites, with the help of the government, meet and shape growing demand in the global marketplace on their own terms.

In an effort to preserve tequila's national image, various social actors hail Mexican citizens and consumers as actively responsible for maintaining its integrity as a uniquely Mexican product. Such tactics are indicative of at-tempts to breathe new life into the themes of national unity that were used during the 1990s when the PRI enacted reforms that championed the benefits of cultural loyalty.[78] Yet, Mexico requires a certain kind of collective under-standing of nationalism to prosper in the local and global marketplace—na-tional pride must be able to foster a robust business climate.[79] By blurring the lines between the commercial and civic realm, citizens are recruited to safeguard commodities and the values associated with them. In the case of te-quila, market agendas are forwarded through the language of national pride. Nonetheless, important questions remain: Do consumers support these offi-cial campaigns? Does drinking tequila exclusively signify the celebration and defense of Mexican identity? What are the variations among Mexican tequila drinkers? In the following chapter, I examine how consumers make sense of their tequila drinking practices.

CONSUMING COMPLEXITY

Tequila Talk in Mexico and the United States

On a recent trip to Miami, Florida, NCTI President Francisco González was interviewed by a local newspaper reporter. He talked about tequila's Denomination of Origin, the proper way to drink tequila, and the development of tourism in Tequila. "Today," González noted, visiting Tequila "is like going to Napa Valley or Champagne."[1] After addressing tequila's popularity in the United States, he discussed its international significance:

> It very well represents Mexico because everybody that I know outside of Mexico associates tequila with Mexico. When you talk about Mexico, everybody asks about the tequila. We say in the industry, "Tequila is Mexico like Mexico is tequila." So we cannot separate them. I feel very proud to be a *tequilero* and to have the best ambassador of Mexico in the world, because tequila is the best ambassador of Mexico.[2]

Promoting tequila as Mexico's "best ambassador," González has good reason to feel proud: Global sales have increased at an impressive rate, and the more lucrative 100 percent agave tequila category (as opposed to tequila *mixto*, made of 51 percent agave) has also made significant gains, amounting to tens of millions of dollars in profit.

Members of the NCTI and TRC elevate tequila as indelible to Mexico. While I believe their actions—and the changes that they have instigated—merit close scrutiny, I do not wish to portray them as purposefully making deleterious decisions. Their job is to support and protect the industry, which, from a purely commercial and economic perspective, they have done very well. However, as I discussed in the previous chapter, success has come at a price for those less powerful manufacturers and local residents.

In addition to supporting and protecting the industry, tequila officials must also manage tequila's reputation. Top among these concerns are efforts to shape consumers' understanding of tequila. For example, as González explained in the same interview, "It's okay to drink margaritas or tequila in other mixed drinks, but the way to appreciate it is straight and slow. You see a lot of young people chug it and follow it with a lime, but that's not the proper way."[3] As he and many of the self-described aficionados I spoke with commented, there are right and wrong ways to "appreciate" tequila. Do consumers follow the guidelines promoted by officials and experts on how to "properly" drink tequila? How do tequila consumers interpret their manners and routines of drinking? Do people's habits and understandings vary across cultural contexts?

This chapter explores how tequila is consumed in everyday practices from a transnational perspective. Drawing on interviews with Mexican-origin tequila consumers in Mexico and the United States, I argue that consumption communicates the shared codes of cultural identity and provides a language through which individuals challenge traditional gender scripts and track social change. With this in mind, instead of claiming that accounts about tequila reveal an inherent notion of "Mexicanness," I focus on how consumers convey a multitude of meanings that illustrate how people interpret personhood and nationhood. Not everyone I spoke with discussed tequila through an exclusively "ethnic" lens; for instance, some described their experiences by drawing on examples such as family interactions and media representations. Therefore, by "shared codes," I refer to the patterns that emerge when consumers narrate a diverse range of circumstances that contribute to their understanding of being and feeling Mexican.

The shared codes communicated in my interviews also point to the shifting connotations associated with tequila that offer insight into how registers of gender, race, and class figure in the expression of collectivity. By analyzing what I call "tequila talk," I draw attention to how dialogue about commodities and their consumption reveal the lesser known terrain of identity as it is sustained and re-created every day under politically and historically specific circumstances.[4]

As individual and collective imaginings of Mexican identity continue to evolve across borders, theorizing these changes as they develop under new global policies requires paradigms that are attuned to unanticipated connections.[5] One useful approach is Néstor García Canclini's work, which considers the intersections of market forces and cultural trade. Specifically, he argues that treaties such as NAFTA not only extend the reach of multinational corporations but influence the character of national identity. For Canclini, public debate in Mexico over NAFTA has focused too intently on whether it would affect notions of tradition and, as a result, has overlooked the possibility that innovative intercultural exchanges were also possible. To avoid this situation in the future, he calls on scholars to "help with the task of rethinking national identities as multideterminant scenarios where diverse symbolic systems intersect and interact" by exploring connections within groups that are "not only *social spatial*, but *socio communicational*."[6] Although Canclini contributes an important theoretical framework for approaching globalization and national identity, this chapter provides an empirical base from which to discuss the intercultural and cross-cultural dialogues taking place through consumption—dialogues that traverse across borders and depart from traditional approaches to interpreting the shared codes of communication.

Challenging Gender Expectations: Consumers in Mexico

Tequila talk often elicited references to tequila's close connection to traditional notions of Mexican masculinity, especially those images celebrated in *comedias rancheras* of the 1940s and 1950s. This was the case when those I interviewed described where they thought most people drank tequila; for instance, common responses included "in cantinas," "at bars," or "at *charreadas* (rodeos)," places that are associated with men's consumption practices. Ironically, however, when asked where they drank tequila, most discussed drinking in their or their friends' homes.

Veronica, a biology professor from Guadalajara, preferred to drink tequila "*derecho*," or straight up. As she put it, "There are many types of tequila drinkers. For example, some like to drink tequila straight and fast to get drunk quickly and efficiently. Others want to relax, while others want *desmadre* (to get rowdy)." She recalled that when visitors came to her house when she was a child, her mother always offered tequila:

> I think a lot of people in Mexico have the same experience; probably 75 percent of us only drink alcohol in our homes. Women drinking in bars [at that

time]? No. The introduction to alcohol, and tequila specifically, always takes place in the home. At parties, on Mother's Day, everything that has to do with family, you can enjoy a *tequilita* (a small tequila).[7]

In the preceding quotation, Veronica explains how drinking tequila was commonplace in the intimate setting of her home. Interestingly, in Spanish, the word *tequila* is preceded by the masculine pronoun *el*; however, she describes a drink of tequila as a *tequilita*, a diminutive term that switches tequila's gendered association from *el* (a masculine pronoun) to *la* (a feminine pronoun). Her recollection calls attention to the gendered connotations associated with language and the places where tequila is consumed.

Riding with a group of friends on a trip to the town of Tequila, I sat next to Lupe, a retired city employee. She preferred her tequila served with grapefruit-flavored soda[8] and usually drank at home when family or friends visited from other parts of the country. A native of Mexico City, Lupe is the only member of her family, aside from her two sons, who lives in the state of Jalisco. She told me the story of a memorable evening with her brother who was visiting from Morelos. As she cooked dinner, he prepared tequila and cola. In her words,

> The next thing I knew, I had already had two drinks and still hadn't eaten because I was cooking. So when I sat down to eat, I was feeling a little tipsy. I ate, and he prepared two more drinks. I didn't notice anything. Then, the next day, my eldest son called. He said he was calling to find out what had happened to me. But I didn't answer the phone; my youngest son did and told him that I was still asleep. He asked him why he wanted to talk to me and he said, "Last night Mom called and left a message on my voicemail saying "Mary Poppins! Mary Poppins! Mary Poppins!" My son told him, "Well, she was drinking tequila with my uncle last night." When I woke up, I noticed I had fallen asleep with my tennis shoes on.[9]

After pausing to laugh (and patiently waiting for me to regain my composure), Lupe explained that now every time she drinks tequila with her sons, they jokingly chant, "Mary Poppins! Mary Poppins! Mary Poppins!" Although unsure why she repeated "Mary Poppins," on her son's answering machine, Lupe seemed certain about what led to her actions: drinking tequila with her brother.

As Veronica's and Lupe's stories show, accounts about tequila operate as a type of autobiographical narrative[10] that departs from conventional representations related to women and alcohol in Mexico. According to anthropologist Stanley Brandes, alcohol is closely associated with gender identity: "In a word, it is not shameful for Mexican man to get drunk, but inebriation is very shameful for a Mexican woman."[11] This double standard is rooted in the notion that the consumption of alcohol could impede women's roles as wives and mothers or possibly lead to sexual promiscuity.[12] Their stories are also indicative of broader changes related to women's increased presence in socioeconomic spheres within Mexico. In other words, today women are more visible than ever in Mexican public and political life.[13] Not just in Mexico, but in Latin America more broadly, women are attaining higher levels of education, moving into the labor market in greater numbers, and playing bigger financial roles in the well-being of their families.[14] As women continue to make important strides, they still face challenges in "determin[ing] their own identities within the construction of nationhood."[15] Tequila's masculine connotations, together with the rigid double standard regarding alcohol, often render women invisible as symbolic participants in the shaping of Mexicanness. However, as these examples illustrate, middle- to upper-middle-class women such as Veronica and Lupe create their own relational meanings through the consumption of tequila, disrupting dominant discourses that obscure women's contributions and sense of belonging to the nation.

Veronica's description suggests that she was aware that social conventions were being challenged in her home. Lupe's actions likewise contested idealized representations regarding women's "proper" comportment. As she celebrated the occasion of her brother's visit by having a few drinks, tequila functioned symbolically not only in commemorating and creating family ties but in highlighting her ability to break free from cultural scripts that regulate her role as a sister and mother within the traditional Mexican family structure. As acts of negotiated resistance, the consumption of tequila, and the stories that people tell of these events, are not just ways to mark occasions but are themselves accounts of belonging in which individuals can acknowledge their own pleasure and contest enduring gendered associations in particular social contexts.

Tasting Pride

Engaging in tequila talk led many to reminisce about when they began to see tequila "in a different light." Lupe, for example, recalled that she always thought of tequila:

. . . like any other drink, like wine, whisky, gin, but when I went to Europe in 2000, I noticed and was surprised that tequila was really expensive and it wasn't good quality. So when I came back here, to the land of tequila, I had a newfound interest in tequila, the flavor of tequila, knowing that it was very expensive in other parts of the world and that I have access to very good tequila and it's not that expensive. It's like French wine. Here it is very expensive, but there it's not. The French probably don't think about it much either.[16]

Lupe gained a new appreciation for tequila when on vacation, an appreciation that was elevated through the acknowledgment of the cultural capital associated with coming from "the land of tequila."[17] Like Lupe, Aranza, a policy consultant, recalled her first experience with tequila outside of Mexico, when she was a graduate student in the United States:

Aranza: I made it a point to convert numerous foreigners to the rituals of tequila when I was in Chicago. I prohibited all of my friends from drinking tequila that wasn't good tequila, so then I took on the responsibility to bring some back from Mexico. They practically kept me in immigration because I had like fifteen bottles of *Herradura Antiguo*. I told them [at immigration], well, I have a lot of friends, and that's why I have a lot of bottles, they're gifts. But instead, I had a big party at my apartment. So, I got everyone drunk. We ended the night, a group of us, sitting in the snow outside, laughing, talking until the police came. The next day, no one was hung over because we were all drinking good quality tequila. I converted everyone there to tequila.

MSG: Now your American friends drink tequila?

Aranza: Well, I cured my friends of their fear of tequila because most of them had only had really bad tequila. Even I'd be afraid under those circumstances. But once they tried tequila that wasn't like bathroom cleanser, they started understanding more and actually liking it.

Risking potential problems at U.S. customs, Aranza saw it as her responsibility to teach others about the diversity of tequila—a diversity that acknowledges tequila's changing connotations. Like Lupe, Aranza's privileged social location, which enables her to travel internationally, provides her with the opportunity to recognize and challenge the multiple representations of tequila in the global marketplace.

Acknowledging the existence of poor-quality versions that were like "bathroom cleanser," Aranza wanted her friends to experience it the way she experienced it: a drink that tasted good, that could be consumed to observe occasions, and that could be enjoyed without getting sick. Aranza's observation about converting "foreigners" to tequila is likewise telling. When in the United States, she is the foreigner; however, in her recollection of events, those who are not properly educated about tequila are, in fact, the foreigners. Here, tequila is used to signal a direct association with her national identity, highlighting her understanding of what it means to be Mexican while in the United States. Furthermore, as Aranza's story shows, tequila served as a vehicle for promoting intercultural education, celebrating cultural difference, and illustrating that Mexican products are not just less developed (like bad tequila). These examples reveal that meanings associated with tequila are being transformed through the transnational experiences of middle- to upper-class Mexicans.[18]

Victor, a thirty-three-year-old surgical technician, recalled an experience when he worked at a hotel in the beach resort, Puerto Vallarta:

> It was one of those all-inclusive hotels where most of the tourists were almost all North American [American and Canadian], and at the bars they served them whatever type of tequila, because, well, they don't know the difference. But what happened is that during Holy Week [Easter week], lots of *paisanos* were also there. They did not accept the same tequila that was being served to those guests from other countries. They started a small protest right there on the beach at the bar because they wanted Cazadores tequila, and they were serious. All of the personnel were taken aback, wow. All of the Americans were being served Charro Negro, ech!, and other cheap brands. We were like, okay, here you go, but be quiet, because the other customers are also going to start requesting Cazadores too.

The protest made by Mexican holiday-goers for higher-quality tequila than that offered to North American tourists was a metaphor that operated at several levels. From as far back as its independence from Spain (1821), the Mexican government's preferential treatment of wealthy foreigners has been a source of resentment for citizens from diverse class backgrounds.[19] Further fueling aversion toward Americans is the widespread awareness of U.S. anti-immigrant sentiment. Simply put, many are dismayed by how Mexicans are treated in the United States. Perhaps the most telling source of antagonism in relation to the scenario in the preceding quotation is the U.S. policy toward Mexican travel. Although Americans can freely visit Mexico with just their passports, Mexicans of all social classes must first apply for a visa to enter the United States—a process that is both costly and time consuming.

Demanding better-quality tequila enabled Mexican tourists to make cultural distinctions that separated them from other tourists. Although tourists themselves, Mexican holiday-goers insisted on superior treatment that allowed them to exhibit their insider knowledge in a setting that typically caters to foreigners over locals. In doing so, they were able to identify themselves as more sophisticated consumers and characterize their tastes as uniquely Mexican. As Victor's story shows, even within Mexico, middle-class Mexicans strategically grapple with the symbolic meanings attached to tequila—meanings that manifest themselves through transnational flows (for example, international consumption) and within transnational spaces (for example, international holiday destinations). Privileging some brands over others, Mexican tourists used their tequila preferences to stake their claims as citizens who deserve higher-quality goods.

Recognizing Change

Many of the people I talked to saw tequila as deeply connected to Mexican national identity. Much like sociologist Colin Jerolomack's research, which illustrates how the act of caring for pigeons allowed Turkish immigrant men to communicate perceptions of ethnicity and culture, people's interactions with tequila, including when, how, and with whom they drink, offer individuals the opportunity to express what it means to be Mexican and to describe changes they see taking place in Mexican society.[20] This was apparent when people explained the characteristics of tequila consumers. For Juana, a tequila drinker has a "strong personality, good taste, and an eye for tradition." Typically, she envisioned this person to be a man. However, she elaborated,

> Juana: Lately, women also enjoy drinking tequila. Before, because of our culture, because of the idiosyncrasies of the *pueblo Mexicano*, probably only a few women drank tequila, but now even girls who are eighteen drink tequila and like it.
>
> MSG: Why do you think this change took place?
>
> Juana: Because of liberty, the freedom of expression. Because now we're leaving behind the image of the Mexican with his sombrero on. The culture is growing and changing. Women are moving forward; well, I'm very feminist, and I love going out with my girlfriends and hav-

ing a drink. Well, I don't personally drink much, but I'm glad I know how to.[21]

Juana's comments suggest that the perception of tequila as a drink for men, one that celebrated the logic of working-class masculinity associated with the "*pueblo Mexicano*," has evolved. Similarly Pablo, a college student, observed, "When you think of a tequila drinker, you inevitably think of a *charro* or an older person. At a certain point, this changed, and now young people also drink tequila, so when you think about tequila, you think of young people who are sophisticated and bohemian."[22] As Pablo points out, tequila's shifting class connotations provide new possibilities not only for women but also for young people to convey attachment to Mexican identity.

Guillermo, an engineer originally from Chiapas, also noted changes in tequila's image. He stated, "Obviously, it's the national drink, and everyone drinks it, but, in the last ten years, tequila has been in fashion and a bit *fresa* (stuck-up)."[23] Guillermo likewise remembered when tequila "was what *el pueblo* (country people) drank . . . if you were *fresa* you drank whisky or gin or even rum, but not tequila. It always stuck with me as a drink from the Mexican countryside, but now that's not the case, but that's the image that stayed with me." He explained that, outside of Mexico, "Tequila has the same reputation as burritos and tacos from Taco Bell, which are disgusting, with the horrible hard-shelled tortillas that are seen as Mexican icons." From Guillermo's perspective, tequila's reputation is changing inside Mexico, but outside Mexico he sees it as remaining static and negative.

Dávid, an office assistant in his early thirties, identifies the shift in meaning as having regional distinctions. As he describes it:

> I have family in the state of Mexico, and they see tequila as a *corriente* [common] drink. They prefer drinks made from grapes, or beer. They see tequila as gross. And using their own words, it's a "drink for *Jalisquillos*" [a pejorative name for people from Jalisco]. But now it's clear that things are changing in the state of Mexico, probably the most important state in the republic, they are selling more tequila, and now there are more people enjoying it. Now I think that most people see tequila as a traditional drink, a drink that people respect more. It's a very good drink.[24]

The description of how people from the state of Mexico view tequila as a "drink for *Jalisquillos*" is a reference to the long-standing rivalry between residents of Mexico City and Guadalajara. During my time in Guadalajara, friends often commented on how "*chilangos*" (slang for people from Mexico City) regarded "*tapatíos*" (slang for people from Guadalajara) as less modern or less sophisticated. In other words, city rivalries were often described along an urban (Mexico City) and rural (Guadalajara) continuum. Based on Dávid's observations, people from the state of Mexico's perceptions of tequila as a drink from the countryside had changed and therefore so to had their perceptions of Jaliscans. From this example, we see how meanings assigned to commodities are often transferred to meanings about people.

Stereotypes about tequila also functioned as a common frame for tracking change. Sergio, a Spanish-language teacher in his late thirties, explained that one of the biggest misconceptions about tequila was its reputation as "a drink for machos." As the stereotype goes, tequila is perceived as, "a drink for men, men, men, because its flavor is strong and not easy to tolerate, no? And whoever drinks more tequila, the more macho you are." I asked Sergio why he saw this as a myth, and he responded, "Because it's not true. Because you don't have to drink a lot of tequila to be macho. Because what you need is to have a tolerance, you need to know how to drink it, know how to distribute it in your throat, and drink it tranquilly, and enjoy it."[25] Like Sergio, José, a day care administrator, noted tequila's "macho" image when I asked him if he thought there were any misconceptions about tequila. In his words, the biggest of all myths was

> . . . the idea that it makes you a hard man. "Oh, I drink tequila because I'm so hard, I'm such a man, because I am a macho, and machos drink tequila straight up, in shots." It's a mistake, in my opinion, but that's the myth. The macho, misogynist, and the fighter don't drink champagne, they drink tequila right? It supposedly gives you this feeling of "life's worth nothing" [*la vida no vale nada*] . . . but that's a myth, that tequila gives you strength, vigor, that it makes you very manly, and only strong men drink tequila. I don't know, but in my opinion, it's very stupid.

Tequila talk highlights how notions of masculinity, and its ties to alcohol, are interpreted in different ways. What is more, it shows how men are able to maneuver within the parameters of gendered associations and apply multiple layers to their identities that include qualities such as "tolerance" and taste appreciation. Thus, dialogues regarding consumption serve as a language in which more complicated understandings of Mexican identity are articulated. Such understandings extend beyond static representations that celebrate the past; instead they incorporate fluid interpretations that acknowledge the complexity of the present. It is important that cultural context also matters, as dialogues shift when they cross borders and enter new commercial spheres. In the following section, I highlight these dynamics by turning to my interviews with tequila consumers in the United States.

Drinking Tradition: Consumers in the United States

Drinking tequila was often described as a familial tradition for Mexican, Mexican-American, or Chicano and Chicana tequila consumers living in the United States. Elena, a self-identified Mexican American in her early twenties, explained that tequila was her drink of choice when she went out to clubs or bars with friends in her hometown of Tucson, Arizona. Like her friends, she ordered shots or tequila-based mixed drinks. For her, a tequila drinker was "someone who likes to be around other people, someone who likes to have fun." In addition to having social qualities, Elena also saw tequila as rooted in Mexican tradition: "It's part of the culture of Mexico. It's distilled there. It's a tradition; it has a lot of history." Birthday parties and weddings were two occasions in which she drank with her family. In one memorable instance during her grandfather's ninety-fifth birthday, a bottle with a glass was passed around together, where family members, "helped themselves to a shot." In her words, "As Mexican Americans and as Mexicans who came here, we still carry on the tradition of drinking tequila."[26]

Lorena, an education consultant in her mid-forties, identifies herself as a "Chicana who embraces the diversity" of her ethnic background. Although she does not drink much alcohol, she occasionally drinks tequila when she is with family: "I'll drink it at family reunions, weddings, one shot. It's readily available at all of my family reunions. I rarely ever go out to bars with friends, but if I do I order tequila, and it has to come with salt and *limón*." When I asked Lorena to describe the characteristics of a tequila drinker, she offered, "Well, it could be my *tías* [aunts] or my uncles. Because I was introduced to it in a family-gathering atmosphere, I don't associate tequila with you know, a young, hip crowd, or anything like that. I associate it with about any member of my family." In addition to family, Lorena also associated it with special occasions and friends. As she explains, "Whenever I give an alcoholic gift, I always buy tequila."[27]

Like Elena and Lorena, Mando, who was born in Mexico but now lives in Southern California and works as a substitute teacher, explains that even though he sometimes drinks tequila with friends, "It's more of a family thing. Usually when I drink it's a family members' home, and it'll be that there are several people there, and someone always brings a bottle of tequila. We sit around and talk. Talk and drink, talk and drink. We'll also drink it at *bodas* [weddings] or at funerals." When drinking with his family, he makes sure to drink only certain brands of tequila—tequilas brands that are "more refined" and Mexican owned. As he puts it, "We don't drink Patrón or Cabo Wabo or any of that, it doesn't come into the picture." I followed up by asking him to elaborate on his comments. He responded:

> It's the idea, well, like it's totally unfounded, right? This whole idea that it's not a national product, a Mexican product. *Son las compañías multinacionales que están laborando* [it's the multinational companies who are producing it], so that's kind of seeped into the mentality of the people that I hang around. I'd way rather drink a Cuervo 1800 than that, I mean, just the thought of it turns my stomach.[28]

Both Patrón and Cabo Wabo Tequila, although made in Mexico, are American-owned brands.[29] For Mando, he prefers to drink Cuervo 1800, a top-selling brand of Jose Cuervo, which is a partially Mexican-owned company. Even though Jose Cuervo is not commonly regarded as a high-quality product in the United States, for Mando, it is more important that his tequila has Mexican ties, so much so that he is willing to compromise the cultural cachet associated with drinking top-shelf brands.

Family tradition was a common theme for consumers I spoke with, still others explained that they were among the first members of their family to drink tequila. Ana, whose family is from the state of Sonora, told me that her relatives almost exclusively drink beer. As she put it, "They do drink tequila; maybe you'll find a bottle, but I don't have images of my family pulling out the tequila bottles—it was more beer and cognac."[30] Still, for Ana, although her family did not drink tequila, she sees it as having valuable cultural connotations; for instance, on their last trip to Mexico, she and her husband made it a point to visit the town of Tequila where they took several distillery tours.

Carlos, whose family is originally from the state of Jalisco, prefers to drink tequila straight up, but he sometimes orders it with cola. Like Ana, members of his family drank beer and other mixed drinks—tequila was not a part of his family's tradition. In his words, "My exposure to tequila was as working as a mariachi musician, and at times I would drink with them. We would play gigs every weekend, and people would often send us free tequila when we're on stage . . . Those guys were drinking Cazadores, Herradura, you know, not just Cuervo 1800."[31] More likely to drink tequila while traveling in Mexico, Carlos prefers high-end brands. Similar to Lorena, he rarely buys tequila for himself but purchases it as gifts for other people. Although the custom is not one that originated within their families, Ana and Carlos are among the many new consumers to integrate tequila into their own drinking traditions.

Making Sense of Multiple Representations

Nearly all of the U.S.-based consumers I talked to mentioned the existence of multiple representations of tequila. In Ana's opinion, there were two prominent images associated with tequila in the United States: "The first is the old man sitting at the table with his friends having a couple of drinks, playing cards, or just relaxing. And then the other image of 'Girls Gone Wild.'[32] You know, naked girls, tequila shots, people asking for another round of Cuervo."[33] Often, one image was rooted in moderation, and the other was rooted in over-indulgence. For Ana, the different meanings are related to different occasions, even in Mexico. On a recent trip, she explained:

> We were in Isla Mujeres, which is very touristy. You know, I think I saw a handful of Mexicans. The rest were Americans, Western Europeans, and Canadians. So, people are there at the bars ordering their rounds, their shots of tequila, their beer backer, and then another shot of tequila. When we were at bodegas and going into tequila tastings, that was a different experience, it was more informational; it was educational; it was going through the process and the history. So, you weren't there to get drunk, you weren't there to forget, you were there to really taste a variety of tequila and, for the bodega's sake, buy something.[34]

As Ana sees it, consumers seek out different experiences: Some "want to drink to learn" and others "want to drink to forget."

George, a third-generation Mexican American from Ohio who now lives on the East Coast, drinks tequila about once a month. Like Ana, he also noted a duality in tequila's image. His description both differed and overlapped with her observations. In his words:

> There's this profusion of tequila bars here, a bunch of places advertising, "We
> have seventy-eight types of tequila here." That seems to be for a spiffily dressed
> clientele; they're trying to go out for the night—usually pretty young, affluent-
> looking folks. My other image of tequila is my collegiate experience, where
> it's just drunken idiots, the drinking tequila to get really drunk and the whole
> "tequila makes her clothes come off"[35] thing, the Sammy Hagar, Cabo Wabo
> kind of nonsense. Those are the two groups I've seen in my life.[36]

For George, two versions exist: a high-end image of "young, affluent-looking
folks" and an overindulgent image consisting of "drunken idiots."

Implicit in the representations described by Ana and George are narratives regarding the intersection of respectability and social class. For some
consumers, tequila is sought out to be enjoyed, whereby it *is* the central aspect
of the consumption experience. For others, tequila is a *means* to a particular
end—one in which getting drunk is the goal. This juxtaposition of meanings
shows how, through consumption, different cultural associations are deployed
to meet certain needs or desires. Context and setting also matter: In bodegas
or tequila bars, consumers are seen as partaking in an educational experience (read: upper-class, appropriate), while in Mexican tourist destinations or
on U.S. college campuses, they are described as seeking out irresponsible encounters (read: lower-class, inappropriate). Ironically, despite these classifications, all of these locations cater to individuals from economically privileged
backgrounds.

Drinking Patrón Tequila over other brands allows Juan, a Chicano student
and teacher from Southern California, to "savor the smooth taste." Although
he used to drink rum and coke, in the last few years he has switched to ordering chilled shots of Patrón. As he sees it, tequila in general is becoming
"more popular and more mainstream, more outgoing." When I asked why he
thought this was the case, he responded, "Before, you would go to the club,
and the songs would talk about drinking Courvoisier, but now they're talking about drinking Patrón. Mainly you hear it in West Coast hip hop, or like
Lil' John."[37] The name-dropping of a brand of tequila in hip-hop music is an
example of what George Lipsitz calls "conscious inter-referentiality," where,
as in this case, musicians "shout out" the name of nonmusical products in
a move that nods to the shared experiences among black, Chicano and Chicana, and Mexican American youth as certain objects and styles associated
with their ethnic backgrounds become increasingly commodified.[38] Despite
tequila's trendy image, Juan explained that another image also exists:

Well, in the U.S. the stereotype of the drunk and lazy Mexican drinking tequila with every meal is pretty predominant. I mean, you see it a lot. An image
that comes to mind is *The Three Amigos*, that movie from the 1980s with these
three American actors who went to Mexico to be these *caballeros* [gentlemen],
these heroes, and everybody was drinking tequila everywhere. Even though it
was a satire, I think that kind of image is pretty popular in the United States
about what Mexico is really like, fiestas every day; everyone is drunk and
passed out.[39]

Images such as those made famous in *The Three Amigos* illustrate how the
mass media exacerbate stereotypes about Mexicans as unable or unwilling to
drink tequila in moderation. Further, Juan's comments provide an example of
the real-world effects of what happens when, through seemingly innocuous
humor, racist caricatures of Mexicans become embedded in popular culture.
Building on media scholar Julianne Burton Carvajal's observation that "perverse texts invite perverse readings," it is fair to say that in this case, perverse
texts also carry with them oppressive dimensions for those whose identity
(Chicano) and cultural practices (drinking tequila) are depicted as deviant.[40]

Social class likewise plays a role in matters of representation. For Mexican-
origin consumers in the United States, the cultural capital associated with
tequila's shifting connotations is tenuous. On the one hand, its "hip" reputation allows them to consume tequila in more exclusive social spaces (bodegas, bars, and clubs), but on the other hand, while in those locales, they must
reckon with well-established stereotypes that imply that Mexicans seek excess
and eschew moderation. As a consequence, for U.S.-based Mexican-origin
consumers, tequila's new status is tempered by a racialized legacy that portrays their consumption choices and customs as evidence of their inferiority.

Drinking Tequila Away from Home

Tequila consumers living in the United States, like those living in Mexico, discussed in great detail drinking tequila away from home. Monica, a California-
based Mexican American product manager, told me that, on a recent trip to
Hawaii, she purchased a bottle of Patrón Tequila to drink in the evenings with
her Mexican-born mother after dinner. Mando explained that on a family vacation in Canada, when he and his cousins went out for the evening, they
always ordered tequila, because, in his words, "You have to represent." When

Ana traveled to Germany to visit her husband's family, her German sister-in-law ordered a round of tequila. As she described it:

> She took me to this tapas bar. She ordered tequila, and they brought out orange slices instead of lime. So, instead of salt and lime they gave us orange slices and cinnamon, which is more common with mezcal, which I learned later after traveling to Oaxaca. Yeah, that was a little strange, but the tequila wasn't that different than what you get here at a bar.[41]

Ana recalled her experience at a German tapas bar as a curious yet memorable occasion in which her sister-in-law sought to connect with her by ordering a round of tequila.

Working for several years at the Vatican during the 1990s, Lorena, like Ana, had an "unforgettable experience" with tequila in Europe. As she explained:

> I remember when I was at the Vatican, and whenever a *Mexicano* would come over and visit us in the Vatican, they would always bring us a bottle of tequila. So now I associate it with priests drinking tequila [laughs] . . . I had this one colleague from Michoacán who was studying there, and he had never had tequila. And someone came and brought us this really powerful tequila from Mexico, from Guadalajara, and he said, "Well, I could drink the whole bottle," and he drank the whole bottle. He was usually pretty good at holding his liquor, and wow, I think he got poisoned—he was sick for days. Tequila is a drink that people share; it's a ritual drink.[42]

Drinking tequila in the Vatican served multiple purposes: It affirmed the visitor's notions of self and national identity at the same time that it allowed those Mexicans who were already there to bond with the visitor and acknowledge their shared cultural heritage through the act of consumption. For Lorena, this type of interaction was evidence of the complex qualities people associate with tequila, ones that not only highlighted the connection between place and self but nourished the relations between community and cultural meaning.

Carlos described his experience when working as a waiter at a Mexican restaurant in Puerto Rico:

> There, one of the things was to have tequila. It was a very kind of exotic ritual for the Puerto Ricans to have their tequila. You know, go to the Mexican restaurant and have their tacos and a tequila shot with sangrita.[43] It was expen-

sive too, really expensive. Mainly it was yuppies who would go to this restaurant. They drank it mainly in shots with sangrita, but of course there were margaritas too.[44]

An "exotic ritual" in Puerto Rico, drinking tequila, from Carlos's point of view, represented a form of "conspicuous consumption" for "yuppies" who could afford tequila's "really expensive" price. Middle- and upper-class U.S.-based tequila consumers, like those in Mexico, both observe and contribute to the transformation of tequila's meaning through their transnational transactions. In this case, witnessing the different connotations associated with tequila's consumption through a viewpoint distinct from his own provided Carlos with a new perspective of tequila's cultural significance. In his words, "Just like mariachis, it's totally an icon of the nation, it's an incredible product, it's a pretty big thing."[45]

Transnational Tequila Talk

Consumers' interpretations reflect tequila's shifting role in the global marketplace. Tequila's increased popularity has heightened its association with Mexico, not just in the United States but worldwide. Not surprisingly, those whom I talked to described tequila's symbolism in relation to cultural identity and tradition. Their perceptions, rooted in different national origins, "filter information and guide situational interpretations and actions."[46] In Mexico and the United States, consumers have experienced tequila as a material and symbolic product "that is highly charged and potentially transformative."[47] Their narratives about consumption choices reflected nationalist themes through the linking of their "personal . . . experiences with broader political issues."[48] These assessments accentuate their relationship to tequila and highlight the "discursive resources" that allow them "to enact and achieve their self-definitions of ethnicity."[49]

Tequila drinkers in Mexico described their consumption practices in relation to long-standing family traditions along a continuum that acknowledged *and* challenged the conventions of these relationships. Familial narratives departed from common gendered associations attributed to drinking tequila. In these circumstances, women, whose consumption of alcohol is often considered inappropriate, were able to speak back to stereotypes, commemorate family ties, and affirm their agency as both consumers and citizens with access to the terms of their own pleasure. "Seeing tequila in a different light" was another recurrent theme with consumers in Mexico. Specifically, many relayed stories of "discovering" pride in feeling Mexican *through* tequila when away from home. Consumption choices were laden with political meaning; this was especially evident in Victor's description of the protest at the Puerto Vallarta beach resort, where Mexican tourists demanded, and were served, better-quality tequila. Finally, consumers were also able to track cultural change and recognize instances of shifting social norms within the country. Tequila served as a metaphor through which to elaborate what they saw as positive changes in society.

For Mexican, Mexican American, and Chicano and Chicana consumers in the United States, drinking tequila was only sometimes described as an ongoing family tradition. However, despite this, many consumers whose families did not drink tequila still associated it with their own personal drinking rituals and considered tequila a salient Mexican symbol. Perhaps the most striking difference between the two sets of groups was how, in the United States, consumers were cognizant of the divergent meanings associated with tequila, one that was seen as celebrating its cultural aspects and another that was seen as using it as an excuse to get drunk and act irresponsibly. Some also mentioned tequila's new "trendy" image that highlighted its shifting class connotations. Unlike consumers in Mexico, U.S.-based consumers expressed more concern about how these representations might translate to misguided beliefs about Mexicans. Drinking tequila away from home in foreign settings allowed middle- and upper-middle-class consumers to proudly "represent" their ethnic identity and experience affirmative connections to their Mexican heritage. What is more, it provided them with a new outlook on tequila, ranging from the complex qualities associated with its consumption to its status as an emboldened symbol of Mexico.

Tequila talk calls attention to the complicated set of conditions within which notions of national and cultural identity are rendered meaningful. Popular associations attributed to tequila, either produced through everyday rituals with family and friends or expressed via customs that mark special occasions, carry with them both subtle and obvious reminders of the enduring effects of inequality that denote the relationship between the United States and Mexico. In spite of dominant representations that depict tequila as closely associated with a masculinized Mexican identity, how consumers perceive tequila is complex: Tequila is described as constitutive of certain accounts of

Mexican culture at the same time it is portrayed as challenging the very social scripts used to uphold these ideals. Thus, through the lens of consumption, we are able to see how tequila symbolically serves as a means of acknowledging the tensions inherent in prevailing depictions of cultural identity that, like commodities themselves, easily and frequently traverse national borders.

Conclusion

Differences and similarities exist with regard to tequila-drinking practices in Mexico and the United States. Culturally and socially mediated, consumption choices "provide a window into how people interpret, use, and define ethnic and cultural categories."[50] In light of the proliferating effects of globalization, the collective identity of consumers is increasingly linked by the shared codes rooted in consumption activities.[51] However, shared codes do not uniformly translate into shared experiences, as the conditions that structure the meanings ascribed to particular commodities are multiple and vary across time and location. For example, in Mexico some consumers widely (and proudly) recognize tequila's significance as a symbol of Mexicanness, and in the United States some consumers honor cultural tradition by drinking tequila at the same time that they (and others) recognize its significance as a racialized signifier of Mexican identity.

Tequila's masculine connotations remain salient in Mexico, but, as my interviews show, changes were taking place, especially with regard to how men and women challenged and, in some cases, rejected rigid definitions regarding the significance of "traditional" consumption practices. Top among the reasons for this shifting interpretation is the way women are redefining their lives both inside and outside the household. In the words of political scientist Victoria Rodríguez, "Mexican women have become a force to be reckoned with—socially, economically, and politically."[52] Although important progress has been made, women have "differing degrees of success in claiming their citizenship" when it comes to the construction and expression of nationhood.[53] Through the shared codes of consumption, women communicate national pride and defy cultural scripts that silence their ability to convey pleasure within and outside the domestic sphere.

As more scholars theorize the role of commodities and "as more people become transnationals," examining consumption as a symbolic practice and material enactment enables a deeper understanding of the precepts of individual and shared identity.[54] Consumption scholars of all disciplines should consider in greater detail how culturally specific realities[55] and unconventional "sites of knowledge and empowerment" influence the terrain of everyday life.[56] Further, closer attention should be paid to the structure of feeling associated with consumption as it is experienced by individuals from lower socioeconomic backgrounds who have limited access to the locations where transnational exchanges take place.[57]

In addition to providing a unique glimpse into the role of the collective consciousness[58] in the global marketplace, this analysis moves beyond the claim that a particular commodity reflects specific or rigid notions of national identity, such as those endorsed by the state, corporate marketers, or industry elites and instead suggests that a more nuanced approach is necessary—one that considers how, through consumption practices, individuals manage complex webs of relations that have diverse social and political implications. Exploring how people understand, challenge, and negotiate meanings pertaining to the consumption of tequila, I have sought to provide an alternative lens through which to consider the multifaceted dynamics that comprise and shape cultural identity within and across national borders.

CODA

On a clear evening in January 2013, seven men were killed in an armed shoot-out on a dusty, yet picturesque, road that connects the town of Magdalena to Tequila. Although the deaths were widely reported, few details were released about the bloody—and likely drug-related—event. The violence left area residents rattled, upset, and very concerned. Just four months earlier, there had been another shootout, this time between suspected members of the notorious drug cartel, the Zetas, and local police. Four officers—from Amatitán, Magdalena, and Tequila—died on a well-traveled highway.

In comparison to other states, like Sinaloa or Michoacán, Jalisco has been spared much of the gruesome savagery associated with the drug trade. However, this reality has changed markedly in the last decade. Most horrifically, in late 2011, twenty-three bound and gagged bodies were dumped near the Millennium Arches, one of Guadalajara's most recognizable landmarks. In March 2013, the Mexican minister of tourism was assassinated in broad daylight while stopped at a streetlight in a popular residential neighborhood not far from the same arches.

The growing unrest—in rural Jalisco especially—can only be understood within the context of broader economic changes, such as the steady rise of poverty and unemployment. A recent government study reports that 2.7 million people in Jalisco, nearly 36 percent of the population, live in moderate to extreme poverty.[1] Jalisco, the heart and cradle of Mexico, currently has one of the highest unemployment rates in the country. In the shadow of these circumstances, multinational tequila companies boast record sales—far exceeding the tens of millions of dollars from decades past. Essentially, every year *billions* of dollars are generated from the tequila region, even as many of its residents struggle to make ends meet. Money flows out with ease. Meanwhile, little heed is paid to the farmers, the workers, or the inhabitants—the people who make tequila.

It would be shortsighted to suggest direct causation: Obviously, the causes of poverty go far beyond the tequila sector. For starters, the conversation would have to begin with the adoption of neoliberal policies that have facilitated multinational corporations' pursuit of wealth and power. Next, the dialogue would have to spotlight the ongoing consumer demand from the United States for drugs, its failed war on narcotics, and its government's backward foreign policies. Finally, the discussion would have to turn to the Mexican government and their acquiescence to transnational businesses and their consistent failure to prioritize better wages and job creation in the region.

This observation brings me back to where I began: Commodities, first and foremost, are about people. Although not always evident, our relationship with things matters. I have argued that commodities have deeply salient "social lives" that not only represent the values of a society but *shape* the commitments held by communities.[2] Commodities like tequila are themselves agents that take part in imagining the nation.[3] They play a pivotal role in enabling a sense of national belonging that helps navigate the "social vertigo of living in a world of random and dreadfully unsteady meanings."[4] Examining the sociality of things provides an opportunity to unearth complexities that we would not otherwise see—how attributes of Mexicanness are shaped, contested, and reconfigured not only by elite actors but also by less powerful individuals.

Throughout this book, I have sought to make sense of the circumstances that helped position tequila as Mexico's national spirit. Tequila's import as the spirit of Mexico did not happen by accident but instead was an outcome of varied conflicts and alliances across time. These struggles, deeply mired in legacies of the past and intensely enmeshed in visions of the future, continue to play out in the contemporary public arena. Powerful tequila industrialists and the Mexican government promote a unified narrative that highlights tequila's importance to the nation. In doing so, they call on the public, both as citizens and as consumers, to defend its integrity in light of growing competition and the increasing manufacture of nonregistered tequila-like products, even though many of these spirits represent the diverse customs associated with mezcal production that have spanned centuries. Yet, regardless of this forceful rhetoric, there remain for ordinary people "mobile pacts for the interpretation of commodities and messages"—room for the negotiation and expression of complex national and individual identities.[5]

Defining the process through which commodities acquire significance is not a new or neutral phenomenon. Predating the colonial encounter and stretching across different historical periods, various meanings were attributed to the agave-based drinks: pulque, mezcal, and tequila. Sometimes seen as too *indio*, and other times deemed too *corriente* (lower class), their symbolic significance was never entirely stable; instead, their associations shifted as changes in the political economy devalued some objects while giving new value to others. These developments continued into the Mexican Revolution era as tequila became closely associated with notions of *lo mexicano* in Mexico and the United States. By portraying Pancho Villa and Mexicans in relation to alcohol, the American media accounted for cultural differences that justified American economic expansion into Mexico at the same time it championed the image of Mexicans as criminally inclined. In Mexico, Pancho Villa and tequila's ties came to symbolize courage and resistance to the status quo in both countries.

Technological advancements prompted new ways of imagining the nation and further elevated tequila's symbolic role as Mexico's spirit. Within the budding Mexican film industry, the birth of the *comedia ranchera* genre created and promoted archetypes about Mexico that were infused with sentimentality. Among the consistently evoked images included the idealization of certain regions, the glorification of traditional (that is, patriarchal) familial ways of being, and the transformative possibilities of individual behavior (for example, making weaknesses into virtues)—conventionally accomplished through drinking tequila.[6]

Audiences flocked to the cinema seeking "to learn skills, to lose inhibitions, to suffer and be consoled in style, painlessly to envy the elites, happily to be resigned to poverty, to laugh at the stereotypes that ridiculed them, to understand how they belonged to the nation."[7] Tequila became increasingly allied with a particular expression of masculinity that was intertwined with romantic, raced, and classed associations situated in the bucolic backdrop of the *rancho grande*. Rituals of consumption enhanced these bonds as "the massification of culture and the commodification of everyday life" brought rural and urban Mexicans together in a common setting with a common tonic that transcended class antagonisms.[8] Although appearing stable and consistent throughout this period, these representations were challenged in films, at cabarets, and on the radio. Actresses and singers such as Sara Garcia and Lucha Reyes interrupted the masculinized narrative regarding tequila consumption—speaking back to mass culture's reliance on static caricatures and queering the boundaries of national identity.

Tequila, and the symbolic economy of identity through which it is brought to life, offers a useful lens into how commodities frame, reflect, and interface with social identities. Contemporary developments also matter in this multidimensional process. The budding tequila tourism industry prompted the reworking and elevation of two figures—the *jimador* and Mayahuel. Each solidified tequila's mestizo and indigenous ties to the nation.[9] In addition, the initiation of formal protective measures, intended to safeguard against the negative effects of globalization—namely the production of tequila in other parts of the world—consolidated the power of transnational tequila industrialists as defenders of the nation's spirit. As a consequence, farmers, residents, and other less powerful actors associated with the manufacture of tequila have been unable to financially benefit from the various measures intended to preserve local knowledge. At the level of production, social identities merge with neoliberal political agendas and economic reforms. Interestingly, national ideologies are also marshaled by industry elites to influence the terms of tequila's consumption, as promotional campaigns call on Mexicans to defend tequila's honor in the marketplace through their drinking preferences and practices.

Individuals—regular tequila drinkers—acknowledge the dominant stereotypes used to describe the Mexican character. This acknowledgment, however, does not rest easily. Although referencing the significance of a national image closely associated with popular cinematic representations of noble, tequila-swigging *charros*, consumers reconfigure official and mainstream depictions of tequila by seeking new terms for its consumption. Consumers are not immune to the campaigns promoted by corporate interests, especially those that emphasize their brand's ties to Mexicanness. However, as my interviews revealed, attitudes vary, and, just as they did in the past, consumers will continue to negotiate what it means to be Mexican in ways that support, extend, and challenge traditional understandings of *lo mexicano*.

I began this book with a vignette describing preparations for the National Fair of Tequila in order to shift the focus away from the celebratory or debaucherous images that often accompany the topic of tequila. I wanted to highlight the individuals who are so critical to tequila's cultural, social, and economic world. The people of Tequila, Amatitán, and Magdalena, and those who live in the surrounding regions, remain invisible—far too often—whenever the word *tequila* is muttered, written, or evoked, whether by a Jaliscan politician or a Mexican American tourist visiting Cancún. This work speaks to the potential of studying commodities—like tequila—as a means of gaining greater insight into how identities absorb significance and how they are employed by different groups of people. Delving deeper into commodities can illuminate the less-recognized processes and people involved behind the scenes in making meaning.

As poverty increases in the tequila-producing state of Jalisco, even as large tequila companies continue to report record profits, new global connections are emerging that seek to counterbalance the seemingly bleak current situation. Academics, activists, agave farmers, and small-scale artisanal producers across Mexico are calling attention to the ecological, political, and cultural impacts of tequila production. They are also highlighting the manufacture of a variety of mezcals—locally made agave-based distilled drinks that have been crafted in Jalisco (as well as other states) for centuries. One such effort that brought these individuals together was the recent move by the Mexican Institute of Industrial Property to essentially trademark the word *agave*. If passed, NOM-186 (as the legislation was known) would have limited the use of the word *agave* to official producers of tequila, bacanora, and mezcal. By law, the formal market for these products allows the use of only six types of agave. Thus, producers who have a centuries-long tradition of using at least forty types of agave in their products would have no longer been able use the word *agave* in their promotional or descriptive materials.[10] This type of standardization (rumored to be revived in the near future) would have further marginalized artisanal producers and hindered their access to new or established markets, as falling outside of the nation's "official" category system ostracizes them.

Much of this activism is sustained through transnational circuits of communication—the ability to raise public awareness through Internet forums, blogs, and Facebook has been fundamental to speaking back to government officials and informing consumers worldwide about their options. There is more than one agave spirit that comprises the nation, they make clear. The increasing international "foodie" movement, in combination with the growing

Mexican and Mexican American middle class in the United States (and their purchasing power), has prompted a renewed and, sometimes new, interest in learning about the history, manufacture, and culture of tequila and diverse types of mezcal. Bars in cities like San Francisco, Philadelphia, Tokyo, Santiago, and Dublin boast of their tequila and mezcal catalogs—many offering several hundred options. Although most customers of these locals are middle or upper class, their search for variety and distinction has turned attention to the products offered by smaller and often family-run brands. Tequila aficionados across the world are quick to thumb their noses at products made by the large industry leaders in favor of more difficult-to-locate brands. Albeit not intentionally political acts, their desires and pursuits support smaller companies.

Tequila is intimately linked to notions of *lo mexicano*—how people interpret *lo mexicano*, experience it, and project meaning onto it. *Lo mexicano* is at the heart of a collective fiction that the nation can and should exist as a unified entity. In this sense, *lo mexicano* is not unique—every nation has its own narratives or myths that underscore the importance of shared sensibilities. Through exploring several historical and contemporary episodes—shots, if you will—I have sought to better understand the complicated circumstances that influence tequila's social life. I considered aspects of tequila's past and present as they diverged and worked in tandem to ultimately enable its ascendance as an esteemed symbol of *lo mexicano*. Yet, tequila's story is far from complete, and many gaps remain. Indeed, my effort here documents only a few of its travels and trajectories. By questioning tequila's status, I paid close attention to how ideologies of race, class, gender, and sexuality were mobilized by different actors to challenge the terrain already covered by tequila and the journeys it has yet to embark on. Commodities such as tequila mark the passing of time and capture change in motion; they simultaneously help us to remember and allow us to forget. They are dynamic, like the spirit of a nation.

REFERENCE MATTER

ACKNOWLEDGMENTS

This project began at the University of California, Santa Cruz, and was deeply enhanced by the intellectual encouragement and sage counsel provided by Herman Gray, George Lipsitz, Olga Nájera-Ramírez, Dana Takagi, and Pat Zavella. Their interdisciplinary insight enriched my thinking and helped sharpen my academic voice. I likewise learned a great deal from talking to and bouncing ideas off Lionel Cantú, James Clifford, Ben Crow, Melanie DuPuis, Rosa-Linda Fregoso, Bill Friedland, Walter Goldfrank, David Goodman, Marcia Millman, Craig Reinarman, Tricia Rose, Helen Shapiro, and Candace West. I am thankful for the community and humor provided over the years by my *colegas* of the Transnational Popular Cultures Cluster of the Chicano/Latino Research Center, including Xóchitl Chávez, Elisa Huerta, Curtis Marez, Olga Nájera-Ramírez, Steve Nava, Russell Rodríguez, Deb Vargas, Isa Velez, Pat Zavella, and Susy Zepeda.

In Guadalajara, Mexico, early guidance from José María Muriá and conversations with Rogelio Luna and Ignacio Gómez-Arriola helped me think about this project in a broader historical context. Ana Valenzuela-Zapata was a crucial advisor during different stages of my stay. David Ruiz, David Suro, and Jaime Villalobos's expertise helped fill in several big timeline gaps. I am thankful for the assistance of archivists, curators, and librarians, particularly María de Jesús Arámbula Limón, José Luis Cervantes, Alicia Rodríguez, and Heriberto Saucedo Campos. Antonia Rojas and Nahún Carriles helped with securing several images from collections housed at the FILMOTECA (UNAM). I am immensely grateful to all those individuals who allowed me to conduct impromptu and scheduled interviews, tag along with them to industry meetings, and trusted me to tell a different story about tequila—I could not have written this book without them. Fantastic friends including Lucia Ávila, Elías García, Monica Garcia, Fernando González, Javier Hernández,

Myrna Machuca, Mario Muñoz, Aldo Prieto, José Obdulio Valdez, María de Lourdes Ramírez, Angelica Rubio, Jana Rupp, Daniel Salzer, and Victor Valdivia made *Guanatos* a home away from home. Mil gracias.

I am indebted to fellow participants of the Eating Culture: Race and Food Group funded by the University of California Humanities Research Institute at the University of California, Irvine, for helping me streamline my research objectives: Robert Álvarez, Julie Guthman, Caroline De La Peña, Melanie DuPuis, Michael Jones, Kimberly Nettles, and Parama Roy. I thank the following colleagues at various institutions for their support and feedback over the years: Enrique Alemán, Sonya Alemán, Sarah Babb, Joe Bandy, Jesse Barba, Barbara Barnes, Susan Bell, Liz Bennett, Sarah Bowen, Elise Boxer, Michelle Camacho, Mariana Cruz, Annelle Curulla, Arlene Dávila, Sergio De La Mora, Jay Demerath, Pat Duffy, Juan Flores, Claudia Geist, Mariana Gerena, Macarena Gómez-Barris, Kim Hackford-Peer, Deborah Heath, Becky Horn, Greg Horvath, Hillary Jenks, Kathryn Kothe, Kim Korinek, Theresa Martinez, Tanya McNeill, Lela Mei, Dhiraj Murthy, Sudarat Musikawong, José Orozco, Vanessa Pérez, Ulices Piña, Susie Porter, Nancy Riley, Michelle Robertson, Dee Royster, Meg Safford, Belinda Saltiban, Fernando Sánchez, Natasha Sarkisian, Caesar Sereseres, Becky Scott, Julie Stewart, Kathryn Stockton, Juan Carlos Toledano, Steve Topik, Becky Utz, Freddy Vilches, Kathy Walker, Daniel Walkowitz, Allen Wells, Enrique Yepes, Elliot Young, Eric Zolov, and Robert Zussman. I am especially thankful to Mary Louise Pratt and Renato Rosaldo for reading and commenting on my entire manuscript-in-progress.

This book benefited from generous institutional support from the Ford Foundation and UC Santa Cruz's Chicano/Latino Research Center, the Department of Sociology, and the Faculty Mentorship Program. Assistance from the University of Utah's Department of Sociology, The College of Social and Behavioral Sciences' Pre-Tenure Sabbatical Program, in combination with and a University of California Institute for Mexico and the United States (UC MEXUS) Postdoctoral Fellowship, allowed me time off to complete the manuscript. At CIESAS Occidente, Guadalajara, José Hernández and Teresa Fernández were welcoming and resourceful. I had the great fortune to work with several first-rate editors, including Matt Pacenza, Erika Stevens, and the team at Stanford University Press, especially Frances Malcolm, Margaret Pinette, and Kate Wahl. Several anonymous reviewers gave thoughtful and constructive feedback.

I appreciate the kindness of my friends who provided much-needed encouragement (and chocolate and wine) throughout this journey—you know who you are. Special thanks to my aunts, uncles, and cousins living in the United States who taught me how to hone my critical thinking skills and to have a sense of humor on many a Saturday evening gathering. The unwavering, long-distance support of family in Kilcar, Ireland; El Tránsito, Chile; and Kingston St. Mary, England kept me going when times were tough. The memory of my sister, Colleen Gaytán, and my mentor, Lionel Cantú, were constant sources of inspiration. Although they never had the opportunity to go to college, my parents, Sarah and Martín Gaytán, were with me every step of the way—teaching me by example how to persevere and keep the faith. Finally, gracias to Gwyn, the most incredible person I know, for his brilliance, patience, and love.

NOTES

INTRODUCTION

1. Appadurai, *The Social Life of Things.*
2. Lacy, *El tequila.*
3. Monsiváis, "Tequila with Lime and Other Table Talk."
4. Quirarte, "The Poetics of Tequila."
5. My use of the "symbolic economy of identity" builds on David Grazian's idea of the "symbolic economy of authenticity" from his book *Blue Chicago: The Search for Authenticity in Urban Blues Clubs*; 17.
6. Ramos, *Profile of Man and Culture in Mexico*: 108.
7. Bartra, *The Cage of Melancholy.*
8. Fischer and Benson, *Broccoli and Desire.*
9. Griswold, *Cultures and Societies in a Changing World.*
10. Muriá, "Momentos del Tequila."
11. Beatty, "Bottles for Beer." Before this time, glass bottles were handblown.
12. Muriá, "Momentos del Tequila": 86–87.
13. Monsiváis, "Tequila with Lime."
14. Límon, *Tequila*: 141.
15. Alfaro, "Tequila and Its Signs": 84.
16. Límon, *Tequila*: 139–141.
17. Bowen and Gaytán, "The Paradox of Protection."
18. Consejo Regulador del Tequila (CRT), "Exportaciones por categoría tequila."
19. Ibid.
20. Bowen, "Geographical Indications."
21. Ibid. These shifts, as Bowen points out, are related to the six- to ten-year cycle it takes agave to mature and conflicts between agave growers and tequila companies.
22. Hundreds of stories were written about the agave shortage throughout the world. Many of these reports are still accessible on the Internet.
23. "A Harvest of Trouble for Tequila Farmers."
24. Bauman, *Hollywood Highbrow.*
25. Appadurai, *The Social Life of Things*: 5.
26. Molotch, *Where Stuff Comes From*: 11.

27. Ibid.: ix.

28. Miller, *Acknowledging Consumption*: 1.

29. Canclini, *Consumers and Citizens*: 47.

30. Appadurai, *The Social Life of Things*: 4.

31. For example, see Douglas and Isherwood, *The World of Goods*.

32. Appadurai, *The Social Life of Things*: 5.

33. For example, see Canclini, *Consumers and Citizens*; Fischer and Benson, *Broccoli and Desire*; and Topik, Marichal, and Frank, *From Silver to Cocaine*.

34. Appadurai, *The Social Life of Things*: 6.

35. I would like to thank Mary Louis Pratt for introducing me to the significance of "sociality" in the context of this work.

CHAPTER 1

1. González Luna, "El paisaje agavero": 13.

2. Researchers disagree on whether distillation technologies existed prior to the colonial encounter. In their 2008 article, "Early Coconut Distillation and the Origins of Mezcal and Tequila Spirits in West-Central Mexico," authors Zizumbo and Colunga assert that the Filipino community in Colima, Mexico, who were accustomed to distilling coconut juice in the Philippines, first introduced distillation to the Americas. Drawing on botanical, toponymic, archaeological, and ethnohistoric data, they argue that locals used the Filipino technique (introduced in 1571), and not Spanish methods, to produce the first forms of distilled agave drinks. These distillation operations were intentionally hidden from Spanish authorities, although some colonial documents mention the production of drinks made in stills. See also Jiménez Vizcarra's *El vino mezcal, tequila y la polémica sobre la destilación prehispánica* for more information.

3. Quiroz Márquez describes mezcal as "the first eminently mestizo drink to arrive on the scene as a result of the Spanish conquest of Mexican soil" (*Lo que quería saber*: 3).

4. Bourdieu, *Distinction*.

5. The word *maguey* comes from the Antilles and was introduced to Mexico by the Spanish (Quiroz Márquez, *El mezcal*). Throughout this book I use the name *agave* for the purpose of continuity.

6. The Agave genus is the largest of the Agaveceae family. The word *agave* comes from the Greek *agaue*, which in English translates to "admirable" (Quiroz Márquez, *El mezcal*). In Mexico there are over 200 species of agave.

7. Quiroz Márquez, *El mezcal*. Codices including the Borgia, Laud, and Magliabecchi drew more specific connections between agricultural cycles and indigenous gods (Dufétel, "El maguey, el conejo y la luna"). In particular, they discuss the Tezcatzóncatl, the collective name of pulque gods.

8. Bruman, *Alcohol in Ancient Mexico*.

9. Ibid.: 63.

10. Dufétel, "El maguey, el conejo y la luna": 1.

11. Sánchez Guevara, "La resmantización del espacio cultural de la Plaza Mayor."

12. Arriola, *The Agave Landscape*: 16. There seems to be little disagreement over the origins of the words *xictli* (navel) and *co* (place).

13. Ibid.

14. Bruman, *Alcohol in Ancient Mexico*: 12.

15. Arriola, *The Agave Landscape*.

16. Bellingeri, *Las haciendas en México*.

17. Parsons and Parsons, "Maguey Utilization in Highland Central Mexico."

18. Evans, "The Productivity of Maguey Terrace Agriculture": 117.

19. Luna, *La historia del tequila, de sus regiones, y sus hombres*: 30.

20. Quiroz Márquez, *El mezcal*: 9.

21. Pagden, *Hernan Cortes*: 104.

22. The term *indio* is problematic—Mesoamericans never considered themselves "Indian." Ethnic populations were diverse, despite the homogenizing effects of the word *Indian*.

23. Godoy, *Tequila*.

24. Bruman, *Alcohol in Ancient Mexico*: 71–72.

25. Toxqui Garay, "El recreo de los amigos."

26. Soustelle, *The Daily Life of the Aztecs*: 164.

27. For more information regarding the salience of segregation during this period, see Mörner and Gibson, "Diego Muñoz Camargo and the Segregation Policy of the Spanish Crown."

28. Cope, *The Limits of Racial Domination*: 3.

29. Botanist and explorer Alexander von Humboldt (*Political Essay on the Kingdom of New Spain*), in his detailed documentation of life in New Spain, explains that pulque had an unusually strong smell even when it was fresh. As he writes, "The inhabitants of the country differ very much in their opinions as to the true cause of the fetid odor of the pulque. It is generally affirmed that this odor, which is analogous to that of animal matter, is to be ascribed to the skins in which the first juice of the agave is poured" (113–114). Bruman also notes that pulque "acquire[s] a most objectionable stench" (71).

30. Taylor, *Drinking, Homicide, and Rebellion in Colonial Mexican Villages*.

31. Smith, *Caribbean Rum*: 453.

32. Florescano, *Memory, Myth, and Time in Mexico*: 66.

33. Ibid.

34. Taylor, *Drinking, Homicide, and Rebellion*: 40.

35. Bourke, "Distillation by Early American Indians": 298.

36. Ibid.

37. For a detailed discussion of this phenomenon, see Aizpuru, "El nacimiento del miedo, 1692."

38. Smith, *Caribbean Rum*. In his research on rum, Smith explains that, even when water was available to European migrants in the Caribbean, they preferred to drink alcohol because of their concerns about contaminated water. The end result was

an "enhanced desirability of alcoholic beverages" (24). According to his findings, one seventeenth-century writer summed up the situation by noting that "only invalids and chickens drink water" when alcohol is available (25).

39. Blocker, Fahey, and Tyrell, *Alcohol and Temperance in Modern History*. Despite concerted efforts, the Spanish were able to produce drinkable wine only in central Chile and western Argentina (Orlove and Bauer, "Chile in the Belle Époque").

40. Smith, *Caribbean Rum*: 548.

41. Wilson and Pineda, "Pineda's Report on the Beverages of New Spain."

42. Pilcher, *Qué Vivan los Tamales*.

43. Quiroz Márquez, *El mezcal*.

44. For instance, during this period the British, French, and Spanish were all involved in Caribbean rum production, and by 1701 nearly 600,000 gallons of rum from Barbados were being exported to North America and Europe (Smith, *Caribbean Rum*).

45. Conroy, *In Public Houses*.

46. Cope, *The Limits of Racial Domination*: 5. See also Mark Christensen's excellent work (*Nahua and Maya Catholicisms*) detailing the multiple versions of Catholicism practiced during the colonial period and across ethnic lines (both Nahua and Maya).

47. Lewis, "The 'Weakness' of Women and the Feminization of the Indian in Colonial Mexico": 68.

48. Smith, *Caribbean Rum*.

49. James Lockhart, *The Nahuas after the Conquest*.

50. Laudan and Pilcher, "Chilies, Chocolate, and Race in New Spain": 63.

51. Von Humboldt, *Political Essay on the Kingdom of New Spain*.

52. Laundan and Pilcher, "Chilies, Chocolate, and Race in New Spain": 64.

53. Katzew, *Casta Painting*.

54. Carrera, *Imagining Identity in New Spain*.

55. Katzew, *Casta Painting*.

56. Ibid.

57. Carerra, *Imagining Identity in New Spain*.

58. Katzew, *Casta Painting*.

59. For a detailed discussion of race, class, and gender under colonialism, see Stoler, *Carnal Knowledge and Imperial Power*.

60. Widdifield, *The Embodiment of the National in Late Nineteenth-Century Mexican Painting*: 128.

61. Pulque, however, was only one of many indigenous customs that the Spanish attempted to restrict. Historian Charles Gibson (*The Aztecs under Spanish Rule*) explains that the Spanish forbade numerous customs that they found uncivilized. For instance, the native ball game (*juego de pelota*), played for 3,000 years throughout Mesoamerica, was outlawed in the sixteenth century because it "was said to involve witchcraft and satanic pacts" (151). Various cultural ceremonies, dances, and celebrations were all condemned by religious and civic authorities. Christian standards regarding marriage, monogamy, and child rearing were also enforced.

62. Taylor, *Drinking, Homicide, and Rebellion*: 16.

63. Ibid.

64. Ibid.

65. Scardaville, "Alcohol Abuse and Tavern Reform in Late Colonial Mexico City."

66. Ibid.: 654.

67. Socolow, *The Women of Colonial Latin America*: 10.

68. Viqueira Albán, *Propriety and Permissiveness in Bourbon Mexico*: 130.

69. Lewis, "The 'Weakness' of Women": 76.

70. Viqueira Albán, *Propriety and Permissiveness in Bourbon Mexico*.

71. Gibson, *The Aztecs under Spanish Rule*: 150. Taylor (*Drinking, Homicide, and Rebellion*: 39) proposes that a significant aspect of preconquest drinking was "the continuation of ritual celebrations as a form of worship in which devotion was measured by the degree of intoxication."

72. Earle, "If You Eat Their Food . . . Diets and Bodies in Early Colonial Spanish America."

73. Taylor, *Drinking, Homicide, and Rebellion*: 41.

74. In his words, "There was nothing insubordinate or carnivalesque in this inebriation; to the contrary, it was entirely 'pro-establishment.' It served, among other things, to punctuate and legitimate the elite's supervisory role in the production and consumption of cosmic energy" (Mitchell, *Intoxicated Identities*: 17).

75. Guedea, "México en 1812."

76. Nemser, "To Avoid This Mixture": 100.

77. Ibid.

78. See Martínez, *Genealogical Fictions*.

79. Kicza, "The Pulque Trade of Late Colonial Mexico City."

80. Scardaville, "Alcohol Abuse and Tavern Reform."

81. Toxqui Garay, "El Recreo de Los Amigos."

82. Scardaville, "Alcohol Abuse and Tavern Reform": 647.

83. Kizca, "The Pulque Trade of Late Colonial Mexico City."

84. Viqueira Albán, *Propriety and Permissiveness in Bourbon Mexico*: 131.

85. Nemser, "To Avoid This Mixture": 106.

86. Alberro, "Bebidas alchólicas y sociedad colonial en México": 356.

87. Cope, *The Limits of Racial Domination*.

88. Ibid.

89. Scardaville, "Alcohol Abuse and Tavern Reform."

90. Viqueira-Albán, *Propriety and Permissiveness in Bourbon Mexico*.

91. Scardaville, "Alcohol Abuse and Tavern Reform": 646.

92. Taylor, *Drinking, Homicide, and Rebellion*.

93. Viqueira Albán, *Propriety and Permissiveness in Bourbon Mexico*: 130.

94. Valadez Moreno, "Vinateros y talladores."

95. Viqueira Albán, *Propriety and Permissiveness in Bourbon Mexico*: 159.

96. Scardaville, "Alcohol Abuse and Tavern Reform."

97. Kicza, "The Pulque Trade of Late Colonial Mexico City": 202.

98. These practices were not limited to Mexico. See Lockhart and Schwartz, *Early Latin America*, for a deeper discussion of Spanish interest in coca and *chuño* (a variety of potato).

99. Piña, "Lords of Agave."

100. Humbolt, quoted in Scardaville, "Alcohol Abuse and Tavern Reform": 650.

101. The sales tax on pulque brought in 600,000 pesos annually in the 1780s and 800,000 pesos annually in the early 1800s.

102. Scardaville, "Alcohol Abuse and Tavern Reform."

103. Van Young, "Urban Market and Hinterland": 594.

104. Lindley, *Haciendas and Economic Development*: 11.

105. Ibid.

106. Van Young, *Hacienda and Market in Eighteenth Century Mexico*: 25.

107. There is some doubt among tequila scholars that De Tagle was the first person to introduce the production of mezcal.

108. Luna, *La Historia del Tequila*: 39.

109. Lindley, *Haciendas and Economic Development*: 15.

110. Van Young, *Hacienda and Market in Eighteenth Century Mexico*: 26.

111. Anderson, "Race and Social Stratification": 17.

112. Lindley, *Haciendas and Economic Development*.

113. Van Young, *Hacienda and Market*.

114. Lindley, *Haciendas and Economic Development*: 15.

115. Dotson and Dotson, "Ecological Trends in the City of Guadalajara, Mexico": 368.

116. Orozco, "Esos altos de Jalisco!"

117. The Mixtón War was a series of uprisings led by native groups who sought to end the Spanish practice of enslaving indigenous people. There were numerous clashes during the two-year period, some which were won by indigenous groups, although ultimately the Spanish prevailed.

118. Patch, "Indian Resistance to Colonialism": 181.

119. Orozco, "Esos altos de Jalisco!": 42.

120. This is not to say that racial segregation did not exist at all; however, as scholars, including Rodney Anderson ("Race and Social Stratification") and John Chase and William Taylor (1978), have illustrated, the boundaries of racial segregation in colonial Mexico City were more porous than past historians had once claimed.

121. Cope, *The Limits of Racial Domination*: 20.

122. Taylor, *Drinking, Homicide, and Rebellion*: 72.

123. Viqueira Albán, *Propriety and Permissiveness in Bourbon Mexico*: 153.

124. Lindley, *Haciendas and Economic Development*.

125. According to ethnobiologist Ana Valenzuela-Zapata, the state of Jalisco has the greatest variety of agave species in all of Mexico, and early production of mezcal in the region was comprised of different types of agave (personal communication).

126. Details provided by Alexander von Humboldt (*Political Essay on the Kingdom of New Spain* [abridged version]) show that the Spanish were importing substantial amounts of alcohol such as brandy, red wine, white wine, liquors, and beer.

127. Duncan, "Embracing a Suitable Past."

128. Ibid.: 254.

129. Pilcher, "Fajitas and the Failure of Refrigerated Meat Packing in Mexico": 419.

130. Ibid.: 419.

131. Godoy, Herrera, and Ulloa, *Más allá del pulque y el tepache.*

132. Pilcher, "Fajitas and the Failure of Refrigerated Meat Packing in Mexico": 420.

133. Luna, *La historia del tequila, de sus regiones y sus hombres.*

134. Pratt, *Imperial Eyes*: 112.

135. Taylor, "The Robber Region of Mexico."

136. Luna, *La historia del tequila*: 1991.

137. Gutiérrez Lorenzo, "Fuentes para el estudio del vino mezcal."

138. "Ya va en camino para Mexico."

139. Muriá, "Momentos del tequila."

140. William Taylor (*Landlord and Peasant in Colonial Oaxaca*) notes that in Oaxaca agave was grown "in nearly all eastern towns" but that it was controlled by local individuals instead of communities or outside investors.

141. Taylor, *Drinking, Homicide, and Rebellion*: 8.

142. Kaplan, *The Anarchy of Empire in the Making of U.S. Culture*: 261–262.

143. In the words of Purnell, private property "would serve as the engine of economic development and prosperity," and would "'civilize' the Indian villagers, weaken their communal and religious identities, eliminate the 'savage' customs associated with those identities, and transform them into virtuous and hardworking citizens of the Mexican Republic" ("Citizens and Sons of the Pueblo": 214).

144. Ibid.

145. Sánchez López, *Oaxaca, tierra de maguey y mezcal.*

146. Ibid.: 111.

147. See Valenzuela-Zapata and Gaytán, "Sustaining Biological and Cultural Diversity," for a deeper discussion of how these practices still continue in the state of Jalisco.

148. "Carranza Prohibits Pulque," 3.

149. Ramírez Racaño, *Ignacio Torres Adalid y la industria pulquera.*

150. Ibid.: 46.

151. Moreno Rivas, *Historia de la música popular Mexicana.*

152. Garner, *Regional Development in Oaxaca during the Porfiriato, 1876–1911.*

153. Muría, "Momentos del tequila."

154. For a more detailed discussion of this phenomenon in relation to a range of goods and traditions, see William Beezley's *Judas at the Jockey Club and Other Episodes of Porfirian Mexico.*

155. Cockcroft, *Mexico's Hope*: 74.

156. Turner, *The Dynamic of Mexican Nationalism*: 51.

157. See Benjamin Orlove's edited collection, *The Allure of the Foreign*, for a description of these practices as they unfolded throughout the Americas.

158. Ramos, *Profile of Man and Culture in Mexico*: 40–45.

159. Cockcroft, *Mexico's Hope*: 11.

160. Villalobos Díaz, *Historia del tequila, leyenda e identidad de una nácion*.

161. "Tiene un completo surtido de vino y licores importados y del país": 4.

162. "Lea esto": 2.

163. Kanellos, "A Brief History of Hispanic Periodicals in the United States."

164. Yeager, "Porfirian Commercial Propaganda": 231.

165. Ibid.

166. Importantly, the penchant for European goods was not limited to elite groups; as Orlove and Bauer ("Giving Importance to Imports") point out, ideas about modern newness and the positive attributes associated with foreignness were also held by working class groups throughout Latin America.

167. Beatty, "Bottles for Beer."

168. Benjamin and Ocasio-Melendez, "Organizing the Memory of Modern Mexico."

169. McCaughan, "Social Movements, Globalization, and the Re-Configuration of Mexican/Chicano Nationalism."

CHAPTER 2

1. Poister, *The New American Bartender's Guide*: 422.

2. Benjamin and Ocasio-Melendez, "Organizing the Memory of Modern Mexico": 328.

3. Ibid.: 379.

4. Ibid.

5. *Indigenismo* refers to the treatment and representation of indigenous people from an elite perspective. Its origins date back to the sixteenth century when early European colonizers sought to subdue indigenous communities throughout Latin America.

6. Gamio, *Forjando Patria*: 177.

7. Brading, "Manuel Gamio and Official Indigenismo in Mexico": 83.

8. Vasconcelos, *The Cosmic Race*.

9. González, "From Indigenismo to Zapatismo": 143.

10. Schmidt, *The Roots of Lo Mexicano*: 165.

11. Parra, *Writing Pancho Villa's Revolution*: 23–24.

12. Ibid.: 23–24.

13. Azuela, *The Underdogs*: 84.

14. Ibid.: 93.

15. Orozco, "Estos altos de Jalisco!": 51.

16. Ibid.: 52.

17. Ibid.: 53.

18. Nájera-Ramírez, "Engendering Nationalism": 4.

19. Mulholland, "Mariachi in Excess": 94.

20. As cited in Mulholland, "Mariachi in Excess": 99.

21. Greathouse, 2009. *Mariachi*

22. Rosales, *Pobre Raza!*: 98–99.

23. Limón, "La Llorona, the Third Legend of Greater Mexico."

24. Berlant, *The Anatomy of National Fantasy.*

25. Nájera-Ramírez, "Engendering Nationalism": 6.

26. Ibid.: 6.

27. Sands, *Charrería Mexicana.*

28. Nájera-Ramírez, "Engendering Nationalism."

29. Palomar, *En cada charro, un hermano.*

30. Stevens, "Mexican Machismo": 850.

31. Womack, "Pancho Villa": 27.

32. Katz, *The Life and Times of Pancho Villa.*

33. Paredes, "The Ancestry of Mexico's Corridos": 83.

34. Brandt, "Pancho Villa."

35. Traditional ballad attributed to Miguel Lira (see María y Campos 1962). English translation by the author.

36. Pancho Villa is the rumored composer of the corrido "La Valentina."

37. Flores, "The Corrido and the Emergence of Texas-Mexican Social Identity."

38. Límon, "Folklore, Social Conflict, and the United States-Mexican Border": 217.

39. Mora, *Mexican Cinema*: 3.

40. Womack, "Pancho Villa."

41. Brandt, "Pancho Villa": 154.

42. Womack, "Pancho Villa": 28.

43. Usher, "The Real Mexican Problem": 33.

44. Historian Elliott Young (*Catarino Garza's Revolution on the Texas–Mexico Border*, 2004) illustrates how the U.S. press also defiled Catarino Garza, a well-known Mexican journalist and political activist, as a bandit.

45. Womack, "Pancho Villa": 27.

46. Marez, *Drug Wars*: 215.

47. "Villa a Negro, Soldier Says": 12.

48. Gutmann, *The Meanings of Macho*: 27.

49. Mirandé, "Qué gacho es ser macho": 65.

50. "Near Prohibition Ordered in Mexico."

51. Anderson, "What's to Be Done with 'Em?": 60.

52. Katz, *The Life and Times of Pancho Villa.*

53. Anderson, "What's to Be Done with 'Em?": 65.

54. "Villa a Negro, Soldier Says": 12.

55. Ibid.

56. "Blame Tequila for Execution": 12.

57. Marez, *Drug Wars*: 178.

58. Kaplan, *The Anarchy of Empire in the Making of U.S. Culture*: 28.

59. González and Fernandez, "Empire and the Origins of Twentieth-Century Migration from Mexico to the United States."

60. Kaplan, *The Anarchy of Empire in the Making of U.S. Culture*: 13.

61. Gusfield, *Symbolic Crusade*: 172.

62. Shafer, "Guadalajara": 14.

63. Harshberger, "A Botanical Excursion to Mexico": 591.

64. Pratt, *Imperial Eyes*: 4.

65. Ibid.: 4–7.

66. Hall, "Cultural Identity and Cinematic Representation": 211.

67. Kaplan, *The Anarchy of Empire in the Making of U.S. Culture*.

68. Here, I am referring to the time period before the onset of the 1910 revolution. Tequila production decreased during the revolution and the Cristero War (1926–1929).

69. Luna, *La historia del tequila, sus regiones, y sus hombres*.

70. Ibid.: 83.

71. See Zolov, *Refried Elvis*, for a more detailed examination of these processes with regard to rock and roll in Mexican society.

72. Batalla, "The Problem of National Culture": 63.

73. Joseph and Henderson, "Introduction": 2.

74. Sandos, "Pancho Villa and American Security."

75. Gaytán, "Drinking Difference."

CHAPTER 3

1. Mora, *Mexican Cinema*: 56.

2. Galindo, as quoted in Mora, *Mexican Cinema*: 56.

3. Here, I refer to work by Roger Bartra (*The Cage of Melancholy*), Sergio De La Mora (*Cinemachismo*), Rosa-Linda Fregoso (*The Bronze Screen*) Carlos Monsiváis ("Notas sobre cultura popular en México"), Carl Mora (*Mexican Cinema*), and Zuzana Pick (*Constructing the Image of the Mexican Revolution*).

4. Mora, *Mexican Cinema*: 3.

5. Muriá, *Una bebida llamada tequila*.

6. Mitchell, *Intoxicated Identities*.

7. Muriá, *Una bebida llamada tequila*.

8. Luna, *La historia del tequila*.

9. Monsiváis, "Tequila with Lime and Other Table Talk": 15.

10. Mraz, *Looking for Mexico*.

11. Nájera-Ramírez, "Engendering Nationalism."

12. As I discussed in Chapter 2, throughout Mexico, Jalisco is widely (if mistakenly) considered a state that has more European racial influences than indigenous ones. In other words, Jaliscans, more than people from any other state in Mexico, are believed to possess purer European bloodlines.

13. Gutmann, *The Meaning of Macho*: 176.

14. Zavala, *Becoming Modern, Becoming Tradition*: 231.

15. Monsiváis, Mexican Postcards: 55.

16. Stavans, *The Riddle of Cantinflas*: 29.

17. Ibid.: 34.

18. Monsiváis, *Mexican Postcards*.

19. While this is the popular explanation of the epitaph *"china poblana,"* the history of the term and its original meaning has been debated among scholars (see Gillespie's discussion of Catarina de San Juan in "Gender, Ethnicity, Piety").

20. For a detailed discussion of the evolution of meanings regarding the *china poblana* costume, see Deborah Vargas's *Dissonant Divas in Chicana Music*.

21. Bailey, "A Mughal Princess in Baroque New Spain": 38.

22. Zavala, *Becoming Modern, Becoming Tradition*: 24.

23. Vázquez Mantecón, "La china Mexicana mejor, conocida como china poblana."

24. Monsiváis, "Calendars: Cultural Snapshots and Visual Tradition": 6.

25. Mraz, 19.

26. Mora, *Mexican Cinema*: 57.

27. Muñoz, *Sara García*.

28. Ramírez-Berg, *Cinema of Solitude*: 59.

29. Bracho, "Cine mexicano": 421.

30. Carrillo, *The Night is Young*.

31. Halberstam, *Female Masculinity*: 9.

32. De la Mora, *Cinemachismo*: 71.

33. For more information, see Mitchell and Schell, *The Women's Revolution in Mexico, 1910–1953*; Poniatowska, *Las Soldaderas*; Reséndez, "Battleground Women"; and Salas's Soldaderas *in the Mexican Military*.

34. Monsiváis, "When Gender Can't Be Seen amid the Symbolic." Historians were not the only people to downplay or overlook the role of *soldaderas*—government officials also disregarded their participation. According to Garcia-Orozco (*"Cucurrucucu Palomas"*), women did not receive military pensions or medical benefits like their male counterparts.

35. Olcott, Vaughan, and Cano, *Sex in Revolution*.

36. Camp, "Women and Political Leadership and Mexico."

37. Women's suffrage, however, was not widely supported by male politicians of the time period. For instance, presidential candidate Adolfo López Mateos cautiously commented:

> The right to vote does not uproot women from family and home and lure them into politics. Rather, women's suffrage brings into the home a deeper understanding of greater national issues, a daily inquiry on matters that are of concern to us all. This will prove once again that neither contentious preaching nor deceptive enticement can change women's most intimate sentiments or wean them away from their home and family.

Blough, "Political Attitudes of Mexican Women": 203–204.

38. Garcia-Orozco, "Cucurrucucu Palomas."

39. Vaughan, "Pancho Villa, the Daughters of Mary and the Modern Woman."

40. Hayes, *Radio Nation*.

41. Gradante, *"El Hijo del Pueblo."*

42. Ibid.

43. Broyles-Gónzalez, *"Ranchera* Music(s) and the Legendary Lydia Mendoza."

44. Nájera-Ramírez, "Unruly Passions: Poetics, Performance, and Gender in the Ranchera Song": 460.

45. "Lucha Reyes ha muerto." *Cinema Reporter*, July 1, 1944: 1.

46. Gradante, *"El Hijo del Pueblo."*

47. Medina Ruiz, "Lucha Reyes, la inolvidable." In this 1954 newspaper article, the author writes that Reyes was twelve when the family moved to Mexico City.

48. Gradante, *"El Hijo del Pueblo"*: 1.

49. Inclán, "Se suicida çon veneno."

50. Garcia-Orozco, "Cucurrucucu Palomas."

51. Yvonne Yarbro-Bejarano ("Crossing the Border with Chabela Vargas") and Guadalupe Loaeza (*Ellas y Nosotras*) likewise write that Reyes was rumored to be a lesbian who did not publicly identify her sexuality.

52. In her 2012 novel about Lucha Reyes, *Me Llaman la Tequilera*, Alma Velasco writes that Reyes lost her child after drunkenly falling down the stairs of her apartment.

53. Medina Ruiz, "Lucha Reyes, la inolvidable."

54. Garcia-Orozco, "Cucurrucucu Palomas."

55. Gradante, *"El Hijo del Pueblo."*

56. It is important to note that, although it was considered taboo for women to perform with mariachi ensembles in the 1930s and 1940s, women mariachis today continue to face gendered challenges as mariachi traditionalists "often contest[ ] the new female presence" (Pérez, "Transgressing the Taboo": 151). Further, these women must also contend with issues within their families. For example, Pérez writes that when she joined a mariachi group in the 1970s, her mother "was concerned that my involvement with this group, my turning into a *callejera*, would lead me to compromise my status as a 'good Christian girl'" (151–152).

57. According to Arrizón her article, "Latina Subjectivity, Sexuality, and Sensuality," *estilo bravío* is a style of singing by women performers that is denoted by their purposeful switching of gendered pronouns, the changing of song lyrics, the creation of alternative meanings of songs, or inverting the song's object of desire. Importantly, it calls attention to women singers' transgression of dominant masculine musical forms, especially the *canción ranchera*.

58. Garcia-Orozco, "Cucurrucucu Palomas."

59. "El homenaje de artistas Jaliscienses a Guadalajara."

60. Vargas, *Dissonant Divas in Chicana Music.*

61. "En el teatro nacional": 3.

62. Gradante describes her appearances in films as "*intervenciones musicales,* or brief appearances, generally as a soldadera or cantina singer"; "*El Hijo del Pueblo*": 2.

63. Moreno Rivas, *Historia de la música popular mexicana*: 190.

64. Vargas, *Dissonant Divas in Chicana Music.*

65. Vargas, ibid.: 106.

66. According to Garcia-Orozco, some fans insist that it was Lucha Reyes who wrote "*La Tequilera.*" As the story goes, while in drunken stupor, Reyes sold the rights to the song to Alfredo D'Orsay. In her words, "It was common in Mexico, as in other countries, for transcribers to claim authorship that was not theirs, it is distinctly possible that Reyes did write songs but never held the copyright to those songs," "*Cucurucucu Palomas*": 138.

67. Ibid.

68. Ibid.

69. Nájera-Ramírez, "Unruly Passions": 462.

70. "Lucha Reyes murió ayer."

71. De Lauretis, *Technologies of Gender*: 26.

72. Hershfield, *Imagining la Chica Moderna.*

CHAPTER 4

1. Mundo Cuervo, "Mundo Cuervo."

2. Ibid.

3. MacCannell, *The Tourist*: 112.

4. Tequila Jalisco, "Hotel boutique la Cofradia."

5. Kropp, *California Vieja*: 6.

6. Chávez, "Globalizing Tequila."

7. "El Indio.".

8. Mundo Cuervo, "What Is Mundo Cuervo?"

9. Mulholland, "Mariachi in Excess"; Peregrina, "La adopción de las estampas Jaliscienses."

10. Cárdenas Díaz, "A Train Called 'Tequila Express'": 4.

11. Ebron, *Performing Africa*: 5.

12. Ibid.: 1.

13. Sturken, *Tourists of History.*

14. MacCannell, *The Tourist.*

15. Personal communication with María de Jesus Arámbula Limón of the *Archivo histórico de Tequila* (Historic Archive of Tequila).

16. Palomares-Medina, *Historia del municipio de Tequila.*

17. Ibid.

18. Van Young, *The Other Rebellion*: 6.

19. Knight, "Mexican Peonage."

20. I viewed several documents at the archive in Tequila that mentioned the presence of African slaves in and around Tequila.

21. Wells, "Reports of Its Demise Are Not Exaggerated": 313.

22. Cutler, *The Tequila's Lover's Guide*: 7.

23. De Orellana, "Microhistoria del tequila": 135.

24. Pratt, *Imperial Eyes*.

25. Connell, "The Big Picture": 612.

26. Herradura Tequila.

27. Mendelzon, "Reinventing the Gaucho": 7.

28. Ibid.: 75.

29. McWilliams, *Southern California Country*.

30. Kropp, *California Vieja*: 3.

31. MacCannell, *The Tourist*: 76–77.

32. Geller, *Tequila, Lo nuestro*. Although earlier references may exist, I have thus far been unable to find any.

33. El Jimador.

34. Delaney, "Making Sense of Modernity," 437.

35. Ibid.: 457.

36. See also Daniel Chávez ("Globalizing Tequila") for a discussion of two other tequila-themed *telenovelas* of the 1990s, *La Mentira* and *Azul Tequila*.

37. Goffman, *The Presentation of Self in Everyday Life*.

38. The character Gaviota was played by Angélica Rivera, who is the wife of Mexican President Enrique Peña Nieto and current first lady of Mexico.

39. Bowen and Gaytán, "The Paradox of Protection."

40. Chávez, "Globalizing Tequila."

41. Bowen and Gaytán, "The Paradox of Protection."

42. Ibid.

43. Chávez describes a similar process in relation to images circulated in the telenovela, *Azul Tequila*. In his words,

> The mobilization for national unity and political legitimacy could not come from the familiar image of the suit-wearing talking heads from newscasts, nor could it come from the sunglass-wearing associated with the traditional politician. It was only in the residual images of the *campesino* culture . . . where any positive reaffirmation of nationalism could be placed. (10–11)

44. Chávez, "Globalizing Tequila": 7.

45. Valenzuela-Zapata and Gaytán, "La expansión tequilera."

46. José Hernández-López (*La jornalerización en el paisaje agavero* and *Paisaje y creación de valor*) reports that many workers are also being recruited from Oaxaca, Michoacán, and Tabasco. Like those from Chiapas, they are paid low wages, earning between US$11 and US$20 a day. Workers from Chiapas are often disparagingly referred to as *chiapanecos,* a term that is becoming synonymous with being backward or wild (Hernández-López, *La jornalerización en el paisaje agavero*: 198).

47. Fitzgerald, *A Nation of Emigrants*: 149–150.

48. Ibid.: 150.

49. CONAPO, *Índices de marginación*.

50. Dinerstein, "The Speed of the Snail."

51. Gaytán and Valenzuela, "Más allá del mito."

52. Radding, *Landscapes of Power and Identity*.

53. Ojeda Díaz, "Las diosas del Códice Borgia": 132.

54. Gaytán and Valenzuela, "Más allá del mito."

55. James, "Tequila."

56. Bruman, *Alcohol in Ancient Mexico*.

57. Wolf, "The Virgin of Guadalupe": 37. The significance and symbolism of the Virgin would remain powerful throughout Mexico, especially during times of war and periods of social struggle. For instance, a banner featuring the Virgin of Guadalupe led an army of soldiers as they marched in the Revolution of 1810. In 1914, supporters of Emiliano Zapata carried signs with her image through the streets of Mexico City after the defeat of General Victoriano Huerta. The first president of the republic, Manuel Felix Fernández, changed his name to Guadalupe Victoria—Guadalupe, for the Virgin, and Victoria, for victory. During the initial years of colonization, the Virgin of Guadalupe symbolically, although not entirely, brought together creoles, mestizos, and Indians under a single faith and a united *patria*.

58. Peterson, "The Virgin of Guadalupe."

59. Paz, "Forward."

60. Ibid.: xix.

61. Benítez, "El señor maguey": 84.

62. Wolf, "The Virgin of Guadalupe": 36.

63. Taylor, "The Virgin of Guadalupe in New Spain": 19.

64. Bushnell, "La Virgen de Guadalupe as Surrogate Mother."

65. Ibid.

66. Alonso, "The Politics of Space, Time, and Substance"; Castañeda de la Paz, "Central Mexican Indigenous Coats of Arms"; Florescano, *Memory, Myth, and Time in Mexico*.

67. Bueno, *Forjando Patrimonio*: 54.

68. Ibid.: 55.

69. Carrillo Trueba, "Los destilados de agave."

70. Kropp, *California Vieja*: 6.

71. Mahoney, "Marketer Betting That for Women, Tequila Is the New Vodka."

72. Ebron, *Performing Africa*: 192.

73. Lomnitz, *Deep Mexico*: 133.

74. MacCannell, *The Tourist*: 40.

75. Williams, *Marxism and Literature*.

CHAPTER 5

1. Academia del Tequila.

2. Ibid.

3. *Distintivo T*.

4. Ibid.

5. Canclini, *Consumers and Citizens.*

6. Berlant, *The Anatomy of National Fantasy*: 28.

7. Berlant, *The Queen of America Goes to Washington City*: 10.

8. Lomnitz, *Deep Mexico, Silent Mexico*: 117.

9. "Tequila: A Gift from Ancestral Gods."

10. SECTUR, "Programa Pueblos Magicos."

11. Ibid.

12. Ibid.

13. Hernández-López, "Tequila": 49.

14. The Battle of Mojonero was an uprising between the Mexican army, led by General Ramón Corona, against a rebel army led by Manuel Lozada. Depending on the source, Lozada, a Cora Indian and Maximilian loyalist, was either a bandit or a liberator. Those residents of Tequila who perished in the skirmish helped defeat Lozada.

15. González Torreros, "Modelo turístico sustentable para el municipio de Tequila, Jalisco, México."

16. Ibid.: 228.

17. UNESCO, "World Heritage List."

18. In addition to the thousands of acres of agave landscape, several ancient tequila distilleries, the Tequila volcano, and the pre-Columbian *guachimontones* (circular pyramids) archeological site are also protected under the declaration.

19. Ibid. Only countries that agree to sign the World Heritage convention, a contract in which nations pledge to protect their natural and cultural heritage, may apply for inclusion on the list. After nominating a local site, state representatives organize a committee to prepare an application—a rigorous process that takes years to organize. The final decisions are made by members of the Intergovernmental World Heritage Committee. As part of the process, World Heritage representatives travel and evaluate sites whose applications have advanced to the final round.

20. Velasco and Preciado, "Es patrimonio, paisaje agavero.".

21. In addition to the Tequila landscape, seven other winners included: Sichuan Giant Panda Sanctuaries (China), Malpelo Fauna and Flora Sanctuary (Colombia), Harar Jugol (Ethiopia), Stone Circles of Senegambia (Gambia and Senegal), Chongoni Rock Art Area (Malawi), Aapravasi Ghat (Mauritius), and Kondoa Rock Art Sites (United Republic of Tanzania).

22. Ibid.

23. "Nombra UNESCO a Tequila, Jalisco, patrimonio mundial."

24. Ruta del Tequila.

25. Founded in 1999, the *Academia* is a private organization comprised of individuals, many of whom own their own brands or operate their own distilleries. Each member is also formally trained as a *catador*, or taster, who, as part of the organization, participates in the blind ranking of tequilas based on a range of criteria that include taste, touch, smell, and appearance. The group describes itself as a "totally autonomous entity that focuses its efforts not only for the purpose of maintaining and

protecting the real image of this drink, but the purpose of disseminating its culture through activities and promotion" (Academia Mexicana del Tequila, "Breve historia").

26. All of the interviews collected and referenced throughout the book took place between 2006 and 2008. Unless referred to by their first and last names, all interviewee names are pseudonyms.

27. Baer, "Import Substitution and Industrialization in Latin America": 106.

28. Ibid.: 117.

29. Ibid.:121.

30. Ibid.: 121.

31. Author interview.

32. Author interview.

33. Author interview.

34. Hernández-López, "Tequila": 47.

35. Author interview.

36. Ibid.: 58.

37. Ibid.

38. From 1974 until 1978, tequila's DO was recognized only in Mexico.

39. As cited in Barham, 2003,127.

40. One important exception here is the United States. Although not legally recognized by the U.S. government, products including Vidalia onions (from Georgia) and bourbon (from Kentucky) have registered trademarks that function similarly to GIs (Bowen, *Geographical Indications*).

41. Escudero, "International Protection of Geographical Indications and Developing Countries, Trade-Related Agenda, and Development Equality": 10.

42. Bowen, *Geographical Indications*.

43. Author interview.

44. Author interview.

45. Vandergeest and DuPuis, "Introduction."

46. Hinrich, "Consuming Images": 268.

47. Ibid.: 273.

48. TRC, "The TRC."

49. Ibid.

50. Hernández, "Swearing-in Ceremony": 7.

51. Cámara Nacional de la Industria Tequilera (CNIT), "Who Are We?"

52. Ibid.

53. Consejo Regulador del Tequila (CRT), "Miguel Ángel Domínquez, nuevo presidente del Consejo Regulador del Tequila A.C."

54. Ibid.

55. Ibid.

56. Consejo Regulador del Tequila (CRT), "TRCard."

57. Consejo Regulador del Tequila (CRT), "El CRT-creando alianzas."

58. Consejo Regulador del Tequila (CRT), "TRCard."

59. García, "La investigación aduanera": 8.

60. Ibid.

61. Ibid.

62. MacCannell, 1999 .

63. Negotiated as part of the 1986–1994 Uruguay Round, the Agreement on Trade-Related Aspects of Intellectual Property Rights (TRIPS), tequila became protected under the provisions of geographical indication legislation. According to the WTO, the TRIPS agreement "is an attempt to narrow the gaps in the way these rights are protected around the world, and to bring them into common international rules" (WTO, "Intellectual Property").

64. Calbreath, "Mexico Is China's Final WTO Membership."

65. Ibid.

66. James, "Tequila."

67. Up until 2007, Mexico was the second-largest U.S. trade partner, following Canada. Replacing Mexico, China now holds that position, leaving Mexico in third place (Harvey, *A Brief History of Neoliberalism*).

68. "How Did Ancient Chinese Distill Spirits?"

69. Leonard, "Globalization and the Blue Agave."

70. *Distintivo T*, "Bienvenido al *Distintivo T*."

71. Ibid.

72. Freeman, "Tequilacertification."

73. "Tequila Regulatory Council 2007."

74. Ibid.

75. Berlant, *The Queen of America Goes to Washington City*: 31.

76. Ibid.: 30.

77. Lomnitz, *Deep Mexico, Silent Mexico*: 118.

78. Harvey, *A Brief History of Neoliberalism*: 85.

79. Ibid.

CHAPTER 6

1. Leon, "Talking Tequila with the Industry's Head Honcho Francisco Gonzalez."

2. Ibid.

3. Ibid.

4. Lipsitz, "The Grounded Transnationalism of Robert Alvarez."

5. Abarca, *Voices in the Kitchen*; Pérez, *The Decolonial Imaginary*.

6. Canclini, "North Americans or Latin Americans?": 147–148 (emphasis in the original).

7. Author interview.

8. Tequila served with grapefruit soda or Squirt soda is also known as a *paloma*.

9. Author interview.

10. Zussman, "Autobiographical Occasions."

11. Brandes, *Staying Sober in Mexico City*: 100

12. Pérez-López et al., "La mujer en los grupos de alchólicos anónimos."

13. Rodríguez, *Women in Contemporary Mexican Politics*.

14. Casique, "Mexican Married Women's Autonomy and Power within the Household": 2.

15. Craske, "Ambiguities and Ambivalences in Making the Nation": 79.

16. Author interview.

17. Bourdieu, "Cultural Reproduction and Social Reproduction."

18. Cantú, "De Ambiente."

19. Alfaro-Velcamp, "Immigrant Positioning in Twentieth-Century Mexico: Middle Easterners, Foreign Citizens, and Multiculturalism."

20. Jerolmack, "Animal Practices, Ethnicity, and Community."

21. Author interview.

22. Author interview.

23. Author interview.

24. Author interview.

25. Author interview.

26. Author interview.

27. Author interview.

28. Author interview.

29. Patrón is owned by John Paul Dejoria, cofounder of the hair products company, John Paul Mitchell Systems. Cabo Wabo was founded by Sammy Hagar, the former lead singer of the rock band Van Halen. In 2007, Hagar sold an 80 percent interest in Cabo Wabo to Gruppo Campari for US$80 million.

30. Author interview.

31. Author interview.

32. "Girls Gone Wild" is the name of a popular video series in which a camera crew, usually filming in a spring-break destination, offers women gifts such as tank tops and shorts in exchange for nude shots. In early 2008, company owner Joe Francis announced the release of "Girls Gone Wild" tequila.

33. Author interview.

34. Author interview.

35. This is a reference to Joe Nichols's hit song (2006), "Tequila Makes Her Clothes Fall Off."

36. Author interview.

37. Author interview.

38. Lipsitz, *Time Passages*: 154.

39. Author interview.

40. Burton Carvajal, "Surprise Package": 141

41. Author interview.

42. Author interview.

43. *Sangrita* is a tequila "chaser" usually made of tomato, chile, orange, and lime juices. Not to be confused with *sangria*, *sangrita* (or little blood) is served as an accompaniment to tequila and is meant to be sipped.

44. Author interview.

45. Author interview.

46. Jerolmack, "Animal Practices, Ethnicity, and Community": 890.

47. Cavanaugh, "Making Salami, Producing Bergamo": 149.

48. Caldwell, "The Taste of Nationalism": 295.

49. Jerolmack, "Animal Practices, Ethnicity, and Community": 890.

50. Ibid.: 892

51. Canclini, *Consumers and Citizens*.

52. Rodríguez, *Women in Contemporary Mexican Politics*: 48.

53. Craske, "Ambiguities and Ambivalences in Making the Nation": 117.

54. Jerolmack, "Animal Practices, Ethnicity, and Community": 892.

55. Canclini, "North Americans or Latin Americans?"

56. Abarca, *Voices in the Kitchen*: 5

57. Williams, *Marxism and Literature*.

58. Durkheim, *The Division of Labor in Society*.

CODA

1. Tucker, "Poverty and Wealth Inequality on the Rise in Mexico."

2. Appadurai, *The Social Life of Things*.

3. Anderson, *Imagined Communities*.

4. Molotch, *Where Stuff Comes From*: 11.

5. Canclini, *Consumers and Citizens*: 43.

6. Monsiváis, "Mythologies."

7. Ibid.: 118.

8. Joseph, Rubenstein, and Zolov, "Assembling the Fragments": 10.

9. Negrón-Muntaner, "Barbie's Hair."

10. Valenzuela-Zapata and Gaytán, "Sustaining Biological and Cultural Diversity."

REFERENCES

Abarca, Meredith. 2006. *Voices in the Kitchen: Views of Food and the World from Working-Class Mexican and Mexican-American Women*. College Station: Texas A&M University Press.

Academia del Tequila. 2014. "The Mexican Academy of Tequila Tasters, A.C." Retrieved on January 2, 2014, from www.academiadeltequila.com.mx/English/the-amct.html.

Academia Mexicana del Tequila. 2010. "Breve historia." Retrieved on August 20, 2010, from www.acamextequila.com.mx/amt3/introduccion.html.

Aizpuru, Pilar. 2008. "El nacimiento del miedo, 1692: Indios y españoles en la ciudad de México," *Revista de Indias* 68, no. 244: 25–27.

Alberro, Solange. 1989. "Bebidas alchólicas y sociedad colonial en México: un intento a interpretación." *Revista Mexicana de Sociología* 51, no. 2: 349–359.

Alfaro, Alfonso. 1995. "Tequila and Its Signs: In Praise of the Country Gentleman," in *El tequila: Arte tradicional de México*, Alberto Ruy Sánchez Lacy, ed, 83–85. D.F.: Artes de Mexico.

Alfaro-Velcamp, Theresa. 2006. "Immigrant Positioning in Twentieth-Century Mexico: Middle Easterners, Foreign Citizens, and Multiculturalism." *Hispanic American Historical Review* 86, no. 1: 61–91.

Alonso, Ana Maria. 1994. "The Politics of Space, Time, and Substance: State Formation, Nationalism, and Ethnicity." *Annual Review of Anthropology* 23: 379–405.

Anderson, Benedict. 1983. *Imagined Communities Reflections on the Origin and Spread of Nationalism*. London and New York: Verso.

Anderson, Mark. 1998. "What's to Be Done with 'Em? Images of Mexican Cultural Backwardness, Racial Limitations, and Moral Decrepitude in the United States Press, 1913–1915." *Mexican Studies/Estudios Mexicanos* 4, no. 1: 23–70.

Anderson, Rodney. 1988. "Race and Social Stratification: A Comparison of Working-Class Spaniards, Indians, and Castas in Guadalajara, Mexico in 1821." *Hispanic American Historic Review* 68, no. 2: 209–243.

Appadurai, Arjun. 1986. *The Social Life of Things: Commodities in Cultural Perspective.* Cambridge, UK: Cambridge University Press.

Arriola, Ignacio. 2005. *The Agave Landscape and the Ancient Industrial Facilities of Tequila.* Jalisco, México: Secretaría de Cultura.

Arrizón, Alicia. 2009. "Latina Subjectivity, Sexuality, and Sensuality." *Women and Performance: A Journal of Feminist Theory* 18, no. 3: 189–198.

Azuela, Mariano. (1919) 1963. *The Underdogs.* New York: Penguin Books.

Baer, Werner. 1972. "Import Substitution and Industrialization in Latin America: Experiences and Interpretations." *Latin American Research Review* no. 7: 95–122.

Bailey, Gauvin A. 1997. "A Mughal Princess in Baroque New Spain: Catarina de San Juan (1606–1688), the *China Poblana.*" *Anales del Instituto de Investigaciones Estéticas de la Universidad Nacional Autónoma de México*, no. 71: 38–39.

Barham, Elizabeth. 2003. "Translating Terroir: The Global Challenge of Translating French AOC Labeling." *Journal of Rural Studies* no. 19: 127–138.

Bartra, Roger. 1992. *The Cage of Melancholy: Identity and Metamorphosis in the Mexican Character.* New Brunswick, NJ: Rutgers University Press.

Batalla, Guillermo Bonfil. 2002. "The Problem of National Culture," in *The Mexico Reader: History, Culture, Politics*, Gilbert Joseph and Timothy Henderson, eds., 28–32. Durham, NC: Duke University Press.

Bauman, Shyon. 2007. *Hollywood Highbrow: From Entertainment to Art.* Princeton, NJ: Princeton University Press.

Beatty, Edward. 2009. Bottles for Beer: The Business of Technological Innovation in Mexico, 1890–1920. *Business History Review* 82, no. 2: 317–348.

Beezley, William. 2004. *Judas at the Jockey Club and Other Episodes of Porfirian Mexico.* Lincoln: University of Nebraska.

Bellingeri, Marco. 1980. *Las haciendas en México: El caso de San Antonio Tochatlaco.* México: INAH.

Benítez, Fernando. "El Señor Maguey," in *Maguey*, Margarita de Orellana, ed., 11. México: Artes de Mexico.

Benjamin, Thomas, and Marcial Ocasio-Melendez. 1984. "Organizing the Memory of Modern Mexico: Porfirian Historiography in Perspective, 1880s–1980s." *The Hispanic American Historical Review* 64, no. 2: 323–364.

Berlant, Lauren. 1991. *The Anatomy of National Fantasy: Hawthorne, Utopia, and Everyday Life.* Chicago: University of Chicago Press.

———. 1997. *The Queen of America Goes to Washington City.* Durham, NC: Duke University Press.

"Blame Tequila for Execution." *Los Angeles Times*, February 24, 1914: 1.

Blocker, Jack, David Fahey, and Ian Tyrell, eds. 2007. *Alcohol and Temperance in Modern History: An International Encyclopedia.* Santa Barbara, CA: ABC-CLIO.

Blough, William J. 1972. "Political Attitudes of Mexican Women: Support for the Political System among a Newly Enfranchised Group." *Journal of Interamerican Studies and World Affairs* 14, no. 2: 201–224.

Bourdieu, Pierre. 1973. "Cultural Reproduction and Social Reproduction." In *Knowledge, Education, and Social Change: Papers in the Sociology of Education*, Richard Brown, ed., 71–112. London: Tavistock.

———. 1984. *Distinction: A Social Critique of the Judgment of Taste.* Cambridge, MA: Harvard University Press.

Bowen, Sarah. 2008. *Geographical Indications: Promoting Local Products in a Global Market.* Doctoral Thesis, University of Wisconsin, Madison.

Bowen, Sarah, and Marie S. Gaytán 2012. "The Paradox of Protection: National Identity, Global Commodity Chains, and the Tequila Industry." *Social Problems* 59, no. 1: 70–93.

Bourke, John G. 1894. "Disillation by Early American Indians." *American Anthropologist*, no. 7: 297–299.

Bracho, Diana. 1985. "Cine mexicano: y en el papel de la mujer . . . quien?" *Mexican Studies/Estudios Mexicanos* 1, no. 2: 413–423.

Brading, David, A. 1988. "Manuel Gamio and Official *Indigenismo* in Mexico." *Bulletin of Latin American Research* 7, no. 1: 75–89.

Brandes, Stanley. 2002. *Staying Sober in Mexico City.* Berkeley: University of California Press.

Brandt, Nancy. 1964. "Pancho Villa: The Making of a Modern Legend." *The Americas* 21, no. 2: 146–162.

Broyles-González, Yolanda. 2002. "*Ranchera* Music(s) and the Legendary Lydia Mendoza: Performing Social Location and Relations," in *Chicana Traditions: Continuity and Change*, Norma Cantú and Olga Nájera-Ramírez (eds), 183–206. Urbana and Chicago: University of Illinois Press.

Bruman, Henry, J. 2000. *Alcohol in Ancient Mexico.* Salt Lake City: University of Utah Press.

Bueno, Christina. 2010. "*Forjando Patrimonio:* The Making of Archaeological Patrimony in Porfirian Mexico." *Hispanic American Historical Review*, 90, no. 2: 215–245.

Burton Carvajal, J. 1994. "Surprise Package: Looking Southward with Disney," in *Disney Discourse: Producing the Magic Kingdom*, E. Smoodin, ed., 131–147. London: Routledge.

Bushnell, John. 1958. "La Virgen de Guadalupe as Surrogate Mother in San Juan Atzingo." *American Anthropologist* 60, no. 2: 261–265.

Calbreath, Dean. 2004. "Mexico Is China's Final WTO Membership." Retrieved on July 26, 2007, from www.freerepublic.com/forum/a3a2fb6732bf1.htm.

Caldwell, Melissa. 2002. "The Taste of Nationalism: Food Politics in Postsocialist Moscow." *Ethnos* 67, no. 3: 295–319.

Canclini, Néstor, García. 1996. "North Americans or Latin Americans? The Redefinition of Mexican Identity and the Free Trade Agreements" in *Mass Media and Free Trade NAFTA and the Cultural Industries*, Emile G. McAnany and Kenton Todd Wilkinson, eds., 142–156. Austin: University of Texas Press.

———. 2001. *Consumers and Citizens: Globalization and Multicultural Conflicts*. Minneapolis: University of Minnesota Press.

Cámara Nacional de la Industria Tequilera (CNIT). "Who Are We?" Retrieved on August 20, 2012, from www.tequileros.org/main_en.php.

Camp, Roderic. 1979. "Women and Political Leadership and Mexico: A Comparative Study of Female and Male Elites." *Journal of Politics* 41, no. 2: 417–441.

Cantú, L. 2002. "De Ambiente: Queer Toursim and the Shifting Boundaries of Mexican Male Sexualities." *GLQ: A Journal of Lesbian and Gay Studies* 8, no. 1–2: 139–166.

Cárdenas Díaz, José. 2005. "A Train Called . . . 'Tequila Express, The Legend.'" *Tequila Express: Official On Board Guide*. Guadalajara: Camera de Comercio: 4–7.

"Carranza Prohibits Pulque." *New York Times*, January 17, 1916, 3.

Carrera, Magali. 2003. *Imagining Identity in New Spain: Race, Lineage, and the Colonial Body in Portraiture and Casta Paintings*. Austin: University of Texas Press.

Carrillo, Hector. 2002. *The Night Is Young: Sexuality in Mexico in the Time of AIDS*. Chicago: University of Chicago Press.

Carrillo Trueba, Lauro Antonio. 2009. "Los destilados de agave en México y su denominación de origen." *Ciencias*, Julio–Septiembre: 41–49

Casique, I. 2000. "Mexican Married Women's Autonomy and Power within the Household." Unpublished paper presented at the XXII Latin American Studies Association Meeting, Miami, Florida.

Castañeda de la Paz, María. 2009. "Central Mexican Indigenous Coats of Arms and the Conquest of Mesoamerica." *Ethnohistory*, 56, no. 1: 125–161.

Cavanaugh, Jillian. 2007. "Making Salami, Producing Bergamo: The Transformation of Value." *Ethnos* 72, no. 1: 149–172.

Chase, John, and William Taylor. 1978. "Estate and Class in a Colonial City: Oaxaca in 1792." *Comparative Studies in Society and History*, 19: 454–487.

Chávez, Daniel. 2006. "Globalizing Tequila: Mexican Television's Representations of the Neoliberal Reconversion of Land and Labor." *Arizona Journal of Hispanic Cultural Studies* 10: 1–17.

Christensen, Mark. 2013. *Nahua and Maya Catholicisms: Texts and Religion in Colonial Central Mexico and Yucatan*. Stanford, CA: Stanford University Press.

Cockcroft, James, D. 1998. *Mexico's Hope: An Encounter with Politics and History*. New York: Monthly Review Press.

CONAPO. 2005. *Índices de marginación*. México: Consejo Nacional de Población.

Connell, R. W. 1993. "The Big Picture: Masculinities in Recent World History." *Theory and Society* 22, no. 5: 597–623.

Conroy, David. 1995. *In Public Houses: Drink and the Revolution of Authority in Colonial Massachusetts*. Chapel Hill: University of North Carolina Press.

Consejo Regulador del Tequila (CRT). 2001. "TRCard." *Gaceta* 1: 20–21.

———. 2004. "El CRT-creando alianzas: Pro defensa del tequila." *Gaceta* 4: 16–21.

———. 2005. "Miguel Ángel Domínquez, nuevo presidente del Consejo Regulador del Tequila A.C." *Gaceta* 5: 21.

Consejor Regulador del Tequila (CRT). 2013. "Exportaciones por categoría tequila y tequila 100% agave," Retrieved on September 28, 2013, from crt.org.mx/estatisticas CRTweb/.

Cope, Douglas, R. 1994. *The Limits of Racial Domination: Plebian Society in Colonial Mexico City, 1660–1720*. Madison: University of Wisconsin Press.

Craske, Nikki. 2005. "Ambiguities and Ambivalences in Making the Nation: Women and Politics in 20th-Century Mexico." *Feminist Review* 79: 116–133.

Cutler, Lance. 1998. *The Tequila Lover's Guide to Mexico and Mezcal*. Vineburg, CA: Wine Patrol Press.

De La Mora, Sergio. 2006. *Cinemachismo: Masculinities and Sexuality in Mexican Film*. Austin: University of Texas Press.

De Lauretis, Teresa. 1987. *Technologies of Gender: Essays on Theory, Film, and Fiction*. Bloomington: University of Indiana Press.

Delaney, Jeane. 1996. "Making Sense of Modernity: Changing Attitudes toward the Immigrant and the Gaucho in Turn-of-the-Century Argentina." *Comparative Studies in Society and History* 38, no. 3: 434–459.

De Orellana, Margarita. 1995. "Microhistoria del tequila: el caso Cuervo." In *El tequila: Arte tradicional de México*, Alberto Ruy Sánchez, ed., 28–36. Mexico D. F.: Artes de Mexico.

Dinerstein, Ana. 2013. "The Speed of the Snail: The Zapatistas' Autonomy *de facto* and the Mexican State." Bath, UK: Working paper number 20, *Bath Papers in International Development and Wellbeing*.

Distintivo T. 2012. "Bienvenido al *Distintivo T*." Retrieved on January 2, 2012, from www.distintivot.org.mx/.

Dotson, Floyd, and Lilian Ota Dotson. 1954. "Ecological Trends in the City of Guadalajara, Mexico." *Social Forces* 32, no. 4: 367–374.

Douglas, Mary, and Barron Isherwood. 1981. *The World of Goods*. New York: Basic Books.

Dufétel, Dominique. 2000. "El Maguey, el conejo y la luna." In *Maguey*, Margarita de Orellana, ed., 18–27. Mexico City: Artes de Mexico.

Duncan, Robert. 1998. "Embracing a Suitable Past: Independence Celebrations under Mexico's Second Empire, 1864–6." *Journal of Latin American Studies* 30, no. 2: 249–277.

Durkheim, Emile. (1893); 1997. *The Division of Labor in Society.* New York: The Free Press.

Earle, Rebecca. (2010) "'If You Eat Their Food . . .': Diets and Bodies in Early Colonial Spanish America. *American Historical Review* 115, no. 3: 688–713.

Ebron, Paulla. 2002. *Performing Africa.* Princeton, NJ, and Oxford, UK: Princeton University Press.

"El Indio." 2007. Flyer advertisement.

"En el teatro nacional." *Prensa*, October 9, 1938: 3.

Escudero, Sergio. 2001. "International Protection of Geographical Indications and Developing Countries, Trade-Related Agenda, and Development Equality." *Working Papers 10, South Centre*, July, 2001.

Evans, Susan. 1990. "The Productivity of Maguey Terrace Agriculture in Central Mexico during the Aztec Period." *Latin American Antiquity* no. 5: 113–132.

Fischer, Edward, and Peter Benson. 2006. *Broccoli and Desire: Global Connections and Maya Struggles in Postwar Guatemala.* Stanford, CA: Stanford University Press.

Fitzgerald, David. 2008. *A Nation of Emigrants: How Mexico Manages its Migration.* Berkeley: University of California Press.

Flores, Richard. 1992. "The *Corrido* and the Emergence of Texas–Mexican Social Identity." *The Journal of American Folklore* 105, no. 415: 166–182.

Florescano, Enrique. 1994. *Memory, Myth, and Time in Mexico: From the Aztecs to Independence.* Austin: University of Texas Press.

Freeman, Heather. 2008. "Tequilacertification." Retrieved on March 7, 2008, from www.heatherfreeman.com/webpage/oyamel/Tequilacertification.doc.

Fregoso, Rosa-Linda. 1993. *The Bronze Screen: Chicana and Chicano Film Culture.* Minneapolis: University of Minnesota Press.

Fumas, J. C. 1965. *The Life and Times of the Late Demon Rum.* New York: G. P. Putnam's Sons.

Galindo, Alejandro. 1975. *¿Qué es el cine?* México DF: Editorial Nuestro Tiempo.

Gamio, Manuel. 1916/1960. *Forjando patria.* México: Editorial Porrúa, S.A.

Garcia-Orozco, Antonia. 2005. "*Cucurrucucu Palomas*: The *Estilo Brávio* of Lucha Reyes and the Creation of Feminist Consciousness in the *Canción Ranchera*." Doctoral Thesis, Claremont Graduate University.

García, Octavio. 2004. "La investigación aduanera: busca de alianzas." *Gaceta*, 4: 8–11.

Garner, Paul. 1995. *Regional Development in Oaxaca during the Porfiriato (1876–1911).* Liverpool, UK: Institute of Latin American Studies, 1995.

Gaytán, Marie S. 2014. "Drinking Difference: Race, Consumption, and Alcohol Prohibition in Mexico and the United States." *Ethnicities* 14, no.3: 437–458.

Gaytán, Marie S., and Ana Valenzuela-Zapata. 2012. "Más allá del mito: mujeres, tequila, y nación." (Beyond the Myth: Women, Tequila, and the Nation). *Mexican Studies/Estudios Mexicanos* 28, no. 1: 183–208.

Geller, Luis. 1983. *Tequila, lo nuestro: Tequila Sauza, 1873–1983.* México, D.F.: Reproducciones Fotomecánicas, SA de CV.

Gibson, Charles. 1964. *The Aztecs under Spanish Rule.* Stanford, CA: Stanford University Press.

Gillespie, Jeanne. 1998. "Gender, Ethnicity, and Piety: The Case of the *China Poblana*," in *Imagination beyond Nation*, P. Bueno and T. Caesar, eds., 19–40. Pittsburgh: University of Pittsburgh Press.

Godoy, Luis Sandoval. 1983. *Tequila: Historia y tradición.* México: Aguinaga, S.A.

Godoy, Luis, Teófilo Herrera, and Miguel Ulloa. 2003. *Más allá del pulque y el tepache: Las bebidas alcohólicas no destiladas.* México: Instituto de Investigcaciones Antropólogicas.

Goffman, Erving. 1959. *The Presentation of Self in Everyday Life.* New York: Anchor.

González Luna, Sofia. 2006. "El paisaje agavero." In *The Agave Landscape and the Ancient Industrial Facilities of Tequila*, Ignacio Arriola, ed. Jalisco, Mexico: Secretaría de Cultura: 13.

González, Gilbert, and Raúl Fernandez. 2002. "Empire and the Origins of Twentieth-Century Migration from Mexico to the United States." *Pacific Historical Review* 71, no. 1: 19–57.

González Torreros, Lucia. 2010. "Modelo turístico sustentable para el municipio de Tequila, Jalisco, México: Una perspectiva de desarrollo local." Doctoral thesis. Universidad de Guadalajara.

González, Roberto. 2004. "From Indigenismo to Zapatismo: Theory and Practice in Mexican Anthropology." *Human Organizations* 63 no. 2: 127–136.

Gradante, William. 1982. "*El Hijo del Pueblo*: José Alfredo Jímenez and the Mexican *Canción Ranchera.*" *Latin American Music Review* 3, no. 1: 36–59.

Grazian, David. 2003. *Blue Chicago: The Search for Authenticity in Urban Blues Clubs.* Chicago: University of Chicago Press.

Greathouse, Patricia. 2009. *Mariachi.* Laton, UT: Gibbs Smith.

Griswold, Wendy. 2013. *Cultures and Societies in a Changing World.* Thousand Oaks, CA: Sage Publications.

Guedea, Virginia. 1980. "México en 1812: Control politico y bebidas prohibidas." *Estudios de Historia Moderna y Contemporánia de México* 8: 23–66.

Gutiérrez Lorenzo, María del Pilar. 2003. "Fuentes para el estudio del vino mezcal en la población del Tequila (Jalisco) siglos XVIII y XIX." Unpublished paper presented at the *Segundo Congreso Nacional de la Historia Económica*, México.

Gusfield, Joseph. 1963. *Symbolic Crusade: Status Politics and the American Temperance Movement.* Urbana: University of Illinois Press.

Gutmann, Matthew. 1996. *The Meaning of Macho: Being a Man in Mexico City.* Berkeley: University of California Press.

Halberstam, Judith. 1998. *Female Masculinity.* Durham, NC: Duke University Press.

Hall, Stuart. 1989. "Cultural Identity and Cinematic Representation." *Framework* 36: 68–81.

Harshberger, John. 1896. "A Botanical Excursion to Mexico." *American Journal of Pharmacy.* November: 588–592.

"A Harvest of Trouble for Tequila Farmers." *Boston Globe*, June 19, 1999: 6.

Harvey, David. 2005. *A Brief History of Neoliberalism.* Oxford, UK: Oxford University Press.

Hayes, Joy, Elizabeth. 2000. *Radio Nation: Communication, Popular Culture, and Nationalism in Mexico, 1920–1950.* Tucson: University of Arizona Press.

Hernández, Fanny. 2005. "Swearing-in Ceremony: Miguel Angel Domínguez, New President of the Tequila Regulatory Council." *Gaceta* 5: 4–7.

Hernández-López, José de Jesús. 2009. "Tequila: Centro mágico, pueblo tradicional: ¿Patrimonialización o privatización?" *Andamios: Revista de Investigación Social* 6, no. 12: 41–67.

———. 2014a. *La jornalerización en el paisaje agavero: Actividades simples, organización compleja.* Michoacán: El colegio de Michoacán.

———. 2014b. *Paisaje y creación de valor: La transformación de los paisajes culturales del agave y del tequila.* Michoacán: El colegio de Michoacán.

Herradura Tequila. "Herradura Tequila." Retrieved on May 9, 2007, from www.herradura.com/ing/home/html.

Hershfield, Joanne. 2008. *Imagining la Chica Moderna: Women, Nation, and Visual Culture in Mexico, 1917–1936.* Durham, NC: Duke University Press.

Hinrichs, Carole. 1996. "Consuming Images: Making and Marketing Vermont as Distinctive Rural Place," in *Creating the Countryside*, Melanie DuPuis and Peter Vandergeest, eds., 259–278. Philadelphia: Temple University Press.

"El homenaje de Jaliscienses a Guadalajara." *El Informador*, February 12, 1942: 9.

"How Did Ancient Chinese Distill Spirits?" *People's Daily Online News*, 2006. Retrieved on July 26, 2007, from http://english.newssc.org/system/2006/10/24/010166373.shtml.

Inclán, Ramón. 2005. "Se suicida con veneno." *La Opinión*, 26 July. Retrieved on October 2, 2007, from www.laopinion.com/columnist11/?rkey=00050729200208135656.

James, Josh. 2001. "Tequila." *TED Case Studies*, n. 629, June. Retrieved on June 22, 2008, from www.american.edu/TED/tequila.htm.

Jerolmack, Colin. 2007. "Animal Practices, Ethnicity, and Community: The Turkish Pigeon Handlers of Berlin." *American Sociological Review*, 72, no. 6: 874–894.

El Jimador. 2012. "Our Story." Retrieved on February 20, 2012, from eljimador.com/story.aspx?id=414.

Jiménez Vizcarra, Claudio. 2013. *El vino mezcal, tequila y la polémica sobre la destilación prehispánica*. Guadalajara: Benemérita Sociedad de Geografía y Estadística del Estado de Jalisco.

Joseph, Gilbert, Anne Rubenstein, and Eric Zolov. 2001. "Assembling the Fragments: Writing a Cultural History of Mexico since 1940," In *Fragments of a Golden Age: The Politics of Culture in Mexico Since 1940*, Gilbert Joseph, Anne Rubenstein, and Eric Zolov, eds., 3–22. Durham, NC: Duke University Press.

Joseph, Gilbert, and Timothy Henderson. 2002. "Introduction," in *The Mexico Reader: History, Culture, Politics*, Gilbert Joseph and Timothy Henderson, eds., 1–8. Durham, NC: Duke University Press.

Kanellos, Nicolás. 2000. "A Brief History of Hispanic Periodicals in the United States," in *Hispanic Periodicals in the United States, Origins to 1960: A Brief and Comprehensive Bibliography*, Nicolás Kanellos and Helvetia Martell, ed., 3–8. Houston: Arte Público Press.

Kaplan, Amy. 2002. *The Anarchy of Empire in the Making of U.S. Culture*. Cambridge, MA: Harvard University Press.

Katz, Friedrich. 1998. *The Life and Times of Pancho Villa*. Stanford, CA: Stanford University Press.

Katzew, Illona. 2004. *Casta Painting: Images of Race in Eighteenth-Century Mexico*. New Haven, CT: Yale University Press.

Kicza, John E. 1980. "The Pulque Trade of Late Colonial Mexico City." *The Americas* 37, no. 2: 193–221.

Knight, Alan. 1986. "Mexican Peonage: What Was It? And Why Was It?" *Journal of Latin American Studies* 18, no.1: 41–74.

Kropp, Phoebe. 2008. *California Vieja: Culture and Memory in a Modern American Place*. Berkeley: University of California Press.

Lacy, Alberto Ruy Sánchez. 1995. *El tequila: Arte tradicional de México*. México: Artes de Mexico.

Laudan, Rachel, and Jeffrey Pilcher, 1999. "Chilies, Chocolate, and Race in New Spain: Glancing Backward to Spain or Looking Forward to Mexico?" *Eighteenth-Century Life*, 23, no. 2: 59–70.

"Lea esto." *Cosmopolita*, July 31, 1915, 2.

Leon, Alexandra. 2011. "Talking Tequila with the Industry's Head Honcho Francisco Gonzalez." Retrieved on June 5, 2013, from http://blogs.miaminewtimes.com/shortorder/2011/07/tequila_talk_with_the_industry.php.

Leonard, Andrew. 2006. "Globalization and the Blue Agave." *Salon.Com*, October 19. Retrieved on June 22, 2008, from www.salon.com/tech/htww/2006/10/19/tequila/.

Lewis, Laura. 1996. "The 'Weakness' of Women and the Feminization of the Indian in Colonial Mexico." *Colonial Latin America Review* 5, no. 1: 73–94.

Límon, Enrique. 1999. *Tequila: The Spirit of Mexico*. Bath, UK: Absolute Press.

Limón, José. 1984. "La Llorona, the Third of Greater Mexico: Cultural Symbols, Women, and the Political Unconscious." Tucson: The Renato Rosaldo Lecture Series 2, University of Arizona.

Límon, José. 1986. "Folklore, Social Conflict, and the United States–Mexican Border," in *Handbook of American Folklore*, Richard Dorson, ed., 216–226. Bloomington: University of Indiana Press.

Lindley, Richard B. 1983. *Haciendas and Economic Development: Guadalajara, Mexico at Independence*. Austin: University of Texas Press.

Lipsitz, George. 1990. *Time Passages: Collective Memory and American Popular Culture*. Minneapolis: University of Minnesota Press.

———. 2005. "The Grounded Transnationalism of Robert Alvarez," in *Mangos, Chiles, and Truckers: The Business of Transnationalism*, Robert Alvarez, ed., xxi–xix. Minneapolis: University of Minnesota Press.

Loaeza, Guadalupe. 1998. *Ellas y nosotras*. México: Editorial Ocean de México, S.A. de C.V.

Lockhart, James. 1994. *The Nahuas after the Conquest: A Social and Cultural History of the Indians of Central Mexico, Sixteenth through Eighteenth Centuries*. Stanford, CA: Stanford University Press.

Lockhart, James, and Stuart Schwartz, 1983. *Early Latin America: A History of Colonial Spanish America and Brazil*. Cambridge, UK: Cambridge University Press.

Lomnitz, Claudio. 2001. *Deep Mexico, Silent Mexico: An Anthropology of Nationalism*. Minneapolis: University of Minnesota Press.

"Lucha Reyes ha muerto." *Cinema Reporter*, July 1, 1944: 10.

"Lucha Reyes murió ayer." *El Informador*, June 26, 1944: 1.

Luna, Rogelio. 1999. *La historia del tequila, de sus regiones y sus hombres*. México: Conaculta.

MacCannell, Dean. 1999. *The Tourist: A New Theory of the Leisure Class*. Berkeley: University of California Press.

Mahoney, Sarah. 2013. "Marketer Betting That for Women, Tequila Is the New Vodka." Retrieved on June 11, 2013, from www.tequila.net/tequila-news/latest/marketing-tequila-for-women.html.

Marez, Curtis. 2004. *Drug Wars: The Political Economy of Narcotics*. Minneapolis: University of Minnesota Press.

María y Campos, Armando. 1962. *La revolución Mexicana a través de los corridos populares*. México D.F.: Biblioteca del Instituto Nacional de Estudios Históricos de la Revolución Mexicana.

Martínez, Maria. 2011. *Genealogical Fictions: Limpieza de Sangre, Religion, and Gender in Colonial Mexico*. Stanford, CA: Stanford University Press.

McCaughan, Edward. 1999. "Social Movements, Globalization, and the Re-Configuration of Mexican/Chicano Nationalism." *Social Justice* 26, no. 3: 59–78.

McWilliams, Carey. 1946. *Southern California Country: An Island on the Land*. New York: Peregrine Smith.

Medina Ruiz. 1954. "Lucha Reyes, la inolvidable." *Cinema Reporter*, November 19: 15.

Mendelzon, Manuel. 2005. "Reinventing the Gaucho: Civilization, Barbarism, and the Mythic Argentine Cowboy." Retrieved on December 6, 2005, from www .ausmcgill.com/idssa/latitudes/pdf/gaucho-mendelzon.pdf.

Miller, Daniel. 1995. *Acknowledging Consumption: A Review of New Studies*. London: Routledge.

Mirandé, Alfredo. 1988. "Qué gacho es ser macho: It's a Drag to Be a Macho Man." *Aztlán: A Journal of Chicano Studies* 17, no. 2: 63–89.

Mitchell, Stephanie, and Patrice Schell (eds.). 2007. *The Women's Revolution in Mexico, 1910–1953*. Lanham, MD: Rowman and Littlefield Publishers.

Mitchell, Tim. 2004. *Intoxicated Identities: Alcohol's Power in Mexican History and Culture*. New York and London: Routledge.

Molotch, Harvey. 2003. *Where Stuff Comes From*. New York and London: Routledge.

Monsiváis, Carlos. 1978. "Notas sobre cultura popular en México." *Latin American Perspectives* 5, no. 1: 98–118.

———. 1995. "Mythologies," in *Mexican Cinema*, Paulo Antonio Paranaguá, ed., 117–127. London: British Film Institute.

———. 1997. *Mexican Postcards*. London: Verso.

———. 1999. "Tequila with Lime and Other Table Talk," in *Tequila: The Spirit of Mexico*, Enrique Martínez Límon ,ed., 13–17. Bath, UK: Absolute Press.

———. 2002. "Calendars: Cultural Snapshots and Visual Tradition," in *Mexicana: Vintage Mexican Graphics*, Jim Heimann, ed., 3–8. Cologne: Taschen.

———. 2007. "When Gender Can't Be Seen amid the Symbolic: Women and the Mexican Revolution," in *Sex in Revolution: Gender, Politics, and Power in Modern Mexico*, Jocelyn Olcott, Mary Kay Vaughn, and Gabriela Cano's, eds., 1–20. Durham, NC: Duke University Press.

Mora, Carl. 1989. *Mexican Cinema: Reflections of a Society, 1896–1988*. Berkeley: University of California Press.

Moreno Rivas, Yolanda. 1979. *Historia de la música popular Mexicana*. México: Alianza Editorial Mexicana.

Moreno Rivas, Yolanda, with Alejandro Pérez Sáez. 1989. *Historia de la música popular Mexicana*, 2nd ed. México: Aliznza Editorial Mexicana.

Mörner, Magnus, and Charles Gibson. 1962. "Diego Muñoz Camargo and the Segregation Policy of the Spanish Crown." *Hispanic American Historical Review* 42, no. 4: 558–568.

Mraz, John. 2009. *Looking for Mexico: Modern Visual Culture and National Identity*. Durham, NC: Duke University Press.

Mulholland, Mary-Lee. 2007. *Mariachi in Excess: Performing Race, Gender, Sexuality and Regionalism in Jalisco, Mexico*. Doctoral Thesis, York University, Toronto, Canada.

Mundo Cuervo. 2006. "Mundo Cuervo." Retrieved on May 19, 2006, from http://.mundocuervo.com.

Mundo Cuervo. 2008. "What Is Mundo Cuervo?" Retrieved on May 20, 2008, from http://mundocuervo.com.

Muñoz, Fernando. 1998. *Sara García*. México: Editorial Clío.

Muriá, José María. 1995. "Momentos del tequila," in *El tequila: Arte tradicional de México*, Alberto Ruy Sánchez Lacy, ed., 17–25. México: Artes de Mexico:

———. 1997. *Una bebida llamada tequila*. Guadalajara: Editorial Agata.

Nájera-Ramírez, Olga. 1994. "Engendering Nationalism: Identity, Discourse, and the Mexican Charro." *Anthropological Quarterly* 67, no. 1: 1–14.

———. 2007. "Unruly Passions: Poetics, Performance, and Gender in the Ranchera Song," in *Women and Migration in the U.S.–Mexican Borderlands: A Reader*, Denise Segura and Patricia Zavella (eds.), 456–476. Durham, NC, and London: Duke University Press.

"Near Prohibition Ordered in Mexico." *San Jose Mercury Herald*, May 11, 1918: 9.

Negrón-Muntaner, Frances. 2002. "Barbie's Hair: Selling out Puerto Rican Identity in the Global Marketplace," in *Latino/a Popular Culture*, Michelle Habell-Pallán and Mary Romero, eds., 38–60. New York: New York University Press.

Nemser, D. 2012. "'To Avoid This Mixture:' Rethinking Pulque in Colonial Mexico City." *Food and Foodways* 19, no. 1: 98–121.

"Nombra UNESCO a Tequila, Jalisco, patrimonio mundial." *El Informador*, July 13, 2006: 1.

Ojeda Díaz, María de Los Ángeles. 2003. "Las diosas del Códice Borgia," in *Las mujeres y sus diosas en los códices prehispánicos de Oaxaca*, Cecilia Rossell and María de Los Ángeles Ojeda Díaz, eds. 118–146. México: Centro de Investigaciones y Estudios Superiores en Antropología Social.

Olcott, Jocelyn, Mary Kay Vaughn, and Gabriela Cano, (eds.). 2007. *Sex in Revolution: Gender, Politics, and Power in Modern Mexico*. Durham, NC: Duke University Press: 1–20.

Orlove, Benjamin, ed. *The Allure of the Foreign*. Ann Arbor: University of Michigan Press.

Orlove, Benjamin, and Arnold Bauer. 1997. "Giving Importance to Imports," in *The Allure of the Foreign*, Benjamin Orlove, ed., 1–30. Ann Arbor: University of Michigan Press.

———. 1997. "Chile in the Belle Époque: Primitive Producers, Civilized Consumers." In *The Allure of the Foreign*, Benjamin Orlove, ed., 113–150. Ann Arbor: University of Michigan Press.

Orozco, José. 1998. "'Esos altos de Jalisco!': Emigration and the Idea of Alteño Exceptionalism, 1926–1952." Doctoral thesis, Harvard University.

Pagden, Anthony. 1986. *Hernan Cortes: Letters from Mexico.* New Haven, CT: Yale University Press.

Palomar Verea, Cristina. 2004: *En cada charro, un hermano: La charrería en el estado de Jalisco.* Guadalajara: Secretaría de Cultura, Gobierno del Estado de Jalisco.

Palomares-Medina, Ramón. 2004. *Historia del municipio de Tequila.* Publisher unknown.

Paredes, Américo. 1967. "Mexico, Machismo, and the U.S." *Journal of the Folklore Institute,* 8: 17–37.

Parra, Max. 2005. *Writing Pancho Villa's Revolution: Rebels in the Literary Imagination of Mexico.* Austin: University of Texas Press.

Parsons, Jeffrey R., and Mary H. Parsons. 1990. *Maguey Utilization in Highland Central Mexico: An Archaeological Ethnography.* Ann Arbor: University of Michigan, Anthropological Papers, Museum of Anthropology, no. 82.

Patch, Robert. 2010. "Indian Resistance to Colonialism," in *The Oxford History of Mexico,* William Beezley and Michael Meyer, eds., 175–202. Oxford, UK: Oxford University Press.

Paz, Octavio. 1950 (1985). *The Labyrinth of Solitude and Other Writings.* New York: Grove Press.

———. 1976. "Forward: The Flight of Quetzalcóatl and the Quest for Legitimacy," in *Quetzalcoatl and Guadalupe: The Formation of Mexican National Consciousness, 1531–1813,* Jacques Lafeye, ed. Chicago: University of Chicago Press.

Peregrina, Angélica. 2009. "La adopción de las estampas jaliscienses en el imaginario nacional mexicano mediante la educación." *Educació i Historia: Revista D'Història de L'Educació,* no. 14: 155–172.

Pérez, Emma. 1999. *The Decolonial Imaginary: Writing Chicanas into History.* Bloomington: Indiana University Press.

Pérez-López, Cuauhtémoc, Lourdes González, Haydeé Rosovsky, and Leticia Casanova. 1992. "La mujer en los grupos de alcohólicos anónimos." *Anales del Instituto Mexicano de Psiquiatría:* 125–129.

Pérez, Leonor Xóchitl. 2002. "Transgressing the Taboo: A Chicana's Voice in the Mariachi World," in *Chicana Traditions: Continuity and Change,* Norma Cantú and Olga Nájera-Ramírez, eds., 143–163. Urbana and Chicago: University of Illinois Press.

Peterson, Jeanette. 1992. "The Virgin of Guadalupe: Symbol of Conquest or Liberation?" *Art Journal* 51, no. 4: 39–47.

Pick, Zuzana. 2010. *Constructing the Image of the Mexican Revolution: Cinema and the Archive.* Austin: University of Texas Press.

Pilcher, Jeffrey. 1998. *Qué Vivan Los Tamales: Food and the Making of Mexican Identity*. Albuquerque: University of New Mexico Press.

———. 2004. "Fajitas and the Failure of Refrigerated Meat Packing in Mexico: Consumer Culture and Porfirian Capitalism." *The Americas* 30, no. 3: 411–429.

Piña, Ulices. 2012. "Lords of Agave: Eladio Sauza, Agaristas, and the Struggle for Land in Tequila, Mexico, 1932–1937." *UCLA Historical Journal* 23, no.1: 13–30.

Poister, John. 1999. *The New American Bartender's Guide*. New York: Signet.

Poniatowska, Elena. 2006. *Las Soldaderas: Women of the Mexican Revolution*. México: Conaculta.

Pratt, Mary Louise. 1992. *Imperial Eyes: Travel Writing and Transculturation*. New York and London: Routledge.

Purnell, Jennie. 2002. "Citizens and Sons of the Pueblo: National and Local Identities in the Making of the Mexican Nation." *Ethnic and Racial Studies* 25, no. 2: 213–223.

Quiroz Márquez, Jorge. 2001. *El mezcal: Origenes, elaboración, y recetas*. Oaxaca: Universidad Jose Vasconcelos de Oaxaca.

———. 2005. *Lo que quería saber del mezcal y temía preguntar*. Oaxaca: Universidad Jose Vasconcelos de Oaxaca.

Quirarte, Vicente. 1995. "The Poetics of Tequila," in *El tequila: Arte tradicional de México*, Alberto Ruy Sánchez, ed., 9. D.F.: Artes de Mexico.

Radding, Cynthia. 2006. *Landscapes of Power and Identity: Comparative Histories in the Sonoran Desert and the Forests of Amazonia from Colony to Republic*. Durham, NC: Duke University Press.

Ramírez-Berg, Charles. 1992. *Cinema of Solitude: A Critical Study of Mexican Film, 1967–1983*. Austin: University of Texas Press.

Ramírez Racaño, Mario. 2000. *Ignacio Torres Adalid y la Industria Pulquera*. México D.F.: Plaza y Valdés.

Ramos, Samuel. 1933 (1962). *Profile of Man and Culture in Mexico*. New York: McGraw-Hill.

Reséndez, Andrés. 1995. "Battleground Women: *Soldaderas* and Female Soldiers in the Mexican Revolution." *The Americas* 51, no. 4: 525–553.

Rodríguez, Victoria. 2003. *Women in Contemporary Mexican Politics*. Austin: University of Texas Press.

Rosales, Arturo. 1999. *Pobre Raza!: Violence, Justice, and Mobilization among México Lindo Immigrants, 1900–1936*. Austin: University of Texas Press.

Ruta del Tequila. 2010. "Ruta del Tequila." Retrieved on August 29, 2010, from http. rutadeltequila.com.mx.

Salas, Elizabeth.1990. Soldaderas *in the Mexican Military: Myth and History*. Austin: University of Texas Press.

Sánchez Guevara, Graciela. 2009. "La resmantización del espacio cultural de la Plaza Mayor: las imágenes de los textos de historia." *Entretextos: Revista Elecrónica Semestral de Estudios Semióticas de la Cultura*, no.14–16: 10–20.

Sánchez López, Alberto. 1989. *Oaxaca, tierra de maguey y mezcal*. Oaxaca: Instituto Tecnologico de Oaxaca.

Sandos, James A. 1981. "Pancho Villa and American Security: Woodrow Wilson's Mexican Diplomacy Reconsidered." *Journal of Latin American Studies* 13, no. 1: 293–311.

Sands, Kathleen. 1993. *Charrería Mexicana: An Equestrian Folk Tradition*. Tucson: University of Arizona Press.

Scardaville, Michael. 1980. "Alcohol Abuse and Tavern Reform in Late Colonial Mexico City." *The Hispanic American Historical Review* 60, no. 4, 643–671.

Schmidt, Henry. 1978. *The Roots of Lo Mexicano: Self and Society in Mexican Thought, 1900–1934*. College Station: Texas A & M University Press.

SECTUR. 2012. "Programa Pueblos Magicos." Retrieved on May 27, 2012, from www.sectur.gob.mx/wb2/sectur/sect_Pueblos_Magicos.

Shafer, A. C. 1899. "Guadalajara." *Los Angeles Times*, November 19: 14.

Smith, Fredrick. 2005. *Caribbean Rum: A Social and Economic History*. Gainsville: University of Florida Press.

Socolow, Susan. 2000. *The Women of Colonial Latin America*. Cambridge, UK: Cambridge University Press.

Soustelle, Jacques. 1964. *The Daily Life of the Aztecs*. Middlesex, England: Penguin Books.

Stavans, Ilan. *The Riddle of Cantinflas: Essays on Hispanic Popular Culture*. Albuquerque: University of New Mexico Press.

Stevens, Evelyn. 1965. "Mexican Machismo: Politics and Value Orientations." *The Western Political Quarterly* 18, no. 4: 848–857.

Stoler, Ann. 2002. *Carnal Knowledge and Imperial Power: Race and the Intimate in Colonial Rule*. Berkeley: University of California Press.

Sturken, Marita. 2007. *Tourists of History: Memory, Kitsch, and Consumerism from Oklahoma City to Ground Zero*. Berkeley: University of California Press.

Tequila Jalisco. 2014. "Hotel boutique la Cofradia." Retrieved on February 5, 2014, from www.tequilajalisco.gob.mx.

Taylor, Bayard. 1850. "The Robber Region of Mexico." *The Sandusky Register*, 13, May, 2.

Taylor, William. 1972. *Landlord and Peasant in Colonial Oaxaca*. Stanford, CA: Stanford University Press.

———. 1979. *Drinking, Homicide, and Rebellion in Colonial Mexican Villages*. Stanford, CA: Stanford University Press.

————. 1987. "The Virgin of Guadalupe in New Spain: An Inquiry into the Social History of Marion Devotion." *American Ethnologist* 14, no. 1: 9–33.

"Tequila: A gift from ancestral Gods, [a] drink with a taste of history." 2006. Flyer advertisement.

"Tequila Regulatory Council 2007." Video.

"Tiene un completo surtido de vino y liqores importados y del pais, y el afamado mezcal de Tequila." *Dos Republicas*, May 17, 1892, 4.

Topik, Steve, Carlos Marichal, and Zypher Frank, eds. 2006. *From Silver to Cocaine: Latin American Commodity*. Durham, NC: Duke University Press.

Toxqui Garay, M. A. 2008. "'El Recreo de Los Amigos': Mexico City's Pulquerías during the Liberal Republic (1856–1911)." Doctoral thesis, Department of History, University of Arizona.

TRC. 2007. "The TRC." Retrieved on July 12, 2007, from www.crt.org.mx/eng/home .htm.

Tucker, Duncan. 2011. "Poverty and Wealth Inequality on the Rise in Mexico." Retrieved on January 2, 2014, from http://duncantucker.wordpress.com/2011/08/17/ poverty-and-wealth-inequality-on-the-rise-in-mexico/.

Turner, Fredrick. 1968. *The Dynamic of Mexican Nationalism*. Chapel Hill: University of North Carolina Press.

United Nations Educational, Scientific, and Cultural Organization (UNESCO). 2007. "World Heritage List." Retrieved on April 20, 2007, from http://whc.unesco.org/ en/list/.

Usher, Roland. 1914. "The Real Mexican Problem." *North American Review* 200, no. 704: 45–52.

Valadez Moreno, Moisés. 2002. "Vinateros y talladores. Dos pervivencias indígenas de Nuevo León." *Revista de humanidades*, no. 12: 249–260.

Valenzuela-Zapata, Ana, and Marie S. Gaytán. 2013. "Sustaining Biological and Cultural Diversity: Geographic Indications and Traditional Mezcal Production in Jalisco, Mexico." *Revue d'ethnoécologie* 2: 2–18.

Valenzuela-Zapata, Ana, and Marie S. Gaytán. 2009. "La expansión tequilera y las mujeres en la industria: del símbolo al testimonio." *Sociedades Rurales, Producción y Medio Ambiente*, 9, no. 18: 167–195.

Vandergeest, Peter, and Melanie DuPuis. 1996. "Introduction," in *Creating the Countryside: The Politics of Rural and Environmental Discourse*, Melanie DuPuis and Peter Vandergeest, eds. Philadelphia: Temple University Press.

Van Young, Eric. 1979. "Urban Market and Hinterland: Guadalajara and Its Region in the Eighteenth Century." *Hispanic American Historic Review* 54, no. 4: 593–635.

————. 1981. *Hacienda and Market in Eighteenth Century Mexico: The Rural Economy of the Guadalajara Region, 1675–1820*. Berkeley: University of California Press.

———. 2001. *The Other Rebellion: Popular Violence, Ideology, and the Mexican Struggle for Independence, 1810–1821*. Stanford, CA: Stanford University Press.

Vargas, Deborah. 2012. *Dissonant Divas in Chicana Music: The Limits of La Onda*. Minneapolis: University of Minnesota Press.

Vasconcelos, José. 1925/1997. *The Cosmic Race/La Raza Cósmica*. Baltimore, MD: Johns Hopkins University Press.

Vaughan, Mary Kay. 2007. "Pancho Villa, the Daughters of Mary and the Modern Woman: Gender in the Long Mexican Revolution," in *Sex in Revolution: Gender, Politics, and Power in Modern Mexico*, Jocelyn Olcott, Mary Kay Vaughn, and Gabriela Cano (eds.), 21–34. Durham, NC: Duke University Press.

Vázquez Mantecón, María del Carmen. 2000. "La china Mexicana, mejor conocida como china poblana." *Anales del Instituto de Investigaciones Estéticas*, no. 77: 123–150.

Velasco, Alma. 2012. *Me llaman la tequilera*. México: Suma.

Velasco, Jorge, and Corina Preciado. 2006. "Es patrimonio, paisaje agavero." *El Mural*, July 13: 1.

"Villa a Negro, Soldier Says." *Los Angeles Times*, February 25, 1914: I2.

Villalobos Díaz, Jaime. 2004. *Historia del tequila, leyenda e identidad de una nácion*. Guadalajara: EDICSA, S.A.

Viquera Albán, Juan Pedro. 1987. *Propriety and Permissiveness in Bourbon Mexico*. Wilmington, DE: Scholarly Resources.

Von Humboldt, Alexander. 1811 (1966). *Political Essay on the Kingdom of New Spain (Volume four)*. New York: AMS Press.

———. 1811 (1972). *Political Essay on the Kingdom of New Spain* (abridged version). New York: Alfred A. Knopf.

Wells, Allen. 2006. "Reports of Its Demise Are Not Exaggerated: The Life and Times of Yucatecan Henequen," in *From Silver to Cocaine: Latin American Commodity*, Steve Topik, Carlos Marichal, and Zypher Frank, eds., 300–320. Durham, NC: Duke University Press.

Widdifield, Stacie. 1996. *The Embodiment of the National in Late Nineteenth-Century Mexican Painting*. Tucson: University of Arizona.

Williams, Raymond. 1978. *Marxism and Literature*. Oxford, UK: Oxford University Press.

Wilson, Iris, and Antonio Pineda. 1963. "Pineda's Report on the Beverages of New Spain." *Arizona and the West* 5, no. 1: 79–90.

Wolf, Eric. 1958. "The Virgin of Guadalupe: A Mexican National Symbol." *Journal of American Folklore* 71: 34–39.

Womack, John. 2002. "Pancho Villa: A Revolutionary Life." *The Journal of the Historical Society* 11, no. 1: 21–42.

World Trade Organization (WTO). 2013. "Intellectual Property: Protection and Enforcement." Retrieved on May 27, 2013, from www.wto.org/english/thewto_e/whatis_e/tif_e/agrm7_e.htm.

"Ya va en camino para Mexico el trigo y la harina comprados en Argentina Información General De La Ce. De Mexico Circular a los jefes militares, los carrancistas siguen." *Prensa*, February 23, 1918, 5.

Yarbro-Bejarano, Yvonne. 1997. "Crossing the Border with Chabela Vargas: A Chicana Femme's Tribute," in *Sex and Sexuality in Latin America*, Donna Guy and Daniel Balderston, eds., 33–43. New York: New York University Press.

Yeager, Gene. 1977. "Porfirian Commercial Propaganda: Mexico in the World Industrial Expositions." *The Americas* 34, no. 2: 230–243.

Young, Elliott. 2004. *Catarino Garza's Revolution on the Texas–Mexico Border*. Durham, NC: Duke University Press.

Zavala, Adriana. 2010. *Becoming Modern, Becoming Tradition: Women, Gender, and Representation in Mexican Art*. University Park: The Pennsylvania State University Press.

Zizumbo, D., and P. Colunga. 2008, "Early Coconut Distillation and the Origins of Mezcal in West-Central Mexico." *Genetic Resources and Crop Evolution* 55, no. 4: 493–510

Zolov, Eric. 1999. *Refried Elvis: The Rise of the Mexican Counter Culture*. Berkeley: University of California Press.

Zussman, Robert. 2000. "Autobiographical Occasions: Introduction to the Special Issue." *Qualitative Sociology* 23, no. 1: 5–8.

INDEX

Note: Page numbers in italic type indicate illustrations.